My Mother
THE SPY

Other books by Freda Nicholls

Love, Sweat and Tears
Back of Beyond
The Amazing Mrs Livesey
Outback Teacher

My Mother THE SPY

The daring and tragic double life
of ASIO agent Mercia Masson

CINDY DOBBIN &
FREDA MARNIE NICHOLLS

ALLEN&UNWIN
SYDNEY · MELBOURNE · AUCKLAND · LONDON

First published in 2023

Allen & Unwin
Cammeraygal Country
83 Alexander Street
Crows Nest NSW 2065
Australia
Phone: (61 2) 8425 0100
Email: info@allenandunwin.com
Web: www.allenandunwin.com

Allen & Unwin acknowledges the Traditional Owners of the Country on which we live and work. We pay our respects to all Aboriginal and Torres Strait Islander Elders, past and present.

 A catalogue record for this book is available from the National Library of Australia

ISBN 978 1 76106 728 0

Set in 12/16.4 pt Minion Pro by Midland Typesetters, Australia
Printed and bound in Australia by the Opus Group

10 9 8 7 6 5 4 3 2 1

The paper in this book is FSC® certified. FSC® promotes environmentally responsible, socially beneficial and economically viable management of the world's forests.

CONTENTS

CONTENTS

For Kyle (deceased), Kieron, Shaun and Kelly-ann

PROLOGUE

Once again, Mercia Masson found herself standing in the witness box, waiting to be cross-examined at the start of the day's proceedings of the Royal Commission on Espionage.

It was March 1955, and the extraordinary inquiry that had been enthralling the nation had already been running for nearly a year.

'I have completed my examination of the witness, Your Honour.'

Barrister Ted Hill approached the witness box and started questioning Mercia, in an exchange that was far from cordial. He asked about Rex Chiplin, how long they had known each other, and about how, as journalists, she and Rex would exchange information of a general nature.

'You know Mr Chiplin's family quite well, do you not?'

'I am very fond of Mr Chiplin's family,' Mercia said. 'I still regard Mr Chiplin as he was, a friend. I think I have been doing the right thing by saving the people I like from thinking the wrong way.'

'I understand that, and I do not want to harass you unduly. But the fact is that you have been in his home quite a good deal?'

'That is so.'

Mercia explained that she had even offered her holiday house to the Chiplin family to use, as she was concerned about his wife's health with the Royal Commission underway. And then she emphasised that her offer was still open.

Mr Hill continued to ask about her friendship with Chiplin, and the fact that he had assisted her with her troubles—someone to talk to about her family problems.

'You found Mr Chiplin a very sympathetic person?' he asked.

'He has always been a most sympathetic person. Mr Chiplin has been a very honest person to deal with. I have no wish to do Mr Chiplin any harm. I think I told you that yesterday. This is not easy for me, Mr Hill, none of it. I have lost everything in coming here—everything that I had up until Monday. I have lost my friends—my close friends over the years—and my association with the left wing; I have now lost my left-wing friends. I have probably lost my position. I shall probably have to remove my child from the school and my mother from the house in which she lives. I do not think there is anything else I can possibly lose.'

PART
1

LIFE AS A SPY

1

A MYSTERIOUS MOTHER

Late in the winter of 1975, Cindy sat in a ward in Sydney's St Vincent's Hospital watching over her mother. She had been there all day.

Although she was an only child, neither she nor her mother had corresponded often. Five years previously, she had been living in Canada and had been surprised to receive a letter from her mother in faraway Australia, saying she'd being diagnosed with cancer. Her mother had suffered from stomach ulcers for as long as Cindy could remember, and now they had turned cancerous.

The pair had never had a close mother–daughter relationship, but Cindy had known she now had to leave her new life and return to Australia. So she had resigned from her job and made the long trip back, always intending to return to Canada one day.

Staring at the crucifix above her mother's bed, Cindy had a sudden thought about converting her mother to Catholicism. She felt her mother would like that, as her mother had often spoken of her friendship with the nuns from the Order of Our Lady Help of Christians. She was close to two in particular, Sister Gertrude and Sister Paul, and Cindy knew her mother had been attending Mass regularly with them for some time.

Cindy went down to the hospital office to find out how to organise her mother's conversion. She explained that she felt her mother would want to become a Catholic before she passed. To her amazement, the hospital staff informed her that her mother had already converted, three years before. Cindy recalled all her dutiful hospital visits since then, and how many times she had said to her mother that the crucifix hanging above the bed in the Catholic hospital was probably not appropriate as she wasn't Catholic. Her mother had never said a thing.

The oncologists had initially removed half of her mother's stomach, but then the cancer spread to her breasts. Now, five years later, the disease had metastasised further and was all through her brain. As evening fell, it became obvious that her mother could no longer distinguish reality from fantasy, and did not have long to live.

The nurses suggested that Cindy leave the room for a short time while they gave her mother a bath. Not long afterwards, they told Cindy her mother had slipped away just after she'd left the room.

Cindy's father had passed away the year before she left for Canada. With all her grandparents also gone, she now had no family left.

What followed was a bewildering time for Cindy. The hospital wanted to do a post-mortem examination of her mother's body, which she agreed to, even though it seemed obvious that cancer was the cause of death. The examination showed that an infection had finally caused her death, not the cancer—a fact she personally felt she didn't need to know. Her mother had been so ill towards the end, it was obvious she was going to die.

As next of kin, Cindy dutifully filled out the details for the death certificate.

```
Name: Mercia Leonora Zoe Masson.
    Father: William John Masson.
    Mother: Leonora Irene Luchere Protti.
```

```
Siblings: none.
Occupation: journalist.
```

Cindy put down her mother's date of birth as 25 October 1919. Mercia's birth was registered in 1913, but Cindy thought her mother was only 55 when she died, not 61.

Funeral arrangements were made, but the ceremony was a bit of a blur. The nuns of Our Lady Help of Christians attended, as did many of Mercia's socialite friends and work colleagues. The funeral was held in Sydney's Darling Point, at The Swifts, a heritage-listed mansion that had been bequeathed to the Catholic Church many years before and was also the home of the Cardinal. As well as looking after the priests at St Patrick's College at Manly, the nuns of Our Lady Help of Christians would take turns at spending time at The Swifts and looking after the Cardinal. What had once been a large ballroom had been converted into a chapel, and when Cindy found out her mother had often attended Mass there with the nuns, she thought it would be appropriate for the funeral to be held there.

Mercia was cremated. Cindy arranged for the ashes to be laid next to those of Mercia's mother, in the rose garden at Botany Cemetery.

Telegrams and letters of condolence arrived from those unable to attend the service—friends, colleagues and charitable organisations that Mercia had worked tirelessly for. A life her daughter had only had glimpses of.

The welfare officer from the Australian Broadcasting Commission (ABC) rang to say he was cleaning out Mercia's desk at work, and asked if she wanted any of the contents. Mercia had worked right up until the last. Cindy told him she didn't know what was in the drawer. She remembers him saying there was a dried-up apple core and she asked him to throw it away.

According to a former colleague, Mercia was efficient, thorough and an exceptionally hard-working journalist. She was always fashionably dressed and had an impressive network of friends and acquaintances. Her address book seemed to hold the Who's Who of

Sydney. Her ability to work so efficiently was despite her after-hours alcohol intake—something that had embarrassed her daughter over the years, especially as the amount consumed had increased.

Mercia had lent her car to one of the nuns before she went into hospital for the last time. Cindy retrieved it and drove to her mother's flat in Double Bay. Looking at all her mother's belongings— including numerous little china animals, which she loathed—she set about sorting out what would be kept and what would be thrown away. Two of her mother's friends arrived and asked if they could come and collect something to remind them of Mercia. Her mother must have meant something to them, though one only took her vacuum cleaner.

Two men also arrived at the flat. They were dressed in suits and told Cindy that they had come to collect her mother's filing cabinet from the garage. Cindy happily let them. As far as she was concerned, it was one less thing for her to sort through. It was only later she thought it strange.

Newspapers rang, asking Cindy what she could tell them about her mother. One journalist said he was writing a book about Australian spies, and that he found Mercia to be one of the most interesting he had come across. As with the other inquirers, she told him to talk to her mother's friends, as she didn't know anything.

Cindy found the idea of her mother being a spy ridiculous. The thought of her strait-laced, prim and proper mother being a cloak-and-dagger spy was ludicrous.

Or was it?

2

NO ONE TO ASK

Going through her mother's belongings at the Double Bay flat, Cindy came across faces in the photo albums that she recognised, as well as books and objects she remembered. But there were also faces that she didn't recognise, and strange things that could not be explained among all the papers, photos, newspaper cuttings and miscellaneous items. Things that meant nothing to her—and now there was no one to ask.

Cindy did recognise from her childhood the familiar formal glassware and a silver entertaining tray, dating from a time when Mercia had entertained people in their home. Her mother had been a good cook and hostess, and always loved to socialise and gossip.

Her mother's piano sat in the main living area. She remembered her mother playing regularly. Quite an accomplished pianist, she had insisted that Cindy also learn.

Among the numerous books were bibles and objects from different religions. It made her think that this lonely sick woman must have been looking for some comfort in her life as the cancer took hold—but Cindy just didn't know.

One book she found very odd. It was titled *Leninism*, by Joseph Stalin, and was signed on the inside cover 'Russell Grant, March 1923'. Cindy remembered Russell Grant; they had shared a house with him when she was a child. But why would her mother keep a book about Lenin? Her mother, as far as she knew, never supported Communism. The complete opposite, if anything. Her mother had been a staunch Liberal Party supporter as far back as Cindy could remember, making Cindy join the Young Liberals, and opposed anything left wing.

Cindy flicked through the well-worn pages of the book and noticed that certain passages were underlined. Rather than delve into this mystery, she decided to add the book to the pile of things she would put into storage.

A passport from 1956 showed her mother's height as five foot. She may have been small in stature, but Cindy knew she was strong-willed—her mother had always known what she wanted. A NSW police pass from the 1960s showed Mercia looking older, but with the same determined look on her face.

There was also a press permit from 1945, showing a younger Mercia with her hair coiffured up into a neat French roll. This war-time permit allowed her to enter naval, military and air force camps and establishments. It was a nice photo. Cindy kept it.

On one wall of the flat was a framed black-and-white photo that Cindy couldn't remember seeing before. Mercia was pictured with three other women and a bespectacled man; they were sitting on the wheel arch and running board of a vintage car, parked on a sandy track. Mercia looked to be in her late thirties. All of them were impeccably dressed in post–World War II fashions, with one woman sporting a fur stole casually thrown over her shoulders. Who were they? And what were they doing on Mercia's wall?

Among her mother's papers, Cindy found a jumbled pile of dog-eared transcripts from the Royal Commission on Espionage from 1955, with some sections underlined and highlighted. This puzzled her further. Her mother wasn't mentioned in them, so why did she have them?

Cindy had so many questions, and no answers. She put the jumbled pages back in the box and stashed them with the other things that she had decided to keep.

3

MERCIA LEONORA
ZOE MASSON

Mercia Masson had grown up in Sydney's Coogee Bay. She attended St Jude's and St Catherine's, both 'high church' schools run by Church of England nuns.

In 1923 her father, William 'Bill' Masson, a busy A-grade reporter at *The Sun* newspaper, was driving from Sydney to Melbourne in an 'open tourer' (an early large four- or five-seat open-topped car) to cover a major story that was gripping the nation—the 'Buckley Murder' case, in which a bank manager had been shot and killed in a botched robbery in Melbourne. Bill Masson had been sent down to cover it, but on the way he was involved in an accident. He returned to Sydney a quadriplegic.

Mercia was only ten at the time of the accident. She and her mother, together with his siblings, would visit him regularly at the private hospital in Randwick that became his home. *The Sun* continued to pay his wage, despite his inability to work.

After leaving school, Mercia completed a diploma in physical education in 1938; she had always been athletic and active. Then, on her father's recommendation, she sought a cadetship with *The Age* in Melbourne, as he felt it offered the best possible journalistic training.

And it was in Melbourne, in 1939, that Mercia met and married a masseur, Baden Geeves, who was seven years her senior—a marriage that her daughter, Cindy, never knew about during her mother's lifetime.

The new Mr and Mrs Geeves lived in St Kilda. Baden began working as a fruit exporter for his family's business; Mercia became involved with charity and social groups, entertaining and organising piano and musical recitals as World War II loomed. Baden enlisted in the army in October that year, at the age of 33, and embarked for Palestine with the 2/7th Battalion on 15 April 1940.

A few months after her husband left for the war, Mercia left Melbourne for a new job in another city. One of the items that Cindy recognised among her mother's belongings was an engraved silver cigarette case, with an inscription dated 19 June 1940—given to her mother by staff at the Melbourne *Age* on her last day at work. Moving to Newcastle, Mercia became editor of *The Newcastle Morning Herald*, and began living at the Great Northern Hotel, a five-storey Art Deco–style hotel in Scott Street, which had been completed only two years earlier.

Outside of work, Mercia was also doing her bit for the war, busily recruiting for the Australian Women's Land Army—an organisation (based on a British model) that managed to keep farms running while so many of the nation's young men were busy fighting abroad. The Land Army Girls, as they liked to be called, would sign up for twelve months work on a farm, or in an auxiliary role for seasonal work, to fill the resulting rural labour shortages. The girls were housed in hostels, given formal training in farming, and were paid by the farmer rather than the government or the military. They kept the farms working and the people fed. Each state had their own army of girls, and Mercia was busy recruiting for New South Wales.

Baden returned to Sydney on 9 January 1943 on military leave, moving into the Coogee home of her mother. Mercia left Newcastle for Sydney when her husband returned, but still kept recruiting for the Women's Land Army.

On 24 February 1943, Baden was medically classified as suffering from mild anxiety. He would eventually be discharged from the army on 20 October 1944, being required for employment in a reserved occupation.

When Mercia later remarried, she recorded that she had been widowed on 17 March 1943. It seems that was the day Baden was discharged from Mercia's life as well.

4

'CATHERINE'

Cindy was born in 1944. Her father was Harry Pearce, but she has no knowledge of how her father and mother first met.

The first two years of Cindy's life were spent living with her parents in a humble weekender, which she came to know well and would later often visit as a child and young adult. It was a holiday house at Killcare on the Central Coast, north of Sydney. Mercia's parents had bought the isolated block overlooking the ocean in the 1920s and built a little beach house on it, with an outhouse further up the hill. Cindy always thought that little outhouse had one of the most spectacular ocean views in Australia.

The block was remote and the landscape breathtaking, a perfect place to 'kill your cares' as the locality name suggested. They called the house 'Catherine', after Mercia's paternal grandmother, Catherine McDonald. Mercia was proud of her Scottish ancestry on her father's side—but spoke little about her own mother, Lucy, who had been born in Sydney in 1893 to a young servant girl, Annie Archer. Annie had been abandoned at the Randwick Asylum for Destitute Children at the age of three. It is not known if Mr Protti, Lucy's father, and Annie were ever married, and he disappears from records around 1913, when Lucy would have been about twenty years of age. For Mercia, the Masson side of the family was far more socially palatable when explaining her heritage.

One of Cindy's earliest memories is of sitting and playing out in the sun on the sandy track outside 'Catherine', safe in the knowledge that her father was nearby. Those distant memories are still the most comfortable of her childhood.

Unusually at the time, Mercia had returned to work as a journalist in Sydney after giving birth to Cindy, and Cindy's father looked after her at their little house on the hill. The journey from the city to Killcare was a long and difficult trip. Today with the freeway, it still takes an hour and a half by road, but back then you wound your way through Sydney's northern suburbs, turning off after crossing the Hawkesbury River and following the Scenic Road, back then a sandy track that could take hours for a bus to traverse. With World War II still raging and petrol rationing in place, to get to the city it was quicker and easier for Mercia to walk over and down the steep hill to Killcare jetty and catch a little launch across Brisbane Waters to the Woy Woy Railway Station, where she would then take the 45-mile (72-kilometre) rail journey to Sydney by steam train.

But, at the age of two, Mercia disappeared from her daughter's life. Cindy went with her father, Harry, to live in Newcastle with her teenage half-sister, Judy, at the house of Harry's mother, Ruth.

Harry had become a widower a year before Cindy was born, and had two previous children—his son, who was in the navy, and Judy. Harry's father had started the Pearce Prestige bakery in the Newcastle suburb of Hamilton, and Harry returned to work there as a baker.

Cindy always found it funny that her father baked bread for a living, but at home he liked his toast burnt black. He was a heavy drinker and a gambler, often going to the races. He was rarely around, but Cindy remembers him as a happy drunk.

They lived in a little house in Gordon Avenue, Hamilton, where Cindy shared an old double bed with her grandmother. The mattress sagged in the middle, and Cindy used to wet the bed as a child. Her grandmother would wake up in a damp patch each morning, and there would be hell to pay.

There was always a chair beside the bed, and every night, the little girl would have to say her prayers at it, facing a picture of Jesus on the wall. If Cindy was ever upset or in trouble, she'd have to pray at that chair. Her grandmother would knock three times on the underside of the bed and say, 'Hear that? It's Jesus coming to get you and he will punish you.' It literally put the fear of God into her.

Cindy doesn't remember this home as being a happy place. If there was a family outing and not enough room for her in her uncle's car, she'd be left behind, and the bedroom with her toys would be locked. She was not allowed to bring friends home from school or to visit them. Her only solace at that time was Sunday school, where she'd be left in peace.

Her stepsister, Judy, was fifteen years older than her, and Cindy felt she was jealous of her. None of the Pearce family was affectionate to her, as she recalls. The only one who showed her any kindness was her dad's twin sister, Iris, who would at least acknowledge her. Everyone else pretended she wasn't there, rarely talking to her unless she was in trouble.

One of Cindy's earliest memories was of her father taking her on the train to Luna Park in Sydney as a treat, pointing out the trees as they whizzed by, saying they were chasing each other. In all the excitement at Luna Park, Cindy's weak bladder let go at the top of the ferris wheel, and she felt nothing but shame. On the way back, as night fell, her father pointed out the evening star, and said the stars were all the people she loved who were in heaven. The little girl didn't think she knew that many people.

※

When she was nine or ten, her father took Cindy on another train journey, saying she was going to have a holiday with her mother. The little girl was curious: she didn't really know her mother, but a holiday sounded nice. With her clothes packed in a little suitcase, they caught the train to Sydney and met Mercia at Central Station. Mother and daughter then took the train to Melbourne, changing at Albury in the dead of night.

Cindy eventually realised that she was not going back to Newcastle, though this was never explained to her, as she recalls. She'd thought she was travelling to Melbourne for a holiday and regretted not sneaking some of her toys into her suitcase.

Her mother enrolled Cindy at St Michael's in St Kilda, another high church school run by Church of England nuns, and at the time a single-sex school. To Mercia's horror, Harry had recorded their daughter as Cynthia Violet Pearce on her birth certificate, instead of Cynthia Ann Pearce. Cindy's name was promptly changed by deed poll—and she was now officially Cynthia Ann Masson. Her mother was working professionally as Mercia Masson, and this change in surname also aligned with Mercia having told everyone in Melbourne that she was a war widow. Harry Pearce was no longer a part of their family.

Cindy felt like she had landed in another loveless house. She was given lessons in playing the piano, ice skating, ballet and elocution, but no affection. When she was older, another activity joined the list, with Mercia sending Cindy to live at a riding school in the Dandenong Ranges on weekends.

Mercia was giving her daughter an education and time with other people—but as a little girl, Cindy longed to be held by her mother and told everything would be all right. That didn't happen. Sometimes a housekeeper—rarely the same woman—would come in and cook for Cindy if Mercia was away covering a story for the newspaper.

Cindy felt she grew up quickly, often doing her own washing and ironing—a latch-key child, letting herself into the house in St Kilda after school when no one was around. Her mother was a career woman, not a housewife.

Mercia and Cindy developed a routine, of sorts. Mercia would come home, they'd often share a meal, go to bed, get up in the morning and go their separate ways, Cindy to school and Mercia to work. Weekends were a little different. Every Friday night they would go to the fashionable Hotel Australia for dinner, where Mercia would sometimes meet up with people. Despite her mother insisting she try something else from the à la carte menu, Cindy always ordered a pie and chips, and wouldn't be swayed. Her mother told her she was 'common', her worst insult. One time, when her mother took her to the ballet, and Cindy accidentally dropped her ice cream over the balcony onto the people below, her mother told her she was disruptive.

Sometimes Mercia would take her along to the newspaper where she worked. Cindy has a photo of herself playing with a piece of silver paper while sitting in the printing room. She remembers sitting there while the presses were running, trying not to be disruptive, being quiet in a noisy room while her mother was working somewhere else in the building. Cindy feels that this was her childhood—offloaded, to anybody and everybody.

In Melbourne, Cindy had not been encouraged to mix with other children; her time was instead filled with after-school activities. Mercia didn't mix with any parents at Cindy's school, and Cindy can't recall her attending any school functions. The only adults they socialised with—including the Friday night treats at the Hotel Australia—were Mercia's work colleagues.

On Saturdays they would catch a tram to the Prahran Markets, where Mercia would do the weekly shopping and Cindy would be allowed to wander through the markets alone. The other weekend outing was to catch a tram from Swanston Street on a Sunday morning to pick up the Sydney papers from the airline terminal, buying a baked rabbit for dinner on the way home. Mercia would then sit and read the local and interstate papers throughout the day, ready for work the following week.

Cindy made friends at St Michael's, and took a keen interest in Australian Rules football. She and her friends would watch their local football team—St Kilda—train, but her mother disapproved and told her it was common. So common.

5

SPIES AND THEIR SECRETS

In 1994, a friend gave Cindy a book called *Australia's Spies and their Secrets*, saying it mentioned her mother. Amazed, Cindy found it contained a short two-page section about her mother. She didn't understand all the references, so she started reading the book from the beginning—about the birth of the Australian Security Intelligence Organisation (ASIO), the hunt for Soviet spies, the Petrov defection, and the Royal Commission on Espionage. And then Cindy remembered the dog-eared transcripts she had found among her mother's belongings. With some incredulity, she began to wonder if perhaps her mother *could* have a been a spy. She wanted to know more.

She became angry. If it *was* true, her own mother hadn't confided in her about that tumultuous time. Hadn't told her even the smallest bit about what she'd been going through. Not even when Cindy was an adult. Now, with so much time elapsed, Cindy didn't know anyone who'd been directly connected with her mother who could tell her about that time.

Cindy was, and still is, a part-time exam supervisor at the University of Technology Sydney and has an uncanny knack of knowing when people are cheating. Notes written out on hair ribbons, notes hidden in toilets, down socks—so many weird and inventive ways. Cindy feels she has seen them all.

But yet again, when it came to her own mother, she had more questions than answers. So she decided to track down David McKnight, the author of *Australia's Spies and their Secrets*, to find out what he could tell her. As luck would have it, David was a lecturer at the UTS, the university where she worked, so she sent him an email. David had since moved on, but her email eventually reached him and he agreed to talk with her.

David explained Mercia's espionage involvement as far as he knew it, then suggested she contact the National Archives of Australia, asking to see her mother's ASIO files. As Mercia had been dead for over 30 years and Cindy was a family member, they might release the files to her, which might help answer many of her questions. The question Cindy most wanted answered was: who *was* her mother, really? Who was Mercia Masson? Mercia seemed to be another person, entirely separate from the person Cindy recognised as being her mother.

Cindy had been living for some time at Elanora Heights with her family, and she had loved being a mum and raising her children, though she didn't feel like she had any support from her husband. She used to spoil her kids with treats and attend as many school and sporting functions as she could, something she had not received from her own mother. Cindy lost her first child, a little boy, as a baby—not quite a year after Mercia passed away. By the time she had the conversation with David McKnight, Cindy and her husband were separated and had started divorce proceedings. She still regrets not listening to the one piece of advice her mother ever gave her: don't marry Mr Dobbin. Her mother had never liked him. But when all her friends were married and she herself was approaching thirty years of age, Cindy had disregarded her mother's words.

The separation and divorce was drawn-out and painful, both emotionally and financially. With the divorce proceedings underway Cindy decided not to contact the National Archives right away. She was already dealing with enough.

In 1998, Cindy's son Kieron was going out with an English girl, who told her about a wonderful clairvoyant she had seen, and how this woman had known so much about her family, without being told. Even though she didn't actually believe in such things, Cindy made an appointment to see the clairvoyant: perhaps she'd get some answers this way?

At the beginning of their session, the clairvoyant looked over Cindy's shoulder and said she could see a spirit crying, sobbing, and that it was her mother. She then told Cindy that her mother wanted to know where her rosary beads were. Cindy thought to herself, *Didn't she want to know something more interesting?* Cindy told the woman the rosary beads were by her own bedside table, and that she herself used them at night.

The clairvoyant then held Cindy's hand and said she had never seen a spirit so upset: 'She keeps asking you to forgive her.' Cindy came away from that meeting wondering what on earth the woman had been on about.

※

At the end of the divorce proceedings, Cindy was left with one thing to call her own: 'Catherine', the small weekender at Killcare that her grandparents, and then her mother, had owned. Her children had all left home by this stage and had started lives of their own. When packing for her move to Killcare, Cindy came across some of the strange items she'd kept from her mother's house, including pages and pages of transcripts from the 1954/1955 Royal Commission on Espionage. Cindy re-read the passages that she assumed her mother had underlined— but again, none of it made any sense to her.

Late in 2010, she decided it was time to find out the truth: had her mother really been a spy? She wrote to the National Archives of Australia, asking to view her mother's files.

In May 2011, a letter arrived from an archives reference Officer advising Cindy that she could access any Commonwealth record that was classified 'open access', and not considered to be of continuing sensitivity. However, security records were generally held by ASIO, and to gain access to these, she would need to fill out an application form giving the full name and date of birth of the person she was researching, any alias they used, the city or town or state in which they had lived, and any activities they had been involved in which might have attracted ASIO attention.

Cindy filled out the enclosed application form, mailed it off, and waited.

6

THE MAN FROM ASIO

Cindy came home one night to find a telephone message on her answering machine. The caller didn't give his name, just a telephone number. The following day, she rang the number, and it was answered by a man who said he was from ASIO, and explained that the National Archives had forwarded her letter to them.

Surprisingly, ASIO had actually been planning on contacting her, because they had commissioned a team of historians from the Australian National University to write the history of the organisation and they wanted to include her mother in it. The man went on to say that, even though they couldn't write a great deal about Mercia, they needed family permission to do so.

Cindy now had official confirmation that her mother had indeed been a spy.

As the only family Mercia had, and determined to find out more about her mother, Cindy told him she wanted to see what was in her mother's files before she agreed to anything. He said the files were closed, and not available even to family—but Cindy insisted that if they wanted her permission, they had to let her read the files.

A compromise was struck: if Cindy and one other family member could make their way to the ASIO offices, they would be allowed to read each of Mercia's files in their entirety—but Cindy would only be allowed two separate days to do this.

Cindy asked her eldest son, Kieron, who agreed to come along and who was quite excited at the prospect of his grandmother being a real spy.

On their first trip down, on a wintery Friday in August 2011, Cindy listened in amusement as her son fielded work calls in the car, telling people with some mystery that he was on the way to the ASIO offices in Canberra to review some files.

The suburb of Russell has no residential area—it's just a large cluster of buildings housing the Department of Defence, administration offices for the armed forces, and ASIO. They arrived, late for their appointment, at the then-ASIO office, with Cindy feeling flustered. Kieron parked the car and they made their way into the four-storey building. Outside, the nondescript concrete office building looked run down, and the new office was being built at the time. It didn't look like a high security building as you drove past, and the inside was plain and small.

On entering the building, Cindy and Kieron were directed to put mobile phones, keys and whatever was in their pockets into security lockers. The lockers started at 001, Kieron checked for 007 and as it was free, he placed his belongings in there. They were then directed to pass through airport-like metal detectors and then down a hall and to the left, into the meeting room. The room was a bland white-walled conference room, and they were directed to sit on one side of the conference table, with four people seated on the other side. Introductions were made. There was a researcher for the upcoming book on the history of ASIO. The other three people were ASIO representatives who were there to observe and answer questions.

An ASIO official started the morning's proceedings by delivering an hour-long speech, explaining Mercia's importance to the organisation. In a nutshell, Mercia had originally been identified as a person with the right skills and strong connections to journalists, artists and high-society people, allowing access to the inner workings of a range of networks of interest to ASIO at the time. And Mercia was ultimately one of their longest-serving undercover agents, working for the security services for nearly thirteen years, when most only managed their double lives for two or three years.

'Are you sure we're talking about the same person?' Cindy asked at one point. All Cindy really wanted to do was to look at the files and get some answers.

Before Cindy and Kieron were finally allowed to start reading through the files that were stacked in the middle of the table, they were both firmly warned that nothing could be copied or taken out of the room.

Opening the first file, Cindy immediately found a vast number of redactions—details had been fully obscured using a black pen, or some bits had been cut out of pages, often in large blocks, to conceal details that ASIO still viewed as a security risk. And there was a lot of black, everywhere. Some file contents were missing entirely, the words 'Withdrawn Permanently' being written on the record.

Not everything that Mercia had been involved with could be shared, not even with her immediate family.

The large vanilla-coloured files before them were in chronological order to a degree, though often the same facts were repeated or expanded in the other file. None of it made much sense to Cindy; it was only when she came across reports sent by her mother that memories flooded back. It wasn't the contents that brought back distressing memories to Cindy it was the thought of her mother typing away late at night in Melbourne. Her mother's reports in the files had the same typeface defects that she recognised from the old typewriter her mother had used in their St Kilda home, with certain letters always out of line. Painful memories came back to her—of a distant mother, working day and night, with little time for her daughter.

Kieron remembers that his mother was quiet in the two meetings they had with ASIO, it was the other people in the room who asked most of the questions of her. Cindy was allowed to ask questions as she read through the files, but felt that when she started to get more inquisitive about certain things mentioned in the files, the ASIO staff tended to become more close-lipped.

There were many revelations for her, as well as many unanswered questions.

Cindy was surprised by *who* was mentioned in the files—her family, her neighbours, even her grandmother's neighbours. No one seemed too insignificant.

One of the most astonishing discoveries was that her mother had been married to a Mr Geeves before meeting her father. Learning that her mother had been married to another man before she was born came as quite a shock—the first of many.

'Were my mother and Mr Geeves divorced?' she asked.

'Yes.'

Her next shock was that her *own* parents weren't married.

Cindy returned home exhausted. That night she rang her half-sister, Judy, to ask if she knew that her parents were not married.

Judy's reply hit her hard. 'You mean you didn't know?'

Suddenly the treatment she had received from her father's side of the family made sense. She was an illegitimate child—something that would have brought great shame to the family back in the 1940s and 1950s. Why hadn't anyone told her?

It would take days for her to get over that first visit.

7

THE TRIBUNE

When her husband, Baden Geeves, returned from the war in 1943, Mercia moved from Newcastle and her job at *The Newcastle Morning Herald* to join him in Sydney, working at *The Sun*, her father's old paper, where she became the assistant editor of the women's section. At this time she was also presenting radio programs on classical music and literature, two of her great loves.

And then there was her unpaid work—with Australia's security services.

Mercia became associated with an unnamed officer from the naval intelligence service. At the time, defence and national intelligence were shared between the Navy, Army and Air Force Intelligence Directorates, overseen by the Joint Intelligence Bureau. Mercia began her undercover career by passing on information about groups of interest, including the Communist Party.

Membership of the Communist Party of Australia (CPA) had steadily increased since its inception in 1920, peaking during the Second World War, with many Communists prominent in trade unions, as well as in cultural, theatrical and literary circles, which Mercia mixed in.

Being a journalist offered good cover for her clandestine work. As well as socialising and reporting on people of interest in social situations, as a member of the press she could attend public meetings and rallies, and record speeches verbatim, without raising suspicion.

The power of the written word was also being used extensively by the CPA, spreading both union and Communist news through its newspapers and printed booklets and pamphlets as the war continued.

In mid-1939, the CPA had appointed a new campaign director and sales manager for the largest of their newspapers, *The Workers' Weekly*. Like many members, Walter 'Wally' Seddon Clayton—a tall, thin bespectacled man—had joined the CPA after seeing the impact of the Great Depression years on the working class. Wally was highly regarded within the Party for both his public speaking and his organisational capabilities. He and his wife moved from Melbourne to Sydney to take up the position. That same year, *The Workers' Weekly* changed its name to the *Tribune*.

Wally was also involved with the New Theatre League, which had been started just seven years before, then called the Sydney Workers Art Club. They were performing socialist and pro-Communist plays that were regularly reviewed in the *Tribune*, but tended to be ignored by other newspapers. A name change in the early 1950s would see it become known as the New Theatre and, unlike many other then Communist fringe groups from this time, it is still operating.

In August 1939—to the surprise of many, including members of the CPA—Germany and the Soviet Union, which had been enemies during the First World War, signed a pact to invade and divide Poland. The Soviet Union would supply Germany with oil; in return, the Nazi Party promised to reverse their negative stance against Communists worldwide. Being a Communist publication, the *Tribune* promoted the CPA and sided with the Soviet Union.

By April 1940, the Menzies United Australia government, frustrated with the anti-war messaging coming from Communist publications, and fearing it was weakening the war effort at home, announced that it was going to censor all Communist publications, including one of its largest, the *Tribune*. On 24 May 1940, the *Tribune* was banned from publication, along with other Communist papers.

By June, the government also outlawed the CPA—a move the CPA had been anticipating. Utilising Wally Clayton's organisational skills, its printing presses and high-profile CPA members went underground. The *Tribune* continued to be published illegally from the end of July 1940, using a manual printing press, which the security services failed to find.

In June 1941, the CPA stance on Australia's involvement in the war changed abruptly. Germany had turned on Russia, opening up the Eastern Front of the war; in retaliation, the Soviet Union quickly allied itself with Britain and America. Nazi Germany and Fascism had become the common enemy of both the Soviet Union and Australia, and the Communist publications followed the move.

The CPA's legal standing was restored in December 1942 by the new Labor government, after the United Australia Party was voted out of office, with the new Prime Minister, John Curtin, asking that the CPA assist with the war effort, not hinder it.

On 3 June 1943, the *Tribune* reappeared—this time as *Tribune: The People's Paper,* an eight-page paper printed once a week.

The CPA's membership had started rising after June 1941, when the Soviets became Australia's ally and friend.

We were all on the same side of the war against Fascism.

8

TWO JOBS

Mercia moved from the Sydney *Sun* to *The Daily Telegraph* in 1945 to work under its new editor, Brian Penton, covering parliament, police and general reporting.

As well, she continued assisting the Women's Land Army and was seconded to its main office. In charge of recruiting, and leading a combined team, she felt useful—supporting the war effort, supporting what she believed in.

She was still also involved with naval intelligence. It is not publicly known exactly what 'tradecraft' skills or training she received for her security work—but her courage and tenacity were on public display during the last year of the war.

On 27 May 1945, Mercia and fellow reporter Maureen Byrne were sent to cover a story in Dover Heights, north of Bondi. A car had crashed through a safety rail and plunged 300 feet (91 metres) off a cliff into the ocean the previous night. Early that morning, the two female reporters boarded a press launch and were driven out of the harbour and down the coast towards Bondi Beach, expecting to watch and photograph a police rescue underway.

When they arrived at the scene, they found themselves alone on the water, with crowds of onlookers watching from the clifftop. They were about 50 yards (45 metres) from where they estimated the car had gone in, but they couldn't see it in the deep water.

As Maureen was taking photos of the crowd on the cliff, someone called out, 'There's a body there!' pointing to the swirling water at the bottom of the cliff.

The launch driver moved them in closer and they could see the body of a young woman bobbing on the surface, her long black hair often hidden by her dress, which was washing over her head with the movement of the waves. The strong currents were carrying her body north along the coast. But it would be stopped, minutes at a time, by eddies that whirled around submerged rocks.

Deciding to retrieve the unfortunate woman's body, the launch driver asked Mercia to take the wheel and showed her how to hold a course and to keep the boat's bow pointing out into the ocean, in case they came too close to the rocks and needed to get away in a hurry.

Waves were breaking over the launch, which rolled and pitched as the driver handed a boat hook to Maureen and fashioned for himself a lasso out of a mop and a length of rope. During calmer spells, Mercia backed the launch towards the body being dashed about. The wash was threatening to sweep the body away from them; at other times, it was in danger of being caught up in the launch's propeller.

Maureen managed to snag the dead woman's underclothes with the hook. But it took another 15 minutes for the launch driver, with the aid of the mop, to manoeuvre a rope around the body and secure it. At one stage Mercia had to let go of the wheel and grab Maureen by the skirt to stop her falling overboard, as the rolling waves threw the launch about.

With the body secure against the boat's side, Mercia slowly steered it out into less turbulent water. But, as they stopped to drag the body on board, its added weight caused the launch to roll, and they all narrowly escaped being thrown into the sea by another wave.

31

With the battered body finally on board, they drove along the coast and back into the harbour, where they were met by the police launch, *Osiris*, which took the body and thanked them for their efforts.

The woman, a divorcee from Bondi, had been a passenger in the car. The body of the driver, a married man from Croydon, would later be removed from the submerged car.

In the press report, Mercia was very matter of fact. She detailed what had happened, when and how; any quotes from her held very little, or no, emotion. Good traits to have as a journalist—and a spy.

9

A COLD WAR

At the end of the Second World War, a Cold War—a war without open battlefields—started between the United States and the Union of Soviet Socialist Republics. The USSR, soon to be joined by China, was governed along Communist principles with totalitarian rulers; America and her allies had Capitalist economies, with democratically elected leaders.

The Communist Party of Australia had started in 1920 and was embraced in Australia by many unemployed people during the Great Depression in the early 1930s, and then again as allies against Nazi Germany. As Communism spread across Eastern Europe under Stalin, and Russia worked towards becoming a nuclear power, the USSR was no longer seen as Australia's friend. People involved with the Communist Party were once again of interest to the Australian security services—and subsequently to Mercia, who would move from supplying information to naval intelligence to the Commonwealth Investigation Service (CIS), which took over some of the security intelligence functions from the military. She was also passing information to Dick Gamble of the NSW Police, mostly about fringe groups of the Communist Party, such as the peace movement organisations and their members.

In August 1945, the use of atomic weapons against Japan led to a nuclear arms race, with both America and the Soviets conducting atomic research and tests. Keeping their research secret from each other became a high priority in their quest to further develop their atomic arsenals. The United Kingdom also wanted to test nuclear weapons—asking Australia, with its vast, remote and scarcely populated outback areas, to help by providing a place where these tests could take place.

Australia had already proven to be a lucrative source of intelligence for the Soviet Union throughout the war—a fact that only became evident in July 1946, when the United States finally broke the code to the Soviet communications they had been intercepting between Moscow and its embassies worldwide. The top-secret VENONA program, as it would become known, revealed a web of espionage networks operating throughout Australia, Canada, Britain and the United States—with the Americans successfully deciphering almost 3000 Soviet messages dating back to 1940. So covert was VENONA that the Soviets remained unaware that their code had been broken, and continued sending their encrypted communications.

The leaks from Australia were serious, involving highly secret and sensitive information. From the deciphered messages, the Americans only had cover or code names for those thought to be providing information to the Soviet Union. The leaks appeared to be coming from unknown public servants who were at least sympathetic to the CPA, if not Party members.

Britain was informed about VENONA in 1947 and, together with the US security agencies, they set about trying to identify the individuals involved in their own countries.

VENONA revealed to the Americans the extent of the espionage ring in Australia, and the amount of information emanating from the Soviet Embassy in Canberra to Moscow. And because the Australian Prime Minister Ben Chifley and his Labor Party government had been reluctant to become involved with the escalating Cold War—Chifley later stating that he preferred to 'deal with the Communists in the open'—the United States decided not to reveal VENONA's existence to Australia.

America's fears that information from top-secret security meetings between Australia, the United States and Britain could be leaked to the Soviets were realised when a post-war planning document titled 'Security in the Western Mediterranean and the Eastern Atlantic' came into the hands of the Soviets, having been leaked from Australia's Department of External Affairs.

A location in outback South Australia had now been chosen as the preferred site for atomic experiments by the United Kingdom. However, still concerned about the security leaks in Australia, the British prime minister asked the Director-General of MI5 to brief Chifley about the security problems in Australia, and to discuss ways to improve the situation—without revealing the existence of VENONA.

In June 1948, Britain declared a state of emergency in Malaya, which was then a British colony, after attacks on rubber plantations by left-wing activists associated with members of the Malayan Communist Party. Robert Menzies, the Leader of the Opposition, visited Britain the following month and witnessed the start of the Berlin Blockade. After the Second World War, Germany had been divided into four temporary occupation zones, controlled by the four occupying Allied powers: France, the United Kingdom, the United States and the Soviet Union, who controlled the eastern zone. The capital of Germany, Berlin, was also divided into four and surrounded by the Soviets who closed the land corridors to the city, cut telephone lines and blocked food and water supplies in an attempt to remove the now isolated Allied personnel out of West Berlin. After returning to Australia, Menzies declared that the Communist Party could no longer be tolerated.

On 24 July 1948, during the Berlin Blockade, *The Sydney Morning Herald* broke a front-page story about America's reluctance to share its atomic research secrets, and the possibility of security leaks from Australia. Sharing that same front page were articles about a Communist arrested in America, the banning of Communism in Malaya, and domestic unrest on the wharves and in coal mines. The fear of Communism was rising throughout the general population.

To add to mounting fears about the threat of Communism, that August, the Soviet Union successfully tested an atomic bomb in the desert outside Semipalatinsk, in north-east Kazakhstan.

Then, on 1 October, Mao Zedong proclaimed the People's Republic of China, after victory by the Chinese Communist Party in the long-running Chinese Civil War.

In Australia, in the lead-up to the December 1949 election, banning the Communist Party of Australia became a new policy for Robert Menzies' newly rebranded Liberal Party.

10

POST-WAR RECONSTRUCTION

After she separated from Harry Pearce in 1946, and left Cindy with him, Mercia obtained a job as the public relations officer for the Department of Post-War Reconstruction, which had been established during the war, and was responsible for planning and coordinating Australia's transition to a peacetime economy, as well as looking after returned servicemen and their families.

Mercia was initially responsible for the public relation activities for each of the eight divisions within the ministry, preparing advisory booklets for ex-servicemen. With her public speaking experience, from her time recruiting with the Land Army, she also gave lectures and talks as required.

She had received the position on the recommendation of the previous public relations officer, who had been transferred to Japan. So unusual was it for a woman to be placed in such a key position that the monthly women's journal, *The Dawn*, even made mention of her work in the department.

Mercia became involved with sending out confidential surveys across the country, requesting details about the goods that different companies produced, where and how much, and then helping to collate the information, as Australia was seen by the United States as a potential food bowl for the Pacific in the event of future conflict and war.

Mercia would have felt of use, working for the good of the country.

Her journalistic skills were recognised at a high level when she started to prepare radio scripts and speeches for the Minister for the Department of Post-War Reconstruction, John Dedman—and then weekly speeches for the Labor Prime Minister, Ben Chifley, who began using radio as a means of reaching the public, and Mercia helped him to write his Sunday evening 'Report to the Nation' radio broadcasts. The Prime Minister's first address spoke of the Commonwealth's post-war economic woes and the need for Australia to increase production, both for the nation and for international trade, and urgently called for a production conference of employers and union representatives within a month.

Brisbane's *Courier-Mail* printed some of Chifley's first address, concluding with a quote from the annual report of the Queensland Employers Federation, stating that 'employer–union talks as a means of stepping up production would be worse than useless, while Communists were allowed to dominate the scene'. Communism was seen as threatening Australia's prosperity—and trade unions were seen, at least by employer groups, to be dominated by those loyal to the CPA.

Mercia also continued her intelligence work with the newly formed Commonwealth Investigation Service. Her case officer directed her to infiltrate left-wing activities, initially with journalists, and then public servants who she was working and socialising with—reporting back to her CIS case officer any behaviour she viewed as suspicious or noteworthy.

On the 1949 electoral role, Mercia is listed as living at the Great Northern Hotel in Newcastle. For some reason, she was back in Newcastle again.

Cindy has a black-and-white photo of herself as a little girl, aged about five or six, dressed in warm winter clothing on the roof of the Great Northern Hotel, with its then clear view out to the sea—but she doesn't remember seeing her mother at that age.

In a later job application, Mercia said she transferred to the nation's capital in 1949—at the request of Prime Minister Chifley, who appears to have had an impact on Mercia and her politics; she would later say that her strong belief in the Labor Party stemmed from her time working for him.

A two-page letter signed by Prime Minister Chifley was among the papers kept by Cindy after her mother's death. Dated 19 November 1947, it was addressed to Mr J.K. Jensen O.B.E., a senior public servant and Chair of the Secondary Industries Commission in Melbourne, which was part of the Department of Post-War Reconstruction. In the letter, Chifley urgently requests a meeting with Mr Jensen, expressing his concern about the growing strength of inflationary forces in the economy, and about labour shortages and bottlenecks reducing production output.

Mercia possibly used this letter in preparing one of Mr Chifley's speeches, but it was strange that she brought it home and then kept it among her personal papers until she died.

11

THE MOVE TO ASIO

Mercia must have been concerned about her job with the Department of Post-War Reconstruction if the Liberal Party won office at the upcoming election. On 22 November 1949 she applied for a position as a sub-editor with the Office of Education in Sydney, preparing adult education publications. She had the experience, but was not successful. How different her life might have been had she secured that position.

On 10 December 1949, the Liberal Party led by Robert Menzies swept into government, winning 74 seats with its Coalition partner, the Country Party, to Labor's 47 seats. Throughout the election campaign, Menzies had been publicly accusing the Labor Party of being 'riddled with Communism'—but such was the disdain felt towards the Communist Party in the ongoing Cold War that the Labor Party directed its own preferences to Liberal ahead of Communist candidates.

Within two months of coming into power, Menzies dismantled the Department of Post-War Reconstruction. Mercia moved back to Sydney to work with *The Daily Telegraph*, helping to cover federal politics, and travelling to Canberra regularly as a result. She was getting good at living out of a suitcase.

Operating along the lines of Britain's MI5, the Australian Security Intelligence Organisation (ASIO) had been formed not quite nine months before the election. ASIO took over some of the security functions that had previously belonged to the Commonwealth Investigation Service, and recruited heavily from within its ranks, something that irked those who remained in the CIS.

ASIO also recruited from military and police ranks—Dick Gamble from the New South Wales police force, George Ronald 'Ron' Richards from the Western Australia Police Special Branch, and Ray Whitrod—who would become Mercia's case officer—from the South Australian police.

ASIO's initial focus was on gathering information on the Communist Party in Australia, as well as finding any government leaks. By the time ASIO was formed, VENONA had identified about a dozen individual cover or code names in the deciphered messages between Moscow Central and Canberra. Two of these were BUR and TURIST—thought to be individuals in Australia's Department of External Affairs, which was referred to in the deciphered messages as NOOK, and was the source of the leaked US post-war planning document two years previously. It was thought that BUR and TURIST had handed over copies of these documents to another person, identified only as KLOD, a Russian variant of the name Claude.

In the first year of ASIO's operation, Ray Whitrod and his team initially pulled together clues from previous intercepts and surveillance. The team then followed members of the Australian Communist Party and its Central Committee, finding out who they were associating with and trying to identify sympathisers within the Australian Government public service and elsewhere.

With her experience infiltrating Communist-front organisations, Mercia was one of the agents who moved from the Commonwealth Investigation Service to ASIO. She was introduced to Ray Whitrod by her old CIS case officer and joined the B2 team, tracking down members of the espionage network that had developed in Australia during the war. She became involved with the peace movement through the Australian Peace Council, which was thought to be a fringe group of the CPA.

Another member of Whitrod's B2 team was Moya Horowitz, a young woman who had been in naval intelligence with Mercia. In one early surveillance effort, Ray Whitrod and Moya sat in a car, staking out a person of interest; it was felt that a man and a woman being together in a car looked less suspicious than a man sitting alone.

Mercia's work was not nearly as cloak and dagger. She was gathering information and reporting on social gatherings, as well as on events and rallies organised by groups of interest. ASIO's formal character assessment of Mercia at this time concluded that 'her motivation for working as an agent was partly patriotism and partly out of frustration'—attributing her 'frustration' to the fact that she was a separated woman, and therefore needed to feel wanted. Needed to feel important.

When Mercia was asked by ASIO what agent pseudonym she wanted, she chose her paternal grandmother's name: 'Catherine McDonald'.

12

THE TARGET

One of Ray Whitrod's first counter-espionage targets was the TASS journalist Fedor Nosov. The Telegraph Agency of the Soviet Union (*Telegrafnoye Agentstvo Sovetskogo Soyuza*) was, and still is, a major state-owned Russian news agency. As TASS was an official organisation of the Soviet State, it was entitled to full diplomatic immunity, and had access to diplomatic pouches, in which documents were able to be sent in and out of the country without interference.

Fedor Nosov was thought to be TEKHNIK (TECHNICIAN) in the VENONA files. As a journalist, Nosov was given access to certain government information, but ASIO also noted that he was responsible for contacting Soviet couriers, and that he had access to the diplomatic pouches on their arrival and departure from Australia, and on their journeys from the Soviet Embassy in Canberra to Sydney. The sharing of information between journalists was not uncommon, but ASIO's main fear was that national security secrets were being passed back to Moscow under diplomatic protection.

Nosov's residence was put under surveillance from 7 December 1949. And the next day, ASIO's very first audio surveillance was carried out in Nosov's Kings Cross flat, in an investigation led by Ray Whitrod. On 8 December, Whitrod gained access to the apartment above Nosov's flat while the TASS man and his wife were out, and he attempted to drill a hole through the floor to install a listening device into Nosov's ceiling. However, the flats were old, and the ceiling below was flaky, and when Whitrod looked through the hole he had created, he saw that bits of ceiling had dropped off onto the floor below. He quickly inserted a microphone, then hastily persuaded the building caretaker to let them into Nosov's flat to clean up the mess. Whitrod, when interviewed years later for the ABC television show *Timeframe*, remembered the event and his inexperience with a laugh.

Observations of Nosov's flat gave ASIO leads to follow. Some were fruitful, some not. ASIO discovered that on 6 December 1949, an Australian journalist, Rex Chiplin, met Nosov at his flat and had taken delivery of photographs and articles relating to Soviet Constitution Day, which subsequently appeared in issues of the *Tribune*. Rex worked at the *Tribune* with two other journalists, Len Fox and Bill Brown (whose wife, Freda Brown, was a member of the Central Committee of the CPA). ASIO noted that Rex had also been linked with other Sydney CPA members.

TASS was the only newspaper source for Soviet news in Australia, and Rex would often go to Nosov's flat to look at news photos, stories and features that could be used in the *Tribune*. ASIO would have been concerned that Rex was a potential source—or even a courier—for information to the Soviets, and he was immediately under suspicion.

On 4 January 1950, ASIO also noted that the Vice-Consul of the Czech Consulate received some files from Rex Chiplin, consisting of information relating to court procedures. ASIO then became aware that Chiplin was going to call on Nosov a few weeks later, at 9 a.m. on 7 February 1950, to collect a Russian Central Statistical Board report from the previous year. Nosov would go on to ask Chiplin to obtain some information concerning Australian parliamentary statistics, which Chiplin subsequently did.

Rex was well and truly on ASIO's radar.

Rex Chiplin appeared on the list of *Tribune* staff from July 1949, writing a regular column for the paper. In March 1950 he turned up at the press gallery at Parliament House as the *Tribune*'s parliamentary reporter, attending two or three times a week when parliament was sitting.

Rex told members of the press gallery that he was replacing the *Tribune*'s reporter Rupert Lockwood, who had left for Stockholm to cover the Council of World Federation of Trade Unions. Rex thought it could be a short trip, or not, as Lockwood was also writing for trade union papers while overseas, making enough cash to get through.

ASIO's later description of Rex is anything but flattering:

Large and fat, with a thick mop of untidy black hair pushed straight back. Small eyes, horn-rimmed glasses. Close-cropped moustache. Smokes a pipe. Untidy. The eccentric city newspaperman type, flashy, hail-fellow-well-met, very approachable, great vitality, effervescent, exuberant, never still, always joking and ridiculing. He is erratic and boisterous and lives in a whirl of confusion. He has a smart turn of phrase, a malicious pen, and is regarded by some as a good hack journalist. He seems incapable of or is not entrusted with serious ideological exegesis. He is shrewd, irresponsible, unscrupulous, and conspiratorial.

For Mercia, travel between Sydney and Canberra was a regular occurrence for her work at *The Daily Telegraph*, staying in a hotel when parliament was in session. With Mercia's espionage experience, her knowledge of Canberra and her work as a journalist, she was perfectly placed to find out more about Rex and other possible CPA members in the press gallery.

Canberra was, and still is, a small capital city; all the journalists knew each other. At the time, all press gallery journalists had to be members of the Australian Journalists Association—the trade union for journalists, which Mercia would also become involved with.

She met up again with her old friend and former fellow cadet at *The Age*, Russell Grant—or 'Rus' as he was known among his friends. He was now married and living in Sydney with his wife, and he too would travel down to Canberra to report for *The Daily Telegraph*. Another political reporter Mercia was friendly with was Fergan O'Sullivan, a young Irish journalist who had recently moved to Australia with his Australian father, who was also a journalist. Ten years her junior, Fergan was working for *The Sydney Morning Herald*; he would later be described in the press as short, slightly built and dark haired.

Around February 1950, Mercia was introduced to Rex Chiplin at a function at the Hotel Civic in Canberra by their mutual friend, Russell Grant. In a rare statement from Mercia that is in the public domain, she explained that she 'cultivated this acquaintanceship in her capacity as a journalist on a constitutional newspaper, and as a loyal Australian', because she 'wanted to keep abreast of the activities of the Communist Party'.

13

SON OF A JUDGE

When Cindy went to ASIO to read Mercia's files, she took with her the framed black-and-white photo of her mother with four people that had hung on her mother's wall. She showed the photo in the meeting room, asking if anyone knew who the people were.

Much discussion ensued. One of the ASIO staff took the photo to another floor to look through their records. They told Cindy and Kieron that the bespectacled gentleman in the photo was Rex Chiplin, but the other three women weren't known to them.

Asked if she remembered Rex, Cindy said his face and name meant nothing to her—despite the files showing they had met.

Reading Mercia's files, she was about to find out a bit about him.

Rex had first come to the notice of the Commonwealth Investigation Service in April 1948, as the organiser of the CPA paper *Waterfront News*, and then the editor and publisher of *Progress*, another CPA publication. And it wasn't just Mercia keeping an eye on him. Reports on Rex were appearing from multiple sources.

Rex had been born in Kempsey in March 1915, the third of four children to Grace and Percy Chiplin. His father was the Crown Lands

Agent and Clerk of Petty Sessions at Warialda in north-west New South Wales.

When Rex was just four, his father shot himself after an auditor came to inspect the courthouse accounts. Rex and two of his brothers were home with a young housekeeper at the time, with his mother in hospital with their youngest child. His father had come home during the lunch hour, said goodbye to his three sons on the back verandah, written a suicide note and shot himself behind a shed when the auditor came to check on why he hadn't returned to the courthouse.

Early ASIO files on Rex show that his father was thought to be a judge. Possibly Rex had alluded to the fact that his father had worked in the legal field, or even given this occupation for his deceased father to those around him, and that information had then made it into the ASIO records.

The Chiplin family next appears in 1931, on the electoral roll for Kensington in Sydney's inner east. Six years later, Rex is registered at the same address as his mother, with one older brother, and is listed as having no occupation. In the middle of the Second World War, he was involved with the progressive and left-leaning New Theatre, where he was described as 'a lousy actor but a good writer'. Rex married Annette 'Annie' Moore in 1944 and lived at 75 Miller Street in North Sydney. He was attending the CPA National School in November 1945, and again in February 1948.

Rex was being observed by ASIO in earnest from 1949, after he visited Nosov's flat. While he was helping to organise public CPA meetings in The Domain—a large park near Sydney's CBD—it was his dealings with the Russian TASS news agency that truly piqued their interest.

Rex is described in ASIO files as a political writer, and when parliament was in session, he visited Canberra regularly. He would usually travel by train from Sydney on Tuesday, returning on Thursday, and chose to stay with the secretary of the Canberra branch of the CPA. An ASIO informant reported that Rex would appear at Parliament House on Tuesdays for the opening of the week's parliamentary proceedings—but did not attend the usual interviews with ministers, as other press representatives tended to do, or even those given by the Prime Minister.

His ASIO file noted that at Parliament House, Rex was particularly friendly with two other reporters: Harry Mills of Sydney's *Daily Mirror*, and Russell Grant of *The Daily Telegraph*. ASIO also observed that Rex and the TASS correspondent, Fedor Nosov, did not give any signs of recognising one another while in Parliament House—even though they were well known to each other.

Things were hotting up for the Communist Party in federal parliament. Having won the 1949 election, and having promised to outlaw the CPA, on 27 April 1950 the Liberal and Country Party coalition introduced the Communist Party Dissolution Bill to the House of Representatives. If the bill was passed, the CPA and other Communist organisations would be declared unlawful, and their assets could be seized.

In the proposed bill, the definition of being a 'Communist' was broad, and included anyone who simply supported the principles of Communism. Furthermore, if you were a Communist, you would be ineligible to hold a Commonwealth position, an office in a trade union, or work for any defence-related industry.

With public sentiment against the CPA growing, opposition to the Dissolution Bill from the Labor Party was minimal—though some in the Labor Party saw the bill as a threat to the trade union movement, which had CPA members in their ranks. The bill passed through the House of Representatives, but stalled in the Senate, where the ALP held the majority. Labor senators agreed that the CPA should be dissolved, but they wanted to make amendments to the bill.

The Communist Party's papers, including the *Tribune*, ran scathing attacks against the proposed Dissolution Bill, and against the ALP for its failure to oppose it.

14

THE QUEST FOR PEACE

On 28 February 1950, four copies of a document stamped 'Restricted' were presented to Percy Spender, the Australian Minister for External Affairs and External Territories, by the American ambassador, Pete Jarman.

The documents were a fresh draft of the proposed Treaty of Friendship, Commerce and Navigation between Australia and the United States of America—an idea first proposed by the US Government in March 1947, when the original draft was presented as a basis for discussion. The draft had been read, polite correspondence entered into with the American Government via its ambassador, and then the document sat dormant for the next two and a half years.

Now, in February 1950, America was trying to breathe life into the stalled treaty.

On 2 March 1950, Percy Spender sent a copy of the ambassador's letter and the draft treaty to his Cabinet colleagues the Treasurer, the Minister for Trade and Customs, and the Minister for Commerce and Agriculture. After analysis and discussion with them, Spender wrote to the American ambassador on 7 June 1950, saying that 'the

Government had given the draft careful and sympathetic study, and a number of questions had emerged that appeared to require clarification as to the intention of the United States'. There were 'Questions of principle on which a frank explanation of the Australian position might facilitate subsequent negotiations'.

His letter was polite, but to the point: further clarification and negotiations were required.

In May that year, it was reported that Rex had separated from his wife, and was living with another woman, Vivienne Bon, at 59 Blues Point Road, McMahons Point—the same address, ASIO noted, where CPA lectures were being held. Lectures and film nights were often held in the homes of Communist Party members as fundraisers, information nights and for those interested in finding out about the Party.

Mercia frequented the Russian Social Club through May and June of 1950, reporting to ASIO her meetings with Rex and his new partner, Vivienne. Mercia also reported meeting the new Russian press attaché from TASS, Mr Pakhomov, who would be taking over from Fedor Nosov.

The Russian Social Club was in the basement of 727 George Street, Sydney. The club may have been in a dimly lit basement, but it could hold 200 people and was used for Saturday night social dances, Russian-language film nights and private functions. The club was frequented by Russian migrants sympathetic to the Soviet Union, while anti-Communist Russians were able to look down on them—literally—from Russian House, or 'White Russian' house as it was jokingly called, across the road on the second storey of 800 George Street. Down the road from both buildings, at 695 George Street, was Marx House, home of the Communist Party of Australia.

Mercia was already involved with the Peace Council, but under instruction from ASIO, was trying to infiltrate the CPA as an active member—a difficult task with an organisation that was under the threat of the Dissolution Bill.

At one of the Russian Social Club evenings, Mercia started up a conversation with Rex. With the Cold War raging, she explained that with journalism her only skill, her craft, she wanted to be doing something to help the quest for peace. She was already helping the Australian Labor Party with pamphlets and other written material in her own time. And she'd been interested in the Council of Civil Liberties in Melbourne when she lived there before the war.

'I think I ought to be doing something more active, and I'm thinking of joining the Party,' she told him. 'What do you think?'

'Sure,' Rex replied. 'There's always a place for people like you.'

When she asked how him she might go about it, Rex replied, 'Go and see my friend Harold Rich, and tell him I sent you.'

ASIO was already aware of Harold Rich, a practising solicitor involved with the Democratic Rights Council (DRC)—which along with the Australian Peace Council, was seen by ASIO to be a front or fringe organisation for the CPA. One of the dangers ASIO saw in these groups was that non-Communist members were joining them without realising they could be affiliated with the Communist Party—and might even be recruited by CPA members to gather information for them, or become agents themselves.

The previous year, Harold Rich had been the instructing solicitor for the General Secretary of the Australian Communist Party, Lawrence Louis Sharkey—who was also the editor of the *Tribune*, and had been charged with uttering seditious words. As the General Secretary, Sharkey had been asked by a *Daily Telegraph* journalist what the CPA would do if Communists invaded Australia. Sharkey had been quoted as saying, 'If Soviet forces in pursuit of aggressors entered Australia, Australian workers would welcome them.'

This was enough for an indictment to be laid against him, under Section 24D of the Commonwealth *Crimes Act 1914*. The jury in the trial had found Sharkey guilty, and the judge had sentenced him to the maximum penalty of three years imprisonment, which was reduced down to eighteen months on an appeal led by Harold Rich.

❊

Mercia met Harold Rich at his office in Sydney's Railway Square. After a short discussion, in which Mercia probably did most of the talking, she was instructed to go to the building next door and see the DRC about becoming one of its members. Her plan to join the CPA had been stalled—but the DRC, being a Communist-linked organisation, could be another way in.

So, Mercia joined the DRC and, from that moment on worked as much as she could for them, ingratiating herself with everyone she met, and hosting some film nights. Film was still a relatively modern phenomenon, a novelty to have in one's home, and the DRC film nights were a means of both communicating the message of the Communist Party and a chance to get together with like-minded people.

Mercia's role in these events was to provide a venue and be the hostess for the evening. One or two DRC members would bring the film and projector and set everything up, then pack up and take them away at the end of the evening. Mercia reported that the black-and-white movie reels mostly came from Communist Eastern bloc countries such as Czechoslovakia and Yugoslavia, and were offered by their embassies.

She continued to regularly meet Rex and Vivienne at private social functions organised by the DRC and the Russian Social Club. Mercia hadn't managed to join the CPA, but she knew that a lot of people ASIO would be interested in were associated with both the CPA and the DRC. Having a natural curiosity and with her mission in mind, she socialised, mingled and gossiped—and dutifully reported it all back to ASIO.

Mercia became the editor of the women's section of both *The Sunday Telegraph* and *The Daily Telegraph*. This promotion at the newspaper was not helpful for her counter-intelligence work in

Canberra—but Rex was attending federal parliament in Canberra while it was in session, and other agents and informants would be reporting on his activities and movements while he was there. Mercia and Rex would still meet up socially in Sydney, and she was also attending events organised by the Labor Party and the Russian Social Club.

Mercia continued to organise events for the DRC and, as with the ALP, she used her journalism skills to help the DRC prepare literature for publication and distribution.

She was still a paid-up member of the ALP. ASIO had not directed her to become an ALP member; she had joined the party after working with Chifley, and she was an ardent supporter.

15

WHAT WOULD PEOPLE THINK?

The Communist Party Dissolution Bill was still being held up in the Senate by the Labor Party. Meanwhile, the threat of war in Korea was fuelling yet more anti-Communist sentiment in Australia and her allies.

At the end of the Second World War, the Soviet Union and the United States had divided up the Korean Peninsula, resulting in a Communist government in the north, and a pro-Western government in the south. The North Korean leader, Kim Il-sung, wanted to invade the south, and with aid from the new Chinese Communist leader, Mao Zedong, the invasion of South Korea started on 25 June 1950.

The United States committed troops to the region two days later. The Menzies government committed an Australian naval frigate to the conflict the following day, and then an RAAF squadron on 30 June, and sent an infantry battalion at the end of July. Australia was once again officially at war. A war against Communism.

In August 1950, ASIO was made aware through Mercia that Rex had urgently left for Brisbane for ten days, to meet up with Max Julius, a Queensland barrister and another known Communist.

Max Nordau Julius was also on ASIO's radar. He had joined the CPA in 1936 and, like Rex, became involved with socialist theatre productions. He also helped start the Brisbane branch of the Eureka Youth League, another Communist-linked group. The following year he had tried to join the Queensland Bar, but was blocked for being a Communist. He took the matter to court and won, and was admitted to the Bar in June 1941. He received few briefs from the Brisbane legal fraternity because of his open involvement with the CPA, and he was now working on the legal challenge to the Communist Party Dissolution Bill.

The following month, Mercia was approached by one of the ladies in charge of the Democratic Rights Council (DRC) in Sydney, who asked her to entertain the journalist Wilfred Burchett and his father, George, who were coming to Sydney. Wilfred Burchett was an Australian war correspondent who had been the first journalist to file from Hiroshima after the dropping of the atom bomb in 1945, vividly and for the first time describing the effects of radiation sickness and death. His reports were heavily censored in the United States, but they helped set the mood for nuclear deterrence, and the quest for peace.

Though never a member of a Communist Party, Burchett was a Communist sympathiser and dared to report the Korean War from 'the other side'. Viewed as highly controversial in conservative circles, in Communist circles he was viewed as a bit of a hero.

Mercia was in her element. She organised and attended parties and talks given by Burchett, including one held on the garden rooftop of the Ironworkers Club. She dutifully reported back to ASIO those who attended, and any conversations she thought worthy of mention.

At this rooftop party, she reported that Rex Chiplin approached her early in the evening, asking to have a private chat with her later. When she could escape her hostess duties, she sought him out and was stunned by his suggestion that she drop any work with the Democratic

Rights Council. Rex feared this work would draw public attention to her. Mercia did not want to; she was enjoying the work, and told him as much.

Rex insisted, saying she was not even to go near any DRC members in future. Mercia again refused, asking him: what would the people she was working with think about her if she stopped working with them? He replied that those who should know, would know why, and hinted that he had earmarked her for some secret work for the Party. That was enough for Mercia to agree, albeit reluctantly.

Not long after this meeting, the Australian Labor Party declared what ASIO suspected: that the DRC was a Communist Party auxiliary. All ALP members had to resign any membership of the DRC, or face expulsion.

16

DISSOLUTION

Mercia and Rex met again after the ALP declaration, and she told him she had withdrawn from her work with the Democratic Rights Council, as he had asked. Leaving the DRC cut off a large part of her friendship group; she had immersed herself almost entirely in the organisation, letting other friendships drop away. She was deeply unhappy about the situation, but waited to see what Rex had planned for her.

Their conversation started in a general way, catching up with what was happening in each other's lives before talking about their mutual interests—the Communist Party and politics. Rex must have known of her open allegiance with the ALP, but she also still wanted to join the CPA. Rex told Mercia, who then reported it to ASIO, that he was concerned that the CPA would soon be declared unlawful—and that if she wanted to help the Party, she could move to Melbourne to join an ALP movement that the CPA hoped eventually to take over.

This would have been of interest to ASIO, but Mercia at this stage was not paid for her work with them, so a move of this nature—to a different city, without employment or the means to support herself—would seem strange to those who knew her. Besides that, she told Rex that she didn't want to leave.

So Mercia kept working in Sydney, in both her paid and unpaid jobs—with Australian Consolidated Press, and with ASIO.

Meanwhile, Mercia and other agents continued reporting on Rex Chiplin's movements. He was regularly travelling from Sydney to Canberra, on one occasion to obtain an early copy of a speech that the Prime Minister had broadcast on defence, and that was only released in the ACT.

His plans to go on holidays to Queensland with his partner were also reported. Their travel itinerary was shared, but when ASIO checked on Vivienne and Rex's movements, the couple hadn't visited all the places itemised, and their exact movements couldn't be verified.

Rex was again seen in Canberra at the reopening of parliament, and was observed in close contact with visiting delegates of the now-outcast Democratic Rights Council, who were in Canberra with trade union leaders and delegates from the Council of Civil Liberties and the Australian Peace Council to talk to members of parliament about, among other things, totally rejecting Menzies' 'fascist' bill. This was later reported by Rex in the *Tribune*.

Rex was also in Canberra when the federal executive of the Labor Party directed its senators to withdraw their opposition to the stalled bill to dissolve the CPA. The Communist Party Dissolution Bill was passed on 19 October 1950. That same day, it was noted that Rex Chiplin had returned to Sydney: the bill's passing had triggered a series of events.

The day after the *Dissolution Act* became law, the Communist Party of Australia became an unlawful association. The Party was dissolved, and its property was forfeited without compensation. The Act also gave the Governor-General the ability to declare bodies such as trade unions and Communist affiliates unlawful.

The Governor-General could also declare a person a Communist; as such, they could not be employed in the public service, or any union or industry deemed vital to Australia's defence and security. Outraged unions immediately launched eight separate actions in the High Court against the Commonwealth and persons associated with the Act, claiming the Act was unconstitutional.

Three days later, federal police raided the Communist Party offices in Melbourne, Sydney, Perth, Hobart and Darwin, the first Commonwealth action under the *Communist Party Dissolution Act*. At exactly 4 p.m. on 23 October, eight officers, together with three uniformed Victorian police constables, entered the Victorian headquarters of the Communist Party. The three female typists in the office denied that the offices were occupied by the Communist Party, saying they were the Political Rights Council. This did not stop the raid. The officers stayed for four hours, breaking into rooms and a filing cabinet before confiscating documents and other articles.

In Sydney, two CIB officers, Detective Inspectors Alfred Wilks and Devereaux McDermott, raided the three floors and basement at 40 Market Street—the offices of both the CPA and the *Tribune*, as well as a Communist bookshop on the ground floor. Several known Communists and a solicitor were present, but did not interfere with the two-hour search. Books and documents were examined and seized.

The CPA waited for a decision by the High Court. They hoped the court would determine that the *Communist Party Dissolution Act* was unconstitutional and would restore their lawful status. *Tribune* articles continued to condemn Menzies, and the *Dissolution Act*.

17

THE FIFTH COLUMN

In December, Rex visited Mercia alone at her home in Randwick. When Mercia asked him if the ban on her involvement with the Democratic Rights Council was still in place, he replied, 'Yes, you're doing just what I told you.' She emphasised in her report to ASIO that Rex was anxious for her to continue to assist the Communist Party.

At the end of January, Mercia attended a film night held at a flat in Darlinghurst, the home of Glennis Fox. Glen, as she was commonly known, was a fellow journalist, who was then working as a public relations officer for the Far West Children's Home in Manly. She was married to Len Fox, a man also on ASIO's radar, who worked at the *Tribune* with Rex. Mercia was still working for *The Daily Telegraph*. At the film night, Glen asked her if she was able to hold cottage meetings or more film nights at her home, saying it was 'desirable that as many be held as possible'. Mercia agreed, despite Rex's ban, and in early February she received a telephone call from a man who introduced himself as 'Claude', about hosting a film night.

When Mercia reported this to ASIO, it must have raised some eyebrows, as the VENONA code name KLOD was Russian for Claude.

Wally Clayton, who had gone underground the previous year, was suspected of being KLOD—but perhaps it would be someone else entirely.

Mercia reported that this Claude had a foreign surname, and that he came to both her home and her office at Australian Consolidated Press to talk about the film nights at her home, suggesting he could get a good selection of films from the Czechoslovakian Consul in Sydney. Claude was the chief organiser of the film nights and would operate the projector on the night.

As promised, Claude brought the equipment and ran the projector while Mercia busily entertained. This Claude would leave Australia not long afterwards and return to his native Germany—he didn't appear to be the KLOD from the VENONA intercepts.

Mercia relayed to ASIO that the film had showcased Czech welfare institutions, and was followed by a talk from a Mr Wright, who had recently returned from Moscow. Mercia also reported on a union official of interest who was present. Anything she deemed as being of interest, she was informing ASIO, for her country.

Rex did not seem to attend any of the cottage meetings or film nights that Mercia hosted in Sydney, but ASIO was still keeping an eye on him. On 16 January he was observed at a talk on the Warsaw Peace Congress in the Ironworkers Hall; on 1 February he attended a meeting of the CPA defence committee. In February, he was also spotted in Canberra, attending parliament once again, the informant noting that Rex had been absent for some time.

In February 1951, ASIO watched the arrival in Sydney Harbour of the ocean liner *Orcades*. Alighting from the ship were six new staff for the Soviet Embassy, including a married couple, Vladimir and Evdokia Petrov.

ASIO watched as the new arrivals were greeted by two members of the Soviet Embassy, Valentin Sadovnikov and the relatively new

TASS correspondent, Ivan Pakhomov. ASIO knew of the Petrovs, having been advised by MI5 that Vladimir Petrov had been active in the intelligence field and had been the Russian link with the Swedish Communist Party while stationed in Sweden.

ASIO watched as the Petrovs and the four other new embassy staff were whisked off by car to the Soviet Embassy in Canberra.

❀

On 9 March 1951, the High Court of Australia ruled that the *Communist Party Dissolution Act 1950* was unconstitutional. The Act was rejected by a majority of six to one, with only the Chief Justice dissenting. They ruled that, as Australia was not in a state of war, the government did not have the power to proscribe organisations. The bill and its resulting crackdown on the CPA hadn't even lasted six months.

The following day, Menzies addressed parliament, saying 'On behalf of the Government, I say that this is not the end of the fight against Communism, it is merely the beginning.'

The next federal election was then set for 28 April 1951.

During another fiery campaign, where the threat of Communism was again a major theme, Menzies said the Liberal Party believed Australian Communists were 'the fifth column for a potential enemy'—a fifth column being a group within a country that is sympathetic to, or working with, that country's enemies.

The Liberal–Country Party coalition again defeated the Labor Party. Their majority in the House of Representatives was moderately reduced, but they gained a majority in the Senate. The Menzies government now had control of both chambers of parliament.

Menzies decided to put the issue of Communism directly to the people. A constitutional referendum was to be held on 22 September 1951, seeking to change the Australian Constitution to allow the government to ban the Communist Party of Australia.

Following this announcement, the CPA, trade unions, democratic rights organisations and the ALP, led by the new Leader of the

Opposition, 'Doc' Evatt, campaigned strongly for the 'No' campaign. Rex and all those working at the *Tribune* were pushing the 'No' campaign constantly through the paper.

Dr Herbert Vere 'Doc' Evatt was a dynamic politician. He had served as a judge on the High Court of Australia from 1930 to 1940, the youngest (and remains so to this day) to be appointed at just thirty-six years of age, before entering politics a decade later. He had held the position of Attorney-General and Minister for External Affairs up until the Labor Party defeat by Robert Menzies in 1949. Evatt's rise to Leader of the Opposition had come suddenly, after the party's leader, Ben Chifley, died on 13 June 1951.

Chifley's death was an event that would have greatly saddened Mercia, who had taken up a new position with another government department just the day before he died.

18

NATIONAL DEVELOPMENT

Early in 1951, the Secretary of the Department of National Development approached ASIO with security concerns, having received reports that Communist sympathisers could be working in their ranks. Leaks from federal departments were a major threat to Australia's security and a chief concern for ASIO, the still relatively new security service.

The Department of National Development was undertaking a survey of the immediate shortages in basic commodities within the nation. It was similar to the survey previously undertaken by Mercia in the Department of Post-War Reconstruction; she was perfect for the job. ASIO was not having much success cracking all the code names in the VENONA program, and, as Ray Whitrod would later say in an interview with David McKnight in the early 1990s, 'Then we cook up a plot to snare Chiplin.' He told McKnight, 'We think if we can get Mercia in a government department with some classified material, we might get an approach from someone in the Communist Party which might make a contact with her.' This could then help them identify individuals who were sharing information with the Soviets. That this might be perceived as a form of entrapment seemed to be either acceptable or not considered on this Cold War battlefield.

ASIO made moves to secure Mercia a position in the Department of National Development to help it track down Communist employees, with the additional prospect of helping to identify the code names in VENONA. Ray Whitrod persuaded her to 'up sticks and move to Melbourne'.

Mercia let Rex Chiplin know that she had been applying for the position; when he knew she was successful, she reported back to ASIO that Rex expressed satisfaction. He especially wanted to know more about her new boss, Commander Jackson.

Commander Robert Gillman Allen Jackson, or 'Jacko' to his mates, was tall, dashing and blond; according to one newspaper report, he had penetrating blue eyes. The newspapers loved him—a decorated Australian war hero, back helping his country.

He had enlisted in the Royal Australian Navy at the age of seventeen and had been quickly promoted to lieutenant after four years at sea. According to another newspaper article, early in 1938 he had undertaken an intensive study of the German language as war threatened.

By the time he was thirty, he had received an OBE for his work supplying Malta in the Second World War. His military and civilian logistics were credited with making a major contribution to Britain's successful defence of the island nation. He then became the Director-General of the Anglo–American Middle East Supply Centre in Cairo, ensuring military and civilian supply needs were met through the rest of the war. His plan to make the Middle East self-sufficient became the post-war model for the world.

Towards the end of the war, the British Government 'lent' Jackson to the United Nations Relief and Rehabilitation Administration, which ran nearly 800 resettlement camps, housing over 700,000 displaced people. At the beginning of 1950, he was again lent out, this time to his native country as head of the new Department of National Development for two years, with a £200 million budget. He advocated for Australia to increase immigration and to exploit her natural resources to secure national security. In particular, he supported the Snowy Mountains Hydro-electric Scheme.

At the end of 1950 he returned to England to marry Barbara Ward, a well-known public figure who had previously been foreign editor at *The Economist* and a governor of the BBC. Docking at Fremantle on their trip back to Melbourne in January 1951, the press were photographing him and his new wife when Commander Jackson pulled out a small camera and took a snap of them, handing his photo to the stunned photographers one minute later. The staring press photographer found that the photograph was completely dry, with deckled feathery edges. This type of early 'polaroid' was not mainstream at the time, so unusual that the description of the process made it into the article about Commander Jackson's return to Australia.

Unlike her previous employers, Jacko was aware that Mercia was an ASIO agent.

Mercia's case officer would once again be Ray Whitrod, who had moved to Melbourne the previous October. After informing *The Daily Telegraph* of her intention to resign, on 10 April she travelled to Melbourne to find somewhere to stay and be fully briefed by Whitrod. She was due to start her new position in early June. It was to last only six months, as Commander Jackson's two-year tenure would be up at the end of the year, and they would be leaving Australia in December. Most of the information she would have access to at the Department of National Development was highly classified.

Mercia left *The Daily Telegraph* on 25 May and began preparing for her move the following week. But before she left Sydney, she met up with Rex and told him she didn't want to lose contact with people who thought as they both did.

'We won't leave you alone,' he told her. 'Someone will contact you.'

Before she was due to leave, her case officer in Sydney submitted a somewhat unflattering assessment on her. Concerned, he told ASIO that she had been unable to get near the inner circle of Party matters, and that there was no continuity in her reports. When she reported on something that 'appeared to have some substance', she would then fail to gain more information, despite him urging her to do so.

Nevertheless, Mercia moved to Melbourne on 5 June 1951, leaving her daughter still living with Cindy's father and grandmother in Newcastle. She had found a house to rent at 300 Yarra Street, Warrandyte, owned by a 'fellow traveller'—a Communist sympathiser.

Warrandyte was an old gold-mining town, about an hour's ride on a bus from Melbourne. Set in the bush on the banks of the Yarra River, it was then a picturesque country town. House prices, rents and general inflation had increased markedly after the start of the Korean War; perhaps this was why she chose to live out of Melbourne, or perhaps it was because of the owner's link to the CPA. Mercia joined the local Labor Party branch, helping out with meetings, socialising and making friends in the branch.

She would eventually share the house with Russell Grant, whose marriage had broken down and who had moved back to Victoria. Mercia took up her position as the Personal Assistant to the Secretary of the Department of National Development, Commander Jackson, on 12 June 1951.

19

PEACE COUNCIL

No longer in Sydney, Mercia was still reporting on Rex from afar.

On 1 June, a report reached ASIO that Rex and Vivienne had travelled to Melbourne on a TAA flight. They were going to stay with Vivienne's sister in Malvern until the end of the month. It was also reported that Rex was organising the publication of some special documentation for distribution. As a side note, the report added that divorce proceedings had commenced between Rex and his first wife, Annette Moore, who had already changed her name by deed poll two years before.

Mercia had arrived in Melbourne with good credentials among her left-wing friends, having worked with the peace movement in Sydney, and set about making contact with fringe groups in Melbourne. She introduced herself to the Australian Peace Council in Flinders Lane, becoming involved with the group and helping wherever she could. But no one approached her from the CPA, as Rex had suggested would happen.

Besides looking for any Communist sympathisers in the workplace, her role at the department was to assist with economic research, and help compile Australian industry reports. Monthly reports were being prepared from all divisions in the department, with a more concise report being prepared for the government for the end of the year. Commander Jackson would also be taking a copy of the final 'GAPS' report, as it became known, to England when he returned at the end of the year.

Mercia reported once a week to her case officer, Ray Whitrod, with any information she obtained, being debriefed in the back pews of the large St Paul's Cathedral near Flinders Street Station. These meetings were always followed up with a written report.

To Whitrod's delight, Mercia managed to infiltrate and report on a Communist study group within the public service. She knew how to talk the talk, readily quoting Lenin and Marx, and was busily increasing her network of socialist friends and colleagues, both socially and in her role with the Department of National Development.

One young woman in the study group, Valda Seamons, was of particular interest to ASIO as she was a stenographer secretary to the Permanent Head of the Department of Defence Production, a position that gave her access to information that would have been of interest to the Soviets. Valda was put under surveillance.

Mercia's political talk at work came to the attention of a fellow employee, who dutifully contacted Brigadier 'Black Jack' Galleghan to inform him that a woman, Mercia Masson, who was in Commander Jackson's employ, was sympathetic, at the very least, towards Communism.

Such was the hysteria surrounding the Communist Party that everyday people would contact politicians or officials—usually in the form of a letter, some signed, some anonymous—to express their concerns about anyone they suspected of being Communist, often from simply something a person may have mentioned in passing— whether they be a friend, colleague, or just someone they knew casually in their community. These tip-offs would then be passed on to ASIO and investigated.

Meeting up with Rex when she travelled to Sydney or Canberra on research work for Commander Jackson, Mercia eagerly shared details about her new role as they gossiped about shared friends and acquaintances. Now that she was no longer in Sydney, Mercia was always keen to hear what was going on. And Rex was keen to know what she was working on.

Rex was still busy reporting on the constitutional referendum Menzies was putting to the Australian people. If the 'Yes' vote won, it would allow the Australian Constitution to be changed to give parliament the power to ban the CPA. The *Tribune* staff were working tirelessly, encouraging their readers and the wider community to vote 'No'.

On 22 September 1951, the proposed constitutional amendment was rejected by the Australian people, with 49.44% voting Yes. It was close, but not close enough. For the constitution to be amended, it needed a majority of all electors nationally to vote yes, together with a majority of the states. Only three states—Queensland, Tasmania and Western Australia—voted 'Yes'. Had only 30,000 people in South Australia and Victoria voted Yes, rather than No, the proposal would have been successful.

Rex couldn't help having a dig at Menzies and his political party. The following week, his column, 'Rex Chiplin Says', started with a satirical advertisement:

FOR SALE: One brand new dictator's uniform, complete with whip, one gross of hand cuffs, 20 rolls of barbed wire, 8 dozen bottles castor oil and one complete home kit for making smoke screens. Apply Liberal Party headquarters, Ash Street, Sydney.

Above organisation also willing to trade one rather worn red herring and flock of publicity men for crate of headache tablets.

20

WORKING FOR THE PARTY

On 25 September, Mercia flew to Canberra once again, to gather more material for her research. She had come across a somewhat disturbing mystery while searching for some industrial development files she knew existed from her earlier time at the Department of Post-War Reconstruction. Some of the divisions of the old department had been merged into National Development, which had originally been based in Canberra before moving to Melbourne.

In Canberra, she searched for these files in the National Archives, but they were missing—along with all the documents from an entire filing cabinet. Even more worryingly, archives staff told her they'd been searching for them, too.

Returning to her room at the Hotel Kingston, Mercia found a handwritten note had been slipped under her door. She recognised the handwriting: Rex. In part, the message read: *I will ring you in the morning about 9–9.30 a.m.—particularly want to see you honey.* He signed the note: *Love etc R.C.*

Mercia and Rex obviously had a solid friendship; but the possibility that this was developing, or had already developed, into a more intense relationship between the pair, as indicated by the language used in his note, is hard to miss. When in Canberra, they were both away from their homes, and Rex was away from his partner—though the 'etc' in his sign-off does seem somewhat flippant.

The following morning, Rex rang and Mercia met him in the lounge of the hotel. They greeted each other and he asked her about her job. She told him about the work she was currently handling, the type of material coming in, that the department were putting together reports from surveys, updating and incorporating the data, starting back from her time in Post-War Reconstruction.

The department was handling a lot of economic information, she explained, coming through from the Industrial Division; it included a good deal of information about foreign capital being invested in Australia. Rex took the bait, asking her to get as much information as she could for him, and as much gossip as possible.

According to Mercia's subsequent statement, Rex already knew about a circular issued to manufacturers and industry about their activities and plans in the event of another war, and he asked her if the Department of National Development was responsible for sending this out. He also asked specifically for any information she could obtain about Defence plans, explaining that the whole picture could not be obtained unless all parts of the plan were known. Rex specifically told her to find out as much as possible about how far American capital had invaded the Australian economy. Mercia explained that this information was out of her divisional area, and could well be highly classified, so she was unsure how much or even what she could get him.

Rex also talked about a proposed Pacific Pact that was in the news, and a Commerce and Agriculture section of the ongoing American Treaty that was being talked about, wanting any information about these. 'It should be possible with a little extra work on your part,' he said to her, 'as capital issues, and investment activities with reports from industrialists, come to your department.'

Mercia then asked again about joining the Communist Party, saying she was anxious to carry on her work for the Party in Melbourne.

Rex spoke about being careful, telling her there were a lot of people like her who could not undertake public activities, that she was in a position to give valuable information to the Party, and would have to be protected as a result.

Mercia said she didn't like the thought of being isolated again, as she felt she had been in Sydney. Rex then told her it would be all right to continue her work with the study group at her workplace, but not to be too openly associated with any left-wing groups, 'Because, from now on you will be working for the Party.'

21

NEWCASTLE

Mercia received a chatty typed letter from Rex at the end of October, from his home at Campsie. They had missed seeing each other the week before, but he would be in Canberra on Wednesday and Thursday, and he mentioned that a telegram care of the press gallery would reach him. He asked about Russell Grant, then added some surprising information: 'Cop this . . . I will become a poppa next year, Vivienne has been told by the docs that she is preggo.'

He then continued: 'You mentioned certain things in your last letter, have you anything further on friendship etc? If you are not coming to Canberra can you send me (to home) the details of the other matters you spoke of, or would you prefer to wait until we meet. If you are not coming up this week, do you have any idea when you will be up? Sorry to appear so demanding, honey, but I am anxious to get the goods.' He signed off in his handwriting: 'Love Rex'.

ASIO's plan to feed information to someone in the CPA, to gain information on the identities of the VENONA code names, seemed at this stage to have only got as far as Rex. He was still after information, particularly something that revolved around 'friendship'.

Mercia continued to meet her case officer, Ray Whitrod, in the back pew of the cathedral opposite Flinders Street Station, passing on information from the public servant study group, and Rex's requests. She passed Rex's latest letter to Whitrod.

It was decided she would share some documents with Rex that were not sensitive and had a low-level security classification; these would be vetted by Whitrod before she handed them over.

Unlike the negative report by her case officer before she left Sydney, Ray Whitrod was delighted with Mercia's work in Melbourne. He wrote in a memo on 2 November 1951: 'During the six months or so that she has been operating under our control, she has, by hard work and ingenuity, finally penetrated a particularly important Communist Party Study Group . . . of undercover Communist Party members.'

Whitrod reported that he saw Mercia's motive for working for the organisation as one of loyalty. He also informed ASIO that she was spending her own money to attend the numerous Peace Council meetings, and suggested they increase her remuneration to cover costs, which they did by an extra £2 a week. He was also concerned that the work was 'producing certain personal problems for her'. Mercia needed a break, telling his superiors that 'nervous tension' was obvious and he had suggested she take a small holiday on an upcoming trip to Newcastle.

Mercia was not one to take holidays; for her to have agreed to this, she must have been feeling the pressure of her busy new life in a city she hadn't lived in since the beginning of the war. Commander Jackson was visiting infrastructure and industry around the country, travelling with his wife, and was planning on being in Newcastle from 7 to 11 November. While there, he was going to visit the port and various industries in the area, including BHP; this was all part of the assessment of Australia's capabilities that Mercia was working on. It was decided that when Mercia joined them in Newcastle, she would stay a few days extra to take a break from her work.

Mercia caught the afternoon flight from Melbourne to Sydney on 5 November. She met Rex in the lounge of TAA's city office in Phillip

Street at 5 p.m. From there they went to the nearby Franchette Café, in an arcade near Martin Place. As instructed, she gave him some graphs she had made on coal production and three reports on American investments in Australian industry, apologising that she had been unable to get anything more than this.

'Don't worry honey,' she reported him as saying. 'I fell on a pile of stuff last week.' Mercia would have been curious to find out what the 'stuff' was and who delivered it, but nothing further was in the statement compiled the following year from her reports.

Rex then asked if she could find out anything about the Commonwealth plans to extend rural food production—particularly the Channel Country in Queensland, the Kimberley and Albany regions in Western Australia, and the Gulf Country—which he said was tied up with Defence. Mercia said she would do what she could.

Rex also warned her to go steady with any left-wing talk in official circles—and on no account was she to proceed with Party membership unless under instruction from him. 'We have lots of people like you whom it is sometimes better to accept as members in name only,' he told her. 'Not that we don't trust you, but there is a panel of special workers too valuable to risk as open members. Your case is under discussion, honey, at a high level.'

He then asked her what she was going to do when Commander Jackson left Australia. The Public Service Board had told her about an upcoming job in External Affairs, which she would apply for—or possibly, she told him, she would be covering the proposed upcoming royal tour of Princess Elizabeth and her husband, Prince Philip, for a newspaper.

King George VI, Queen Elizabeth (the future Queen Mother) and Princess Margaret had planned to visit Australia in 1949, but the trip had been postponed due to the King's ill health. The new tour date was rescheduled for early 1952. Palace authorities had recently announced that, due to the King's ongoing ill health, he would again not be able to tour Australia, and Princess Elizabeth and Prince Philip would tour instead, arriving on 1 March 1952.

'Go for it,' Rex told her. 'In External you would be doing two jobs in one. You would have Defence plans coming into the department, and international policy, and your prestige after the tour would be tops.'

That night in Sydney, Mercia wrote a long report of her meeting with Rex, and had a sleepless night, before catching the 9.05 a.m. train to Newcastle the following morning, 6 November. Mercia reported that the train arrived in Newcastle at 11.30 a.m., and she checked into the Great Northern Hotel on 6 November at 8 p.m. According to the hotel ledger, she checked in as 'Miss Mason (Pearce)'.

Harry Pearce and their daughter, Cindy, arrived at the hotel; Mercia never visited them at his mother's home. Cindy was seven, and there is a photograph of her in a summer dress on the rooftop of the hotel. To this day, Cindy has no recollection of seeing her mother then or any time while she lived with her father, despite the existence of two photos showing her on the rooftop of the Great Northern Hotel at different ages.

On 7 November Commander Jackson and his wife arrived, and from 7 to 11 November Mercia moved to room 418, and was listed in the hotel register as 'Miss Mason'. No 'Pearce' to be seen.

22

ISSUE NO. 715

Not long after his meeting with Mercia, Rex left Sydney for Canberra, attending a cocktail function at the Soviet Embassy on 7 November to celebrate the annual Russian holiday marking the 'Day of the Great October Socialist Revolution'. It was here that Rex first met the stockily built 44-year-old Consul and Third Secretary, Vladimir Mikhailovich Petrov. Rex's contact with the embassy was now through the new TASS news correspondent, Ivan Pakhomov.

The Soviet Union expected Petrov to continue to try to infiltrate Australian Government departments and political parties, as his predecessors had done. The previous April he had been promoted to Third Secretary at the embassy, responsible for cultural and consular tasks, providing cover for his regular travel to Sydney and Melbourne. Petrov was trying to set up his own networks through contacts within the Australian–Russian Friendship Society, with some success.

One of Petrov's contacts, unbeknown to him, was one of Dick Gamble's agents: Michael Bialoguski, a Russian doctor involved with the Russian Social Club and the NSW Peace Council, and a security agent for the Commonwealth Investigation Service and then ASIO.

Unlike many of the other Soviet Embassy staff, Petrov had a relatively free lifestyle outside the embassy.

Returning from Newcastle on the morning of 12 November, Mercia called into Rex's home in Campsie on the way to Melbourne, and said she would be in Canberra again the following week. Rex waited for his pregnant wife to leave the room, then told Mercia he would also be in Canberra the following week and would meet her there. He also said it was best that they were not seen together in Parliament House or any public places.

On Wednesday 14 November 1951, issue no. 715 of the *Tribune* hit the streets.

Rex started his column, 'Rex Chiplin Writes . . . a Canberra Diary', announcing there would be a special meeting of the Commonwealth–State Agricultural Council before the end of the year. The meeting would discuss far-reaching plans to turn Australia into a food bowl to supply 'US led aggression against Chinese, Malayan and Indo-Chinese people'.

The next paragraph spoke of the three great food development projects that were underway: the Kimberley Air Beef Scheme, and those in the Albany area in southern Western Australian and the Gulf and Channel territories in Queensland—the same areas that were mentioned in Mercia's report to ASIO.

On page three of the paper was a large article bylined to Rex Chiplin and titled 'Secret treaty sells us to the US; Menzies must explain'. It spoke about the same treaty with America that had first been suggested back in 1947 and was still under consideration by the Australian Government.

Unlike the general information in his column, this article contained classified information. It started in typical Rex Chiplin language, rallying against the conservative government:

Hidden away in the top-secret files of the Menzies-Fadden
Cabinet is a Treaty which, together with the Pacific Pact

and the terms under which Menzies borrowed $100 million in
1950, completes the bonds which make our country a vassal
state of the United States of America.

It went on to say that a high-placed government official was disgusted by the treaty, and by the thought that any government would sign away the independence of the country in which they were born and profess to love. That was why he (the informant) had revealed it to Rex.

The article then detailed various sections of the treaty, indicating which sections favoured the United States in trade and tariffs, the purchase of property and the treatment of US companies and nationals operating in Australia. The informant explained that the treaty would spell doom to the Australian Constitution, and to Australia's independence and membership of the British Commonwealth of Nations. Rex's article made it sound like the treaty was a done deal.

ASIO immediately started an investigation into the leak. As Mercia was their best-placed source on the author of the article, Rex Chiplin, her reports were now directed straight to counter-subversion and counter-espionage investigations.

With her elevation in importance, Mercia was assigned a new source symbol or pseudonym. She was no longer 'Catherine McDonald'; she was now 'Julie Lee'.

The ASIO files Cindy saw in Canberra showed Mercia to be a dedicated Labor Party member. Cindy couldn't believe that at all, given the disdain she knew Mercia felt for the Labor Party in her later life. As far back as she could remember, Cindy's teenage years had been filled with the Liberal Party, with Mercia insisting that Cindy regularly attend Young Liberal meetings. Mercia always insisted that her daughter mix with the right people, dress conservatively, and be as prim and proper as Mercia projected herself to be.

Cindy simply could not imagine, as she read through the files, increasingly confused, that this was the same woman that she knew as her mother.

Mercia was more of a mystery to her than ever before, and she even started to wonder if her mother had a split personality.

23

LEILA

Since arriving in Melbourne, Mercia had been regularly attending the Peace Council office in Flinders Lane, formerly known as Australia–Soviet Friendship House. She quickly befriended the chief assistant Leila Cohen, spending many of her lunch hours with her. Either Mercia would take her lunch to the Peace Council office, or the two of them would go to a cafe or restaurant, then window shop on their way back to the office.

Cecilia, or Leila as she liked to be known, was the daughter of a Jewish tailor and was similar to Mercia in age, size and looks. She was married to a man seven years her junior, John Hubert 'Jack' Mullett, and the couple were both known to be active members of the CPA, Jack having joined while studying at the University of Melbourne. The witnesses to Leila's wedding in 1942 were Jack's father and Edward (Ted) Fowler Hill—a 27-year-old Communist activist and lawyer specialising in workers' compensation, who would become a leading legal figure in the CPA.

Leila had already been on the security services radar for some time. She was the former treasurer of the CPA's North-West division, and had been the secretary of the New Theatre group. She was also a member of the Federated Clerks Union and had taught English at the recently closed Marx School in Collins Street.

As Leila and Mercia's friendship steadily grew, Leila said she would find a way to help her new friend to join the Communist Party. Mercia didn't stop her, despite Rex's previous order that she on no account proceed with Party membership unless instructed by him.

Leila apologised that she wasn't introducing Mercia to new callers at the Peace Council rooms; she felt it better that others did not know who she was. Leila also explained that Mercia's position in the Party was under discussion, and they were waiting for instruction. Mercia dutifully relayed all of this to ASIO.

Mercia's position at the Department of National Development finished at the end of November, and she was still waiting to hear about a job in the public service. ASIO seemed happy with the inroads she was making, with the possibility she was about to become a member of the Communist Party, and her ongoing meetings with and information-gathering on Rex and other CPA members. With this progress, ASIO wanted her to stay in Melbourne and increased her weekly stipend from £5 to £16, to cover her rent and expenses.

Early in December 1951, she received a phone call at Warrandyte from Leila, saying a 'friend' wanted to meet her, and could she possibly set aside a day for lunch. They fixed an appointment for a few days later—but when Mercia turned up, Leila was disappointed to say that her 'friend' had gone away, and they would have to reschedule, but Leila wasn't sure when that would be.

On 17 December, during one of Mercia's regular visits to the Peace Council rooms, Leila asked if she could keep Wednesday 19 December clear to meet her 'friend'. Mercia readily agreed.

Mercia arrived at the Peace Council offices at the agreed time, 10.45 a.m. Mercia watched as Leila called Head Office, asking for someone called Ric; she gathered that Leila was talking to a girl she knew. Leila signed off, saying, 'He knows what it is all about. We will be leaving here in a few minutes and going to Gibby's Coffee Shop in Little Collins Street, opposite Cann's.' Mercia later told ASIO she had no doubt this appointment was in connection with her membership of the Communist Party.

After ordering coffee at Gibby's, she and Leila sat at a table for two. Soon afterwards, Mercia was aware of a man standing alongside them. Leila greeted him and said, 'Ric, this is Mercia.' No surname was given, but Mercia looked over him as he sat himself down. Tall and with an athletic build, he accepted a coffee.

George Richard 'Ric' Oke was already known to ASIO and the Commonwealth Investigation Service as a staunch Party member. In a 1949 assessment, the CIS described him as a full-time organiser for the Victorian section of the Australian Communist Party in Melbourne, a State Committee member and discipline leader. A 'muscle man' for the organisation, he was assessed as being the most likely person to be contacted by Soviet agents, as he was regarded as the 'Intelligence Officer' for the Party in Victoria. He was said to have a quick mind, which was hidden by an inability to express himself fluently, and made penetrating insights into the character of people he met.

An ASIO assessment stated that Ric had served in the RAAF in Borneo and was known to threaten violence. A further assessment in July 1952 stated he dealt with all matters of security and vetted incoming members of the Party. This last part of the assessment was probably gleaned from Mercia's reports.

After a little general conversation, in which Ric took very little part, he said he would see them outside. He got up, paid his bill and walked out. Mercia looked at Leila, who was already gathering her bag. They paid for their coffee and joined Ric outside.

Leila suggested that they go for a walk, and he replied that it would be better if they didn't. Motioning towards a secluded doorway, he ordered, 'We'll stand in here.'

Speaking in a low voice, Ric asked Mercia what Rex's attitude towards her membership and activities had been. Mercia said she had better give him the background and started to explain. But he interrupted her and said, 'There's no need for all of that. The important thing is what you are doing now.'

Mercia started to tell him what she'd been doing for the Peace Council, but again he interrupted her, asking Leila what Mercia had been doing with the Peace Council, and how many people knew she had been going there.

Leila explained that Mercia had been helping her, but she'd been trying to keep people away from her, as she knew Mercia wanted to join the CPA.

Mercia said she hoped she was not going to be cut off again. 'It happened before in Sydney.'

'We will take care of that,' he replied. 'Sometimes it is better to work alone than out in the open. It's harder, it takes a great deal of determination, and grit and courage, but you won't be lonely.'

Mercia asked him about CPA membership and the costs involved. He explained she would have a special undercover membership and that, with the current economic recession, it was a sliding scale. For people earning more than £5 a week, it would be 52 shillings a year—plus anything she could possibly pay into the Party, because the CPA had been hit very badly, like everyone else.

'Have you got a safe channel for your information to Chiplin?' he asked.

Mercia said she only had his home address, but usually waited until she saw him and gave him anything she had.

'How often is that?' he asked.

'Every few weeks,' she replied. 'But I don't know how this will be affected by my new job, as there is a possibility that I will be going to External Affairs.'

'That's good,' he told her, and asked if she would still be in Melbourne. She said she'd be based there if her job application was successful. She then stated she would be going to Sydney again shortly.

'Right,' he said. Ric then explained that, before she saw him again, she would receive directions as to how to contact him directly. Rex was always to be her first point of contact.

Without saying anything further, Ric left. The whole interview had lasted no more than half an hour.

She walked along the street a little way with Leila, who remarked that from what Ric had just said, her precautions in not introducing Mercia to other visitors to the Peace Council office had been justified.

24

YOU ARE NOW ONE OF US

As Mercia had mentioned to Ric, she had applied for a job as Third Secretary to the head of External Affairs, Richard Casey, but there was also another position in Defence that she could apply for. Both positions would be beneficial for her work with ASIO.

She continued to give reports on Rex Chiplin and others in the back pew of the cathedral in Melbourne, and sometimes in Ray Whitrod's car. While Cindy vaguely remembers the meetings in the cathedral, she isn't sure if these were with Ray Whitrod, and unclear of the timeline. Cindy didn't always go in with her mother, often waiting outside the cathedral, but she was aware as a child that this was when her mother received money.

Rex was still under surveillance by other agents in Sydney, attending various CPA meetings and gatherings, and other events involved with his *Tribune* work. Despite not having employment, Mercia travelled to Sydney in early January 1952, meeting him in one of the Repin's cafés in Market Street on Monday 7 January 1952.

The Repin's chain was part-owned by Mercia's uncle, James Masson, who also held interests in several movie theatre cafeterias. Cindy remembers helping out in those cafeterias in the school holidays with her second cousin—her Uncle Jim's daughter—and had been surprised to see the name of Repin's in the ASIO files.

After some catch-up conversation, Mercia started to tell Rex about her meeting with Ric. He stopped her and said he knew all about it, saying they had been in touch with him. Mercia reported that, even though he had told her not to go ahead with trying to get CPA membership, he was not annoyed—far from it. He told her she could go right ahead, saying she would be admitted to full membership, and Melbourne would look after the formalities. He added that he had been trying to keep her services for his exclusive use, and that her activities had been discussed at a high level within the CPA. Rex then reiterated that, for the time being, he was to be her only contact, and whatever she gave him would eventually reach Melbourne, warning her again not to have any open connection with left-wing organisations, and to keep her membership secret—even from other Party members she knew.

He then asked if Mercia had been able to get the regional surveys they'd talked about at their previous meeting, and asked if she had seen the completed 'GAPS' document that she had been working on.

Mercia told him she hadn't seen the entire document before she left the department, but was expecting to receive a copy from the Commander. Rex wanted to see it as soon as possible; he wanted to look at it overnight. Mercia laughed and told him light-heartedly that this would be difficult, as it weighed over seven pounds.

Mercia returned to Melbourne the following day.

On 9 January, the following 'Rex Chiplin Says' column appeared in the *Tribune*:

Some time ago we wrote from Canberra that the Menzies Government was collecting facts and figures on Australian affairs—from immediately pre-war to the present—for presentation to Britain to be collated with other Empire reports for submission to the US, which wants a capitalist world picture of the war potential.

The job has been finalised and it is being taken to
Britain by Commander R. Jackson, administrative head of
the Department of National Development, who sails on the
Aorangi this Thursday.

The finished report is known as the GAPS report.
It is a complete picture of every Australian industry
and its background; each industry has been broken into
factories, groupings, etc.

After each section there follows a brief appendix on
that particular industry or factory's war potential.

Rex had once again taken some of Mercia's conversation and published it in his column.

The following Tuesday, 15 January 1952, Mercia again called in at the offices of the Peace Council in Flinders Lane and saw Leila, who welcomed her enthusiastically, saying, 'You are now one of us.' Leila added she wasn't surprised at the ban on Mercia's public activities. She also said she had been to the CPA's Head Office the day before and Ric was still away.

ASIO was duly informed about all of this.

ASIO was conducting surveillance of the Russians at the Soviet Embassy on Canberra Avenue. Early in 1952, a telephone intercept revealed that Petrov was going to meet an unidentified male.

Near St Paul's Church, two ASIO officers saw Petrov walking towards Manuka Oval. Following him, they watched Petrov meet with Rex Chiplin.

25

OWN METHOD OF COMMUNICATION

Mercia received a phone call at home from Leila on Tuesday 22 January 1952. After a quick catch-up, Leila asked if she could come to Melbourne, as someone wanted to see her. She didn't say who, but seemed anxious that Mercia see 'him'. Mercia said she would catch the bus to Melbourne from Warrandyte the following day, and telephone her when she arrived.

The next day in Melbourne, she telephoned Leila as promised at around 3.30 p.m. and met her at the Peace Council offices at 4 p.m. When no one else was in hearing distance, Leila quietly said that Ric had wanted to see her, but was now unavailable. Could she possibly come again the following day?

On Thursday 24 January, Mercia again arrived at the Peace Council office just before noon. After chatting briefly, Leila made a phone call and asked her to wait a moment.

A door opened and Ric looked in. He nodded to Leila, without saying anything, and then withdrew, shutting the door behind him. Leila went out after him. A few minutes later she came back and said something to the effect that, if Mercia went into the next room, she would find a friend waiting.

In the adjoining room, Mercia found Ric sitting at a table, by himself. He stood up and led her into the room next door, again without saying a word.

Ric asked if she had seen Chiplin in Sydney. 'Yes,' she replied. She began telling him what had transpired—what Rex had said to her about her full membership and future activities in the Party.

Ric knew all about that; he had received a note from Chiplin giving the details and personal references for Mercia. He asked if Chiplin had given her any directions as to future contact and channels of communication.

She said she had only been told to write direct to Rex at his address at Clissold Parade in Campsie.

Ric was at pains to say that she must see Rex and talk the matter over with him more fully. He said he didn't trust telephones or post offices, and that they had their own methods of communication.

Mercia explained that Rex had said that it would be all right to send mail to him at that address. If anything went wrong, he would give her an alternative address.

Ric then asked when she was going to Sydney, and when she would be returning to Melbourne. Mercia told him she would be leaving on the weekend, and probably return the following Wednesday. He then asked her where he could contact her in Melbourne. Mercia gave him her home telephone number.

'Do you know anyone named Michael?' he asked. Mercia mentioned two Michaels who she knew.

'If someone was to ring and say it was Michael speaking, would you know who it was?' he asked.

'I would,' she replied.

'I will ring you when you get back from Sydney,' Ric stated, then added that she was not to take any public part in activities, and the fewer people who knew about her membership the better.

Ric asked what she had done for the Democratic Rights Council in Sydney, what she was now doing for them in Melbourne, where she was working, and what she expected she could do.

Mercia explained about the cottage meetings and film nights in her home in Sydney, and her work helping the DRC with events, and how much she enjoyed these, allowing her to speak with like-minded people. She also told him of her friendship with Rex Chiplin, and the fact that he had restricted her from social activities in Sydney, leaving her lonely and unhappy.

Ric said he understood, but it was something that had to occur at times.

Mercia chipped in, 'I hope I will not be cut off again.'

'We will take care of that,' Ric replied. He said he had no objection to Leila knowing about her membership, nor their personal association and friendship, but cautioned, 'This takes a lot of determination and courage on your part.'

She replied that she understood this. Mercia was already sacrificing for what she believed in, for the good of her country and its people.

After the meeting, Mercia described her conversation with Ric to Leila, who told her she need not feel lonely as there were many more people in the same position. Leila explained that although you could see the names of some Party members on pamphlets and in the newspapers, 'The most *important* members you will never have heard of, as they are behind the scenes—for instance, Ric. You didn't hear about him, but he's a most important man in the movement.'

Mercia repeated what Ric had said about not trusting postal communications. Leila confirmed they had their own method of communication, outside the ordinary processes of the postal department, and it was very effective.

Mercia reported all this to ASIO, then prepared to travel north.

Mercia would later witness this method of communication, when she was asked to obtain information concerning an anti-Communist ALP supporter, to pass on to Rex urgently. She had to leave it at Leila's flat in the evening; when she arrived, she wrote the information down and left it with Leila, who was quite flustered.

Rex confirmed the following morning that he had received it. Much faster than the postal department.

26

DEFENCE

Mercia arrived in Sydney and was making plans to attend the upcoming CPA Youth Carnival for Peace and Friendship in March, despite Ric's and Rex's suggestions that she lay low.

She met Rex at Repin's Café in the city at 11.15 a.m. on 30 January, handing him a package containing the Division of Regional Development's surveys on the Burdekin and Albany regions, and a Channel Country survey by the Queensland Government, which Rex had previously requested. Ray Whitrod had vetted these surveys while she was still working in the department.

She told Rex her next job could possibly be in External Affairs, but she thought the one in Defence was more likely. Rex was extremely happy with this, saying it would be good that she would be on the 'frontline'—and that, once she started there, they would have a special discussion about her position.

The following day, Mercia visited Rex and Vivienne at their Campsie home. Mercia admired the new typewriter on their dining room table. Rex commented to the effect: 'Have a look at it, I wouldn't part with it for the world. It's a gift from a grateful government.'

Rex said it had been made in East Germany, and something about it having come through the embassy. In her report to ASIO, Mercia said she had no doubt he was speaking about the Soviet Embassy.

Vivienne left the room and Mercia again mentioned her loneliness to Rex. 'You are lucky, you can openly work,' she complained, 'but you have placed me on a lonely footing.'

'Look, you go back to Melbourne and see Ric,' Rex replied. 'Tell him, but I will too, that you are to be left alone and only see me. He'll arrange the collection of your fees and your membership, but you must keep clear of every public activity. It's most important that you keep the knowledge of your membership as restricted as possible.'

Mercia said she was miserable, and he told her, 'I know it's hard, but the most important of our workers are people like yourself. I'm in touch with many of them, and if in your new job you spend much time in Canberra, I will put you in touch with some of them who are in the same boat as you, so that you can spend some time with them socially. You will like them; they are grand people. I have to regularly see them, like you.'

He suggested that, when she returned to Melbourne and started with External Affairs, she should let him have a weekly note of her activities, out of which he could get an idea of her work and make a plan. He said they would have another long discussion once she started in her new job.

When Mercia remarked that she didn't feel as though she was contributing enough to the cause, he said, 'Don't be silly. As a matter of fact, what you have done is highly regarded in circles that would surprise you.' He added, 'I want you to meet Ivan at the embassy. I will arrange it for you. I have always told you that you had so much to give in more ways than you realise.' (Later, Mercia told ASIO that Ivan's Russian surname sounded like 'Popinoff'.)

Rex said he hadn't told Vivienne about her CPA membership—not even Sharkey, the organisation's General Secretary. For one thing, it was not his bloody business, and secondly the people who *did* know about her were more important.

'You are making me feel more isolated than ever,' Mercia complained. 'I am cut off from my former friends because I can no longer tolerate their stupidity, and even my family are becoming less and less real to me.'

'I know it is hard,' he replied. 'But the most important of our workers are the people like yourself.'

Mercia said she still hoped to attend the upcoming Youth Carnival—but again, Rex told her not to, emphasising it was for her own protection; he did not want people to know that she was associated with the CPA in any way. Mercia was upset, explaining that she particularly wanted to attend the festival's film and drama sessions.

Vivienne then returned to the room and Rex changed the subject to their mutual friend, Fergan O'Sullivan. He was annoyed with the young journalist. 'Apparently it is so bad,' he explained, 'that Fergan has had to be recalled to Sydney. He has been to two parties at the embassy and on one occasion he had brought with him two drunken women and was drunk himself—and on the second occasion he was also drunk.'

Unbeknown to Mercia or Rex, Fergan was helping the Soviet Embassy in his own way, and had been given the code name ZEMLYAK (Russian for 'Fellow Countryman').

27

URGENT

On Monday afternoon, 4 February 1952, Mercia was sitting in the Peace Council chambers talking with Leila when a man came to the door and handed Leila a white envelope. Leila looked at it and exclaimed, 'Heck, it's marked urgent! Excuse me.'

She opened it in front of Mercia. There was a second envelope inside it, marked in large letters 'RICK', with some other writing she couldn't read. Leila explained, 'I'm the go-between, and this is bloody urgent.' Because Leila was preoccupied, Mercia left the office soon afterwards, dutifully reporting the event to her case officer.

Other than her work for ASIO, Mercia was still unemployed. Covering the proposed royal tour of Australia had not eventuated, due to the death of Princess Elizabeth's father, King George VI, on 6 February 1952, and it would be another two years before the new Queen Elizabeth II and her husband, Philip, visited Australia.

Mercia wrote to Rex the following week, letting him know she hadn't obtained the job in External Affairs, but was still hopeful for a position in Defence; she also handed a copy of her letter to ASIO.

Back in Canberra, Rex met the TASS news correspondent Ivan Pakhomov in a park in Kingston; he had an urgent message for the embassy. The CPA had learnt that two women, both Russian nationals working at the embassy, were of interest and were being watched. One of these was Mrs Petrov.

As they were about to leave, Pakhomov thought he saw someone photograph them. He reported this to Petrov, who relayed the information in an official report by cable to Moscow. The Russians were concerned for their staff, both inside and outside the embassy.

In June, TASS correspondent Ivan Pakhomov was going to be replaced by Victor Antonov; Moscow instructed Antonov to minimise his meetings with Chiplin in the Canberra press gallery and other places, and that he should only accept information from him in fully advantageous conditions. Moscow was concerned that Rex was being followed.

Rex certainly was still under close surveillance by ASIO; in Canberra he was followed on foot and by car, and on public transport. His movements in and around Parliament House, and the meetings he attended, were all noted and recorded.

Moscow then chastised Petrov about the information he had received from Chiplin, saying he should ascertain Chiplin's source, citing two examples that Chiplin had recently told Pakhomov about— the first being the two women of interest at the embassy, the second about an exchange of enciphered messages between the governments of Australia and America.

Colonel Charles Spry had been appointed head of ASIO in July 1950. In early 1952 he conceived another approach to identifying Communist spies in the public service. Hoping to replicate Mercia's successful intelligence-gathering at the Department of National Development, his plan was to get Mercia a job in the Joint Intelligence Bureau, with the hope that someone from the CPA would approach her about getting classified information. They would then organise the exchange of information in such a way that the Communist agent could then be arrested and charged.

Spry had a meeting with the Secretary of the Department of Defence, who voiced his concerns about the plan's implications for the Australian–American Security Agreement on classified information, saying he would need to discuss it with the Defence Minister and the Prime Minister. The plan did not go ahead.

Meanwhile, Mercia was still looking for a job.

Among her mother's belongings, Cindy came across a carbon copy of Mercia's application for the position with the defence department, dated 18 February 1952. Cindy had kept it because of its impressive array of referees. These included the Governor of the Commonwealth Bank, Dr H.C. Coombs; the Editor of *The Age*, Mr H.A.M. Campbell; the former Director of Public Relations at the Department of Post-War Reconstruction, Dr Lloyd Ross; the Information Officer for the United Nations South-West Pacific, Mr Duckworth-Barker; the Managing Director of Australian Consolidated Press, Mr Frank Packer; and the Leader of the Opposition, Dr H.V. Evatt.

28

ATOM EXPERIMENTS

Mercia was still visiting Leila regularly, and was planning another trip to Sydney. On 3 March, Leila said Ric wanted to see her before she left for Sydney. Rather than use the telephone, they arranged to meet again the following day, and Leila would tell her where and when the meeting would take place.

The following day, when Mercia called in to the Peace Council office, she found Leila in conversation with a girl called Kathie, and another girl from the New Theatre. When they weren't looking, Leila passed Mercia a slip of paper that said, 'Quarter to two, Tafts Fountain Pen Shop Arcade, Collins Street, opposite Hotel Australia'.

As arranged, Mercia went to the arcade at 1.45 p.m. and was met by Ric a few minutes later. They then went to a coffee shop near the Golden Dragon Chinese restaurant and ordered some coffee. The following exchange is from one of Mercia's statements, her interpretation of the exchange between them.

'What are you doing?' he asked.

'I am still waiting for an appointment with the Public Service Board, which with its slowness and muddle is messing me about,' she explained. 'I understand I have missed out on the External Affairs job because an appointment had been made when it was thought I was to go on the royal tour.'

'Is there any security reason why you have not been appointed?' he asked.

'I don't think so,' she replied.

He then asked several questions about her past activities in Sydney. 'Have you ever signed your name to a piece of Democratic Rights Council propaganda, or spoken on a platform?'

'No. There has always been a certain amount of discretion, and I have dropped the DRC work.'

He asked about her activities in the Australian Journalists Association, the trade union for journalists, and then, 'What do you think you will be doing?'

'I think I will probably be going to Defence.'

'On the job, would you know or hear anything about the atom experiments?'

'I think that will be probably in Defence, though I do not know which division would be handling it.'

'It is becoming more and more clear, increasingly so, that your position in the Party must be uninterrupted and clear, and that regular contact be made with you. I am afraid you will have to drop going near the Peace Council and drop your left-wing friends.'

He added, 'I know it calls for a lot of personal courage and sacrifice, but there are bigger things than personal friendships.'

'I realise that,' Mercia replied. 'I will miss Leila.'

'I think we can come to some arrangement whereby you can maintain a friendship with Leila, but you must drop everything else. It would be criminally wrong if anything was to go wrong with your position and your opportunity to maintain contact with us. It would be criminally wrong to stand in your light,' Mercia reported that he then said. 'For the cause of peace it is important that we know what goes on at the atom experiments. It is important to have someone in the midst of it. To have someone who would be among it, is important. I am afraid you will have to drop the idea of the carnival.'

'The Peace and Youth Festival in Sydney?'

'Yes,' he replied. 'When are you going?'

'I was going on Friday.'

'I am quite sure Chiplin will support what I say. In fact, I am certain he will endorse it, and even without my telling you, would give the same instructions.'

'I will be disappointed,' she replied.

'I'm sorry, but that is out,' he stated. 'Will you be back at the end of March?'

'Definitely yes.'

'Can we make a time and place to meet now?'

'Yes,' Mercia replied, pulling out her trusty diary.

'What about three weeks from today?'

Mercia looked in her diary and they organised to meet on the twenty-sixth.

'Do you know Batman Avenue?'

'Yes.'

'There is a kiosk there. Meet me there at a quarter to two.'

'All right, unless I have been appointed to a job, in which case I will be unable to make the time. I will then tell Leila, in case I need to change the time.'

Ric agreed.

After some further discussion about her donating some books to the Left Wing Book Club, she said, 'I have sent a letter card to Chiplin, telling him of my arrival in Sydney, and that I expect him to meet me as usual. I will tell him of my meeting with you.'

Ric nodded.

She then asked again about her membership dues for the CPA. Ric repeated what he had said at their previous meeting—that she could start from their next meeting.

Mercia said she would arrange some exclusive gatherings to raise funds, but wouldn't run anything along the usual lines, as they were too boring—too many people spoke for too long. He agreed to this, despite having told her not to socialise with her left-wing friends.

He asked her where she lived in Warrandyte and she gave him the address.

'You can use the place if you like for Party fundraisers, but you must be discreet,' she said.

'We will talk about it when you come back,' he replied. 'See you on the twenty-sixth.'

29

YANKS AND URANIUM

Back in Sydney, Mercia met Chiplin at 11 a.m. on 10 March 1952, again at Repin's Café in Market Street. She told him Ric had instructed her to obtain information about the atomic bomb experiments, should she gain employment with the defence department, and that she should break off her association with the Peace Council and other left-wing personalities.

'Ric is quite right,' Rex replied, 'but we will talk about it when you get settled.'

They discussed Ric's concern with methods of communicating, and then general political matters. Finally they parted ways, but not for long—she had been invited to Rex and Vivienne's that night for dinner.

Rex spent the next few hours being busy. ASIO observed that he met with William Gallagher, a Scottish Communist Party MP, and also with someone called Leo, to discuss an ongoing Japanese Peace Treaty campaign. He also spent fifteen minutes with a colleague who had tried to justify to Rex his intention to join the staff of Larry Anthony, the Country Party MP who was then the Civil Aviation Minister in the Menzies government.

Mercia arrived at Rex and Vivienne's home at about 6 p.m. In the presence of his wife, he told her, 'I am expecting some Party members tonight to distribute some literature about the Carnival. I want to tell you that there must be no more public meetings in places like Repin's. In future, I will meet you at the Market Street entrance to St James Station. When you ring, just mention the time; but don't mention any name or place.'

'All right,' Mercia replied.

Later, when his pregnant wife had gone to bed, he told her, 'Remember there will be no carnivals for you and no associations. Undoubtedly the delay in your appointment is due to investigation.'

Mercia appeared concerned, but Rex told her not to worry, that it was probably a normal security check.

'Let me know your movements as soon as possible,' he insisted. 'Don't be unhappy and don't feel lonely—we'll get you friends.'

He then added, 'Ric is quite right about the experiments, although there will be only missile tests at Woomera. The rest will be taking place on Christmas Island. That is why they are bringing landing barges with them,' he explained.

Two weeks before, on 25 February 1952, a photograph had appeared in *The Sydney Morning Herald* under the heading 'Equipment for Atom Test on the Way', with the caption beneath reading 'Laden with men and equipment for Britain's first atomic test in Australia, the tank landing ship "Narvik" sailed from Portsmouth, England last week.' In the fuzzy black-and-white photo there appeared to be five large bits of machinery strapped to the front deck: the landing barges. Another clearer reproduction of the same photo appeared three days later in the South Australian newspaper, *The Chronicle*, speculating that the *Narvik* was carrying landing craft on her deck, 'commonly associated with island rather than wharf side landings'.

'Did you know about the bacteriological warfare experiments?' Rex asked her.

'Leila had mentioned it in general conversation,' she replied.

'We had a bloody awful cable from Burchett telling us of bacteria bombs the Yanks are using,' he apparently told her. Mercia wrote in her statement that the bombs were of a cylindrical type; when exploded, a number of different objects were released, including fleas, lice and ants with big horns. There were also insects that discharged fluid. Rex finished off his description of Burchett's cable to her by saying that a Japanese colonel was in charge of the operation.

Two visitors arrived at Rex and Vivienne's home that night. One of them told Mercia he worked in a government insurance office. ASIO later came to believe this man had provided a reference back in 1949 for an international Communist in India who had allegedly arranged for the sale of 42,000 rifles and ammunition from Australia to Burma.

The second man worked at Garden Island, the Royal Australian Naval base in Sydney Harbour. He showed them his security pass, a flat disc with a hole in the centre, and said he had been interviewed by the Naval Police to get the job. He said that, if the security elsewhere was as slow-witted, no one had anything to worry about.

The following day, Mercia wrote up her report on this meeting, while Rex enjoyed the start of the week-long festival, where he was reported on by other ASIO agents.

Five days later, the British tabloid *Sunday Express* printed an article stating that Britain's first two atom bombs would be tested late in the summer of 1952 off Christmas Island in the Indian Ocean.

Their source was apparently in close touch with atomic production, and said the fact that landing craft had been carried on the two atom bomb supply ships, *Narvik* and *Zeebrugge*, gave strength to the belief that the explosion would take place on an island.

The following day, a spokesman for the British Prime Minister's Office said nothing was known about the report that Britain would explode two atom bombs at Christmas Island.

Not quite six months later, on 3 October, the first test of a British atomic device would be detonated in Main Bay, Trimouille Island, in the Montebello Islands, 139 kilometres off Western Australia's Pilbara coast. The successful detonation, code-named Operation Hurricane, made Britain the third nuclear power, after the United States and Soviet Union.

Mercia met Rex again on 19 March 1952, organised as per their new arrangement, where she had to ring him first. During that telephone call, she carried out his instructions, and did not give her name or any details as to why or where she was ringing from. At the arranged time, she met him outside the Market Street entrance to St James Station, opposite David Jones. They then walked to the St James Hotel, on the corner of Elizabeth Street, and went into the lounge.

Rex told her he had two visitors billeted at his home in Campsie that week, for the carnival. Mercia said, 'I hate to be going back to Melbourne because of the loneliness, which would be increasing from now on. I am very unhappy about everything.'

Rex took her hand and said, 'I keep telling you everything will be all right. I can understand how you feel, and that you hate going back. As soon as you are settled, I will see you have people and friends. Get yourself settled. Write to me and let me know what is happening.'

'I am seeing Ric on Wednesday to fix up my dues,' she said, 'and I'll tell him what you've said.'

'Ric will look after you, but you are still to make me the number one contact. Ric is a grand fellow, but a strange one. He has the most wonderful parents,' Rex added, explaining that he had once stayed with them for some months.

'I will send you a list of books,' he added, 'but I want to consult some of our folks first. Anyway, don't get distressed, just drop me a note when you do.'

'I will probably do that next week,' she replied. 'Surely by then I would have something constructive about the job in Defence.'

'It's probably a normal delay for a security check—don't worry.'

'Do you think the job will be terribly dull, as I can't imagine any job in Defence being anything otherwise.'

'You will probably find it most interesting,' he said. 'If you get anything about the Yanks and uranium, let's have it pronto!'

'I'm not liable to hear anything now, except gossip,' she lamented.

'Anyway, keep your ears open, and if you happen to go to Canberra let me know and I'll dash down there and see you.'

Their meeting lasted an hour, before they went their separate ways—Rex to work, and Mercia back to Melbourne.

On 26 March, Mercia made her way to the kiosk at the end of Princes Bridge on Batman Avenue to meet Ric as arranged.

Ric Oke never arrived.

30

WOMEN'S WORLD

Mercia found Leila the next day, to ask if she knew why Ric hadn't met her. Leila apologised, saying that, with her also being in Sydney for the carnival and not knowing when Mercia was to return, she had failed to give Mercia a message from Ric that he could not keep the appointment. She thought he'd gone to Wonthaggi on something urgent, and that these sorts of things could happen. She told Mercia not to worry, and that she'd let her know when a further meeting was possible.

Mercia continued to regularly meet Leila in Melbourne, and was still carrying out her work with the ALP in Warrandyte, and reporting it all back to ASIO.

On 21 May, ASIO recorded that Leila had a conversation with her good friend, Robert 'Bob' Freestone—a journalist who had started his career as an office boy at *The Sydney Morning Herald* and was now working as a public relations officer for TAA airlines. He had attended the recent Youth Carnival in Sydney with Leila, and then a march with some members of the Peace Council to the offices of Australian Consolidated Press, in protest at an article they had recently published.

In a rare miss of the redactor's black pen, Mercia's name appears in Bob Freestone's ASIO file. Despite being told to steer away from her left-wing friends, it was thought she had been seen with the pair at the march. Mercia's name then appears a second time, possibly because of a misspelt surname through an audio surveillance. In this report Leila told him that 'Mercia Mosson' was anxious to see him. Bob's daughter was ill, and in the Alfred Hospital awaiting an operation; Leila explained to him that 'Mosson's' uncle was one of the leading people at the hospital and suggested Bob contact him to ensure his daughter would receive more personal attention. Leila and Robert organised to have lunch at 1 p.m. on 21 May; it was thought that 'Mosson' was to join them.

Cindy has a vague memory of a teacher at her school in Melbourne, a Mrs Freestone. Her mother warned her not to speak with Mrs Freestone if she came to Cindy asking any questions about them.

※

Mercia continued meeting Leila, and various members of the Peace Council. Since she was not currently employed in the public service, the ban on her activities seems to have been lifted, or she was simply defying the order.

At lunch at the Hotel Australia with Leila on 10 April, Leila assured her that her 'friend' was okay. 'I have still not seen your friend, but it is all right. He is a busy man.' She always referred to Ric Oke as her 'friend' rather than name him, particularly in public.

On Tuesday 6 May, Mercia again met Leila at the Hotel Australia for lunch. Leila told her that Ric knew she was coming to the Peace Council rooms regularly, but he hadn't contacted her because he'd been very busy, and he knew he could always contact Mercia through her.

He had asked Leila about Mercia's CPA subscription. Mercia said she would give it to her at the end of the week, as she was in a bit of a financial crisis with her upcoming house move.

On the first Monday in June, Mercia was intending to move from her Warrandyte house to the inner suburb of St Kilda.

'Ric thinks it is all right for you to see me and even to come up occasionally,' Leila said. 'He knows you are not in the Defence job, but immediately you are switched on to more confidential work, you must let us know so we put the shutter down on your movements. You must be protected.'

Back in Warrandyte, Mercia bumped into her neighbour, Betty Vassilieff, who'd had her passport cancelled and was hoping Mercia could help. Betty was born Elizabeth Sutton and had married the Russian-born artist Danila Vassilieff. She was part of a delegation from the Victorian Peace Council hoping to attend the Peking Peace Conference that September, but like many others, she'd had her Australian passport cancelled.

Betty asked Mercia to find out Australia's policy towards those countries that had delegates attending the Conference—Malaya, New Guinea, Indo-China, Philippines, Burma, Thailand, Indonesia, China, Japan, Formosa and Hong Kong. While those with Australian passports were unable to attend, others travelled on British passports, such as one of the founders of the Australian Peace Council, Reverend Victor Montgomery Keeling James, who ended up leading the Australian delegation. He was one of the few Australians who managed to attend the Peking Peace Council in September 1952.

Mercia explained to Betty that such information was kept in top-secret files at External Affairs, and was impossible for her to obtain, especially as she was no longer employed by the government. Betty told her that she was trying to gather as much information as she could, to circulate among discussion groups. Mercia said she would contact her if she found out anything.

By the end of May, Mercia finally had a job, as a journalist with a women's paper, *Women's World*, in Melbourne. While Rex had previously told her that he was going to have a word with someone to try to get her work on a newspaper, in her next report to ASIO she was adamant that Rex had not secured the *Women's World* position for her, and that she had gained it on her own merit.

31

NEST OF TRAITORS

ASIO was still investigating members of the public service who had been involved in the Communist study group that Mercia had infiltrated. Valda Seamons, a government stenographer, had been questioned by ASIO, with her boss Harold Breen also being interviewed. He stated that Valda had worked for him since she was seventeen and he was 'satisfied with her integrity'.

Unfortunately for Mr Breen, he did not think to inform his own boss, the Minister for Defence Production, of the interview at the time.

Not long afterwards, an article appeared in *The Daily Telegraph* stating that security intelligence officers recommended the dismissal of a woman from the Commonwealth Public Service, and that they had compiled a list of Communists in the public service. The article went on to explain that the woman had been questioned as part of an investigation into whether defence information had been leaked.

Two days later Breen's boss, Eric Harrison, the Minister for Defence Production, met with Colonel Spry and Stan Roper, a senior officer at ASIO, to discuss the article and the investigation. Colonel Spry explained that the leak to the press seemed to have come from the minister's own department, but they had no evidence that the young woman had leaked any information—only that she had associated with people she knew to be Communists. Valda Seamons was moved from her position. At the time, this was explained as the consequence of a foolish association she had made—but it was also due to Mercia's reporting and the subsequent investigation.

The Daily Telegraph article was raised in parliament on the same day. The Government Whip asked about the employee, the investigation, and whether the employee had in fact been dismissed. The Acting Prime Minister, Sir Arthur Fadden, replied that he refused to 'discuss the activities of the security service'.

It had been over six months since Rex's article on the American draft treaty of friendship—or the 'Traitor Treaty', as Rex would later call it—had been published in the *Tribune*. A week after Fadden had refused to discuss the matter of the Defence Production employee, Liberal backbencher William 'Billy' Charles Wentworth, a staunch anti-Communist in the Menzies government, asked the Minister for External Affairs, Richard Casey, about the US 'Friendship Treaty' described in Rex's article.

Casey—Mercia's old boss as the Minister for the Department of National Development—had replaced Percy Spender as the Minister for External Affairs. He stood up in the House of Representatives to reply, explaining that there were a number of drafts of the treaty, and that the investigation into the serious matter of the leak was still proceeding.

Later the same day, Wentworth asked in parliament if Casey could give the date of the treaty draft, and also make available the date on which the public servant, Dr Burton, had ceased to be head of the Department of External Affairs, where he'd had access to the document. He finished his question by stating: 'The incident underlines once again the paramount duty of the Government to take action to get Communists out of the Commonwealth public service and out of the defence forces.'

Dr John Wear Burton had been appointed Secretary of the Department of External Affairs in 1947 at the age of just thirty-two. At the beginning of 1951, Burton had taken up the position of Australian High

Commissioner to Ceylon, but had resigned to return home to contest the upcoming federal election. When Casey and Wentworth spoke in parliament about the leak, Burton was the endorsed Labor candidate for the federal seat of Lowe. He had also left the previous week for the Peking Peace Conference—the same conference due to which the passports of so many Australian delegates had been cancelled.

Instead of taking the question on notice, Casey was clearly prepared for it and replied to Wentworth immediately, amid a barrage of interjections from the Opposition. Casey stated that the last draft of the treaty was put on paper around February 1950, and was available to four or five Commonwealth Government departments.

'I don't want the inference necessarily to be drawn that I suspect Dr Burton of this leak,' Mr Casey continued, 'because, after all, there is a period of time between the period in the first half of 1950 and the date of the appearance of this leak in November 1951, which would appear to make it improbable, at least, that Dr Burton had been responsible.' ASIO would, many years later, say they were satisfied that Dr Burton 'was in no way responsible for the leakages' of the draft treaty. Casey concluded:

The unfortunate part of this whole business is the fact that some senior public servant has been so—to put it in the mildest terms—remiss as to neglect his duty and so traitorous to his country as to send this information to a Communist journal.

Casey told parliament there was nothing essentially secret about the treaty, adding: 'But there are traitors in our midst in this country, and in the Commonwealth Government departments.'

Uproar from the Opposition followed, and the Speaker had to repeatedly call the Opposition members to order. Casey continued:

The information that has come my way in recent times, not only on this matter, about which I know a little bit more

114

than I am able to tell this House, makes me wonder where
the truth lies. There are traitors in our midst that we
are doing our best to discover. As I said this morning,
this matter had been under investigation for a number of
months and certain facts have come to light.

The Speaker tried to keep the House in order as Casey spoke about how, when Communism had become unpopular, members of the Labor party had then 'jumped on the bandwagon of popular opinion', before stating that 'The Government is doing its utmost to uncover the nest of traitors that exists somewhere or other in the public service.'

More interjections from the Opposition followed, before Casey repeated, 'The Government is endeavouring to unearth this small but extremely dangerous nest of traitors that exists in the public service.'

The *Tribune* article hadn't caused much of a fuss when it was published—but now, after Casey's 'Nest of Traitors' claim, it was being talked about in the mainstream media, with *The Sydney Morning Herald* spelling out the contents of the *Tribune* article alongside Casey's disclosure in Parliament House.

Two days after Casey's 'Nest of Traitors' assertion, Mercia called Rex from the GPO in Melbourne on his work phone at the *Tribune*. She was upset and asked that he come to Melbourne because she needed to speak with him urgently.

Rex was obviously annoyed and very curt on the phone. He told her, 'I can't possibly come down. I'm tied up,' and the conversation ended.

Little did Rex know that Mercia had rung under instruction from ASIO.

32

RUM BY THE FIRE

Two days later, on Saturday 31 May, Rex called Mercia at her Warrandyte address, saying he was in Melbourne.

Rex had flown to Melbourne the night before under an assumed name, Mr J Matthews, though he gave his correct address in Campsie. Unexpectedly, on the same flight were E.F. 'Ted' Hill and Vida Little, both CPA members. Ted Hill, now a barrister, had been elected State Secretary of the CPA in 1948; Vida Little would later run as an Independent Communist candidate in the Legislative Assembly seat of Albert Park in the 1958 Victorian election.

Unbeknown to all three, ASIO was watching and listening.

Rex told Ted and Vida that he was making a rushed trip to Melbourne to attend a special meeting of the CPA propaganda committee, and that he would also be seeing another person. This meeting, he stressed was very important and hush-hush. He also said his business would only take an hour or so, and he planned on returning to Sydney by plane the following afternoon. ASIO tracked him that night to the home of a married couple in Kew who were believed to be members of the Kew branch of the CPA, and whose home was a known CPA meeting place. It was noted that he had no luggage with him.

Rex caught the bus to Warrandyte the following day and found Mercia in the midst of packing her belongings. She was moving to St Kilda the following Monday.

Rex explained why he had been rather terse on the phone and had practically hung up on her, adding that what Casey and Wentworth had said in parliament should not have been mentioned over the telephone.

Sitting in front of the fire sipping rum, Mercia said she was worried about the 'Nest of Traitors' claim made in parliament, and that he would be made a pivot of the government's attacks, and she was concerned because of the close relationship she had with him.

'Don't worry,' he replied. 'You should not have phoned me up, anyway. I will look after you, I think the world of you. There's nothing I wouldn't do for you. Don't you worry. They can't do a bloody thing to me.'

According to Mercia's ASIO report, Rex then became amorous. Perhaps not for the first time.

Later, the pair walked to the nearby Warrandyte Hotel, where they shared a few drinks in the lounge while they waited for the bus to take him back to Melbourne.

'I am preparing a pamphlet,' he told her, 'on this question of allegations of traitors in the public service that has been made in Parliament.' He was going to incorporate references to witch hunts and persecutions of innocent people, and try to keep a finger on Casey's movements.

He once again warned her to keep away from the Peace Council rooms and public functions, and was angry that Mercia was mixed up with the Friday night group, which was run by Leila, and to which she had been invited. He told her to stay away from other Communists, and that he was to be her only contact.

Back at the airport, Rex was seemingly still unaware that he was being observed by ASIO. Travelling under his assumed name, he took his seat on the 7.40 p.m. plane for Sydney. Little did he know that Ron Richards from ASIO was seated right next to him.

Ron Richards reported that Rex had been drinking and slept most of the journey, though they did share a bottle of beer. Rex mentioned that he had spent his Sunday in front of a fire drinking rum in Warrandyte, a place about an hour's bus ride out of Melbourne in the Dandenong Ranges. He said he was thinking seriously of going to live in the place, which he described as 'most attractive, with a glorious view overlooking the river'.

Richards was certain Rex was unaware of his identity, and that he was not met at Mascot airport on arrival.

The following week Rex wrote an angry article—'How can Govt dare talk of 'Traitors'?'—that appeared in the *Guardian*, another CPA publication at that time.

The article started:

Last week the allegation was made in Canberra that 'traitors' in the Public Service had given me the details of a secret Treaty between Australia and the USA.

The 'secret' document was a secret only because the Government feared to make its infamous contents public. So, are the traitors those who told the people—or those who are the authors of a traitor treaty?

Adopting the US tactic of character assassination, W.C. Wentworth and External Affairs Minister Casey tried to divert attention from the Traitor Treaty by attacking Dr John Burton because he attended the Peking Peace Conference.

Rex went on to state categorically that the 'Treaty of Friendship, Commerce and Immigration' had not been given to him by Dr Burton, and that the treaty would break down existing economic barriers and turn Australia into nothing but a US colony.

Rex then turned his anger on the Labor Party, saying that, by its actions, the Opposition was at one with the government on this issue, with not one Labor member attacking the contents of the treaty or the government, or raising their voice against this 'horse trade':

```
The utter silence of the Opposition leaders on the Traitor
Treaty, and their later foul attacks on Dr Burton for
exposing US germ warfare in Korea, indicate how closely
both parliamentary groups are aligned with the US and its
war-mongering policy.
    The people can judge.
```

The article also appeared in the *Tribune*. Rex subsequently produced a sixteen-page booklet—'Where is the Nest of Traitors?'—containing almost the same material.

The following day, the Deputy Leader of the Opposition and prominent Labor Party member, Arthur Calwell, demanded in the House that the government prosecute the Communist newspaper the *Tribune*, and the author of the article that gave details of the confidential agreement with the United States.

The Acting Prime Minister, Sir Arthur Fadden, promised to have the matter looked into.

33

POLITE PEOPLE

The *Tribune* was not without its friends. Josef Triska from the Czechoslovakian Consulate contacted Rex two days after his article appeared and invited Rex and two other *Tribune* journalists, Len Fox, now remarried, and Bill Brown, to a film night at his home at 11 Roscoe Street, Bondi. The film, titled *Never Again Lidice*, was about the Nazi destruction of an entire town near Prague in 1942, in reprisal for a lethal attack on a high-ranking German official by the Czech resistance.

When ASIO surveilled the Bondi address that evening, it was noted that only Bill Brown and his wife, Freda, attended.

Mercia moved to 549 St Kilda Road, a small two-storey house in the style of an old coach-house. Cindy remembers how the original main house—a large white mansion—sat at the front of the block, with a tennis court out the back; their new home was to be found down the end of the driveway, next to the tennis court. Upstairs were two bedrooms and a bathroom; the entire ground floor was a combined living room and kitchen, perfect for entertaining. At the back of the block ran Alfred Lane, which led to busy Commercial Road; the Alfred Hospital was on the other side of this lane. The block sat between the Chevron hotel and the Blind Institute. Demolished long ago, their house is now the site of a high-rise commercial building.

ASIO national headquarters was located near her new address, at 'Netherby' 8 Queens Road. Built in 1891, the large white 'Netherby' mansion has since been incorporated into the next door hotel and is now used as a stately function centre. Mercia would have been run out of ASIO's Victorian Regional office rather than headquarters. It was situated in the old Theosophical Society building at 181–187 Collins Street, where Mercia's case officer would have been stationed.

Mercia would again be sharing her new home with her old journalist friend, Russell Grant, who was recovering from a bad car accident that had left one of his legs badly broken. He stayed in one bedroom; Mercia in the other. Rus, like many of Mercia's journalist friends, drank heavily. By the time Cindy went to live with them, he had been convinced by Mercia and other journalist friends to join Alcoholics Anonymous. Cindy remembers he would spend a lot of time in his room alone.

In ASIO's file on fellow journalist Bob Freestone is a non-redacted report of a telephone conversation between Leila and Mercia. On 10 June 1952, Leila informed Mercia that she had received a telegram from someone only identified as 'Lex', saying the baby had arrived. The timing would be right for the arrival of Rex and Vivienne's baby.

The report describes an everyday conversation, with Leila inquiring how the new house was, and Mercia replying it was going well, adding that Bob had dropped in to see her the previous evening. He had intended calling in for only a few minutes, but had stayed for about three hours. They signed off, with Mercia agreeing to call in for morning tea the following day.

Mercia was still regularly meeting Leila, both at Leila's work and for lunch. One time at Hoddle Café in Little Collins Street, Leila reiterated caution about Mercia's exposure to the CPA.

'The ban on your attendance at public functions must be enforced,' she emphasised, 'and your home is to be used for entertainment of polite people only. It must not be used for everyday functions, and it must not generally be known that the house is a meeting place.'

'What do you mean by "polite people"?' Mercia asked.

'It means when the Party wants to entertain anyone special, in good surroundings,' Leila replied. 'I have given your name to a group in St Kilda Road, but they have been lax.'

Mercia said she knew general Party work was out, because Rex had told her that again at their last meeting. She was more useful alone, and that she was to work through him.

Despite this conversation, Mercia sent out invitations to a buffet tea at her new home at 549 St Kilda Road on 16 August, to listen to recordings of proceedings of the 'House of Un-American Committee' (sic), entitled 'America Speaks Out'.

The House Un-American Activities Committee in the US House of Representatives had been created to 'investigate alleged disloyalty and subversive activities on the part of private citizens, public employees, and those organisations suspected of having either fascist or communist ties'. Mercia's invitation tantalisingly urged those invited not to miss these most enlightening and revealing recordings.

At one of Cindy's meetings at the ASIO office with Kieron, she was asked if she remembered the house at Warrandyte or socialising with Rex Chiplin's family in Sydney. Cindy only remembers her home in St Kilda Road, so she assumes she arrived in Melbourne around this time. ASIO also asked Cindy repeatedly if she remembered different people in the files. Memories of a child, and the fact that her mother never introduced her to people, meant the answer to many of their questions was 'No'.

Cindy does remember travelling by bus on weekends to Warrandyte to visit a family and playing with another young child and teasing the chickens. Mercia didn't get her driver's licence until the late 1960s, and was an expert on getting around on public transport.

Cindy does tell one story of her mother with a chuckle. They were running to catch a train at Flinders Street Station, and the elastic gave way in her mother's underpants, which fell to her ankles. Mercia just stepped right out of them and kept running to catch the train, leaving her broken underwear on the ramp leading to the platform. Mercia didn't even look back. Cindy was shocked seeing her mother, who always insisted on everything being 'proper', running around without underwear.

Australia in the 1950s was no place for a single woman with an illegitimate child, and Cindy remembers Melbourne being even more conservative than Sydney. When Cindy moved to Melbourne, Mercia made it known that she was a widow; 'Mrs Masson' was much more socially acceptable now she had a child with her. With the change of Cindy's surname also to Masson by deed poll, Miss Masson became a name of the not-so-distant past. Cindy firmly believes Mercia brought her to Melbourne as it looked better professionally for a middle-aged woman to have a child and be 'widowed', rather than be seen as a spinster.

After Cindy moved to live with her mother, she lost contact with her father, Harry Pearce. When her grandmother Ruth died in 1966, she and Mercia went to Newcastle for the funeral and found Harry sitting forlornly in a chair in his mother's house, his home having been stripped by other family members taking anything they wanted. Cindy had felt sorry for the old man sitting in the chair and was amazed to see her mother actually flirting with her old lover, flicking her scarf around her neck, showing him that she still had it. Cindy thought it revealed that there was still a bit of feeling between them.

Harry died two years after his mother, hit by a car one night as he crossed a busy road in Newcastle. Mercia and Cindy went to his funeral, but no one in the Pearce family would go near them. Her father had married again and Cindy now had a younger half-brother; she remembers at the funeral with some hurt how the little boy's mother would not let her son go near Cindy.

Living with her mother in Melbourne, some school holidays Cindy would be sent back to Killcare to be with her maternal grandmother, Lucy—but never again to Newcastle. Mercia didn't really have holidays; she was dedicated to whatever and wherever she was working.

Cindy also remembers, as a young girl, musical afternoons on Mondays at the home of Moya Horowitz in North Yarra. The Horowitz girls, Moya and her younger sister, were both talented musicians, and Mercia would often accompany them on the piano. When Cindy and Kieron visited ASIO on the second visit, she was surprised to see Moya's name in the files, and to discover that Moya was also an agent. Cindy remembers enjoying these musical evenings a lot more than the film nights at her home.

For Cindy, the film nights are a dark chapter of her childhood. Cindy doesn't recall ever going to the picture theatre with her mother. The film nights at St Kilda featured terrible black-and-white war movies that gave her nightmares. One that stuck in her mind depicted Polish soldiers with ferocious dogs; the soldiers were carrying big guns and searching for people in tunnels. There were never any other children at these nights, and she had to sit quietly while the films were screened.

Her mother's familiar silver tray would come out for these afternoon and evening events, full of delicacies that Mercia had created; Cindy remembers there was always a lot of cigarette smoke and plenty of alcohol. Russell Grant was not the only journalist with a drinking problem.

Cindy would be sent to bed when it became late. One film night, not long after Cindy was sent to live in Melbourne, one of Mercia's male guests made his way into the bedroom that Cindy shared with her mother. Cindy slept in one single bed; her mother in another. Cindy was asleep and woke to find a man lying on top of her, his hand between her legs, hurting her. Cindy lay there scared and confused; but the man left when he realised she was awake. She has no memory of who the perpetrator was, only of being hurt and scared.

A lot of her mother's friends were men, generally older men. Cindy never told her mother about what had happened that particular night. At the time she felt that Mercia wouldn't have believed her, that she would have thought that she was just making up a story.

34

THE RED BAITER

On the twenty-third of August, Mercia was in Sydney again and went to Campsie to visit Rex, Vivienne and their new baby daughter. Mercia reported back to ASIO that Rex was careful not to say anything in front of his wife concerning her work for him.

Rex said he had inside information about some proposed legislation; from their conversation, she believed this related to the tightening of secrecy provisions.

After telling her about this, Rex added, 'I am worried about Fergan O'Sullivan and his drinking in Canberra.' He said Fergan was now sharing a flat with Bruce Yuill, a young economist.

Rex then changed the subject: 'I have been searching Australia for Hashim.'

Hashim was a Pakistani journalist who had come out to Australia under the Colombo Plan to study, and Rex wanted to introduce him to the 'right people'. Mercia had met Hashim in Melbourne; he said he was a member of the Communist Party in Pakistan and was hoping to study left-wing movements in Australia. Probably not the academic work the Menzies government thought he was doing when they issued him with a visa.

'I missed Hashim in Canberra,' Rex told her. 'Tell him not to phone the *Tribune* office, but to write to me at Campsie.'

When Hashim later called in at her home in St Kilda Road, Mercia dutifully passed on the information—that he should write and go to Chiplin's home, but not to ring.

Rex had good reason to be cautious, as the events of the next week would show.

※

Earlier that week, in his column 'Rex Chiplin Writes . . . a Canberra Diary', Rex had written about Liberal backbencher Bill Wentworth—whose loathing of the Communist Party, and of Rex in particular, was well known, and who had a reputation for being a 'red-baiter'.

Rex couldn't seem to help doing a bit of baiting back. He wrote in his column three short sentences that greatly upset the Liberal politician:

```
Last week W.C. Wentworth had a long lobby discussion with
Messrs. Frankovich, Oster and Dodd—three of the Yank
uranium experts out here.

All told, there were six Yank uranium men here; three are
to be stationed at Rum Jungle, two at Uranium Hill, and
the other stays in Canberra, just to keep an eye on things.

Incidentally W.C. and German scientist Schliecher [sic] had
some long discussions at Rum Jungle during the parliamentary
recess.
```

Wentworth was furious. He stood up in Parliament on 27 August, towards the end of a discussion on budget estimates, and stated that he wanted to raise the matter of an article by Rex Chiplin in the Communist journal *Tribune*, detailing certain happenings in the lobby of Parliament House. Wentworth reminded his fellow politicians that

Chiplin was the Communist who boasted that he had suborned a high-ranking public service officer to betray secrets. He then read out the three sentences and said the first sentence was significant, before the Deputy Chair interrupted, asking him if he could connect his remarks to the proposed budget vote before parliament.

'I have referred to a happening in this building,' Wentworth emphasised, saying that the three named men mentioned in the article were new arrivals in the country and were not known. 'This suggests that there is Communist espionage at work in this building.' He went on, talking about the United States having interest in the development of uranium in Australia, and that the Soviet Union was concerned to stop it.

Wentworth then corrected the last offending sentence in Rex's jibe, explaining that at the Rum Jungle uranium mine he had spoken with a Czech employee by the name of Slice, not a German scientist named Schleicher, and that the espionage network was not only in Parliament House, but also at Rum Jungle.

He then quoted Section 122 of the Constitution, giving Parliament unlimited sovereignty as far as the Australian Capital Territory (ACT) was concerned, saying that those in parliament had the power to make such laws as they thought proper regarding Communists in the ACT. He spoke of the necessity to exclude from the ACT signed-up members of the Communist Party, such as Rex Chiplin, who he then branded 'a full and complete traitor'.

Wentworth wanted Rex banned from entering the press gallery, the precincts of the chamber, or even the entire ACT, over which they had authority. He then reminded parliament that they had this same authority over the Northern Territory, where Rum Jungle was located.

After he sat down, the politicians went ahead with their vote on the budget.

※

Two days later in Parliament House, the new TASS correspondent, Victor Antonov, appeared in the Canberra press gallery with Vladimir

Petrov and another Soviet Embassy employee. Question Time that day dealt with Papua New Guinea, civil defence, Commonwealth contracts, government loans and finance, housing, road maintenance, textiles, immigration, sugar, industrial production, employment, television, social services—and perhaps of most interest to the Soviets, atomic weapons.

The Labor member for Fawkner asked the Minister for Defence to indicate the extent, if any, of Australia's participation in the atomic tests that were to be conducted in the Montebello Islands, and if it was correct that the British authorities undertaking the tests were reluctant to allow active Australian participation in the work.

The minister gave a somewhat evasive answer, saying that a considerable time ago the British Government had asked the Australian Government whether it was prepared to provide a site for atomic tests. The government indicated that it was prepared to do so, and was then asked whether it would do some preliminary preparation on the site selected. The Australian Government undertook to do that, and completed the work required to be done.

The minister then stated:

The conduct of the tests themselves is entirely in the hands of the British Government, which has not asked us for any further help. If the British Government should need further help, the Government would comply with any request it made. However, the British Government is the authority responsible for the tests, and will itself decide the nature of the tests to be carried out, who shall attend them and the information that will be released as a result of them.

This would have been of some interest to the Soviets.

An hour and a half before the parliamentary session started, the Commonwealth Investigation Service had raided the Left Wing Book Club and printery of the *Tribune* in Sydney's Market Street, the *Tribune* office above it, and Rex Chiplin's home.

35

SECRET POLICE RAID

At 9 a.m., four Commonwealth Investigation Service officers entered the *Tribune*'s office above the Communist Party bookshop in Market Street. The *Tribune* editor, Alfred Watt, protested, but to no avail. The security officers searched files and office drawers for nearly two hours; but they didn't search anyone in the office, despite a warrant enabling them to do so.

They took some cuttings and notes, as well as a letter congratulating the *Tribune* on Rex's 'Friendship Treaty' story the previous November. Alf Watt protested against the removal of any material, but the CIS officers told him the papers seized referred to the matter they were concerned about.

TASS's press agent Victor Antonov also arrived at the *Tribune* office, but quickly left once he realised the premises were being raided by federal officers.

During the *Tribune* raid, three other security men simultaneously entered Rex and Vivienne's home at Campsie—including Alf Wilks, who was involved in the 1950 raid on the Communist Party offices. They searched the house, but did not seize anything.

Rex later said the officers told him they were convinced he sourced his information for his *Tribune* article on trade and immigration from a 'leak' in Canberra. Wentworth's outburst in parliament seemed to have brought some action.

After the raid, *Tribune* staff issued a statement protesting against the 'secret police raid' as 'an attack on the right and liberty of the Labor movement to freely criticise the government of the day, and a serious blow to the freedom of the Press in Australia'.

Rex then wrote a scathing article in the *Tribune*: 'THEY RAIDED MY HOME', the headline blared.

Rex's fury was again obvious:

```
By authorising this raid, Menzies has declared war on the
sanctity of the home; war on women and children. He will not
get away with this. Although there is no suggestion that
Wilks and Co were other than considerate and courteous,
that is not the point. It was only by the greatest good
fortune that my wife was not alone at the time.
```

To Rex's annoyance, the three men had even searched the room where his wife lay ill, nursing their three-month-old baby—including his wife's dressing table and the cabinet containing the baby's clothes. Rex asserted it was the first raid on a private home since the early days of the Second World War, when raids on Australia First, a far-right group, had taken place.

Rex added that Wilks had informed him that the raid was in connection with the *Tribune* articles and the publication of a pamphlet dealing with the 'Secret US Treaty' with Australia. Rex told a *Sun* reporter that he regarded his source of information as inviolate.

Rex couldn't help a touch of humour. He and Vivienne shared their house with its owner, Stan Rust, a widower, whose room was also searched. Rex wrote: 'Through the grimness of the scene shone the indominable spirit of the working class who will never bend the knee to Menzies.' While a security man went through a huge case of newspaper clippings, Stan perched beside him and tried to sell him a copy of the *Tribune*. He failed, observing later that it would have been a 'difficult sale to consolidate'.

It wasn't just Rex that ASIO was focusing on. A former temporary employee at External Affairs had also been brought in for an interview on 1 September, but no further action on it was noted on the file.

Mercia heard about the raid, but—as with the birth of his child— she did not hear it directly from Rex himself. Her flatmate, Russell Grant, received a letter from Rex, which he then shared with Mercia. Mercia took the letter to her room and typed a copy of it. She handed the original back to Rus, and later gave the copy to her case officer.

As a result of the raids, Rex and Mercia were not seen together in public for some time.

36

INTERROGATION

Rex was seen at the annual *Tribune* picnic in Sydney's Clifton Gardens. Reports were made about who he met for drinks, his travel to and from Canberra, and where he stayed. A leaflet titled 'People's Choice', authorised by Rex, was noted on his file, and he was seen at the Soviet Embassy for Soviet National Day celebrations.

However, it was also observed that on his visits to Canberra, Rex was not appearing in the press gallery at Parliament House. He either had other business in Canberra, or perhaps he was wary of Bill Wentworth's threat to expel all CPA members from parliament and the ACT. On 19 November, he was seen in conversation with Fergan O'Sullivan outside Bruce Yuill's flat in the Canberra suburb of Reid. ASIO was watching.

That same month, Petrov received a cable from Moscow, asking him to find out what Australia's reaction would be if a person named Milner were to return to Australia. Ian Milner, originally from New Zealand, had been employed in External Affairs before leaving Australia in 1947 to work at the United Nations. He was now living and teaching English at a university in Czechoslovakia.

Petrov asked Moscow if he could approach Rex Chiplin for help. Moscow agreed.

Investigations by the Commonwealth Investigation Service into the source of the leak continued, with Inspector Wilks, who had led the raid on Rex's home, focusing on the draft treaty and its interdepartmental movements. An internal minute from ASIO's regional director of the ACT, noted that Inspector Wilks had discovered that the Department of National Development was the original source of the leaked treaty document, and every assistance was to be accorded to him.

Inspector Wilks was on his way to Melbourne, where the Department of National Development was based, to investigate further.

Alfred Amos Wilks was described as a hawk-nosed, florid-faced, rotund and heavy-set man. He had joined the NSW Police in 1924, moving to the Australian Capital Police in Canberra in 1945, and then joining the Commonwealth Investigation Service in Sydney, where he was appointed detective inspector in 1947, and CIS acting deputy director of New South Wales from 1957.

Mercia was called in and interrogated by Wilks, in the company of an unnamed ASIO officer. She stated emphatically that she had not leaked any unauthorised document to Rex Chiplin.

Wilks was unaware that Mercia was an ASIO agent, though he did know of her friendship with Rex, and questioned her on that. Mercia stood her ground, telling them she had a right to be friends with whoever she liked, and reiterating that she had not leaked the treaty document.

It was a time for moves.

Ric Oke had been permanently transferred to Wonthaggi in regional Victoria as a CPA country organiser, and Mercia would not have direct contact with him in Melbourne again.

Internal politics between Australia's two security services, ASIO and the Commonwealth Investigation Service, were about to undermine Mercia's good working relationship with Ray Whitrod. At ASIO's inception, the CIS had been stripped of arguably its best operatives, which had led to tension between the two organisations. It would take a special person to improve morale. Ray Whitrod was encouraged to apply for the position of Director of the Commonwealth Investigation Service. He was successful and moved to Canberra with his family.

37

IN FEAR

On 5 March 1953, Joseph Stalin died.

Stalin had ruled Communist USSR for over a quarter of a century, industrialising the nation, collectivising its agricultural sector and consolidating his position by police repression. He helped defeat Nazi Germany, extended Soviet control into the Eastern European states and led the Soviet Union into the nuclear age.

Tribune published a special four-page Stalin Memorial edition of the paper on 9 March, with the front-page headline stating that 'STALIN'S NAME IS IMMORTAL'. It began: 'J.V. Stalin was the greatest man and the dominating figure of our time. For as long as human beings continue to exist on this earth, the name and cause of Stalin, of Communism, will live.' In sharp contrast, two days earlier an editorial in *The Daily Telegraph* had begun with: 'Stalin is dead. So passes a man who brought nothing of value but much of misery to the world.'

In early March 1953, Mercia's new case officer, Stan Roper, instructed her to travel to Sydney and meet with Rex, and inform him of Wilks's interrogation, to record his reaction.

She telephoned Rex to say she was in the city, and they arranged to meet the following afternoon at 5 p.m. Under the same instructions as before, Mercia waited at the entrance to St James Station and, when Rex arrived, they went into the nearby St James Hotel and had a drink and dinner.

Rex said he and Vivienne had moved to Ryde and were building a new home in Gymea Bay.

Mercia then broached the subject ASIO had been keen for her to impart: her interview with Mr Wilks.

'I have been upset and worried about a visit I had from Mr Wilks,' she told him.

'Don't talk about that here,' he ordered.

Rex changed the subject, again complaining that Fergan was causing more headaches, getting horribly drunk and disgracing himself.

After dinner they caught a bus to his home in Ryde. Walking from the bus stop, a good half hour's walk, he turned to her and said, 'Now tell me everything that Wilks said and how he said it.'

Mercia told him how she had been questioned at a room in Collins Street about her work at the Department of National Development, and her association with Rex.

'What did you say about that? You can see that's why I didn't want to be seen in public places with you.'

'I admitted my association with you. After all, it was an established fact, and Wilks seemed to know,' she explained. 'I was challenged about the flagging of the file in which the trade document had been kept. I was quite sincere in saying that I have no idea concerning the contents of files flagged by me. Unless one is particularly interested, it was something not done.'

She turned to him and added, 'You are a complete stinker not to have told me how close I was and to have allowed me to be brought into it.'

'I am really sorry, and distressed,' he told her. 'It is sometimes better for a person not to know, and then they can't tell. It was for your own protection that I kept things from you.'

'I cannot even remember all the names of the people working around me, about whom I have been questioned', she told him.

Rex then asked whether a particular employee was still with the department.

'I don't know,' she replied. 'I think so. I haven't been in touch with the division for months.'

'Don't worry,' he replied, 'but let me know if anything else happens. I may be in Melbourne soon, and I will let you know, and you can put me up.'

She said Wilks had questioned her about her left-wing political outlook, and she'd told him that she made no secret of her political outlook or what her interests were.

Mercia made a full written report about her meeting with Rex in Sydney on 10 March, passing it to her new case officer.

In May, Mercia was back in Sydney yet again. She met Rex using the same mode of communication—a telephone call, and then waiting outside the railway station entrance.

Rex considered it would be desirable for Mercia to continue undertaking left-wing work with Ric Oke's mother, Mrs Mabel Oke.

Mercia then asked, 'Am I to be used as I was before and left in trouble?'

'No, you'll be all right. Have you heard anything more?'

'No, but I lived in fear all the time.'

'Don't do that,' Rex replied.

In the United States, two American Communists, Julius and Ethel Rosenberg, had been sentenced to death. The married couple had been found guilty of conspiracy to commit espionage by providing top-secret information about radar, sonar, jet propulsion and nuclear weapon designs to the Soviet Union.

They were both executed by electric chair at Sing Sing Prison in New York on 19 June 1953.

※

One of the VENONA code names was SESTRA (Russian for 'Sister'). From the VENONA intercepts, both ASIO and Britain's MI5 knew SESTRA had given information to KLOD. By the time SESTRA was identified as Frances Bernie, a young typist who had worked for 'Doc' Evatt, the Labor Attorney-General and Foreign Minister during the war, she had already left Evatt's office, and they were unable to interview her for fear of exposing VENONA's existence. Nevertheless, they kept her under surveillance.

When a refugee gave Frances Bernie's name as a referee, ASIO saw an opportunity to interview her, without giving VENONA away. The head of ASIO approached the Attorney-General and asked permission to offer her immunity from prosecution, if she were to speak about her association with the CPA. This was granted.

Frances Bernie was interviewed in June 1953 by Ron Richards and another ASIO officer at her home in Wahroonga. She admitted she had been a member of the CPA from 1941 to 1944, and had removed material from Evatt's office and given it to Wally Clayton (KLOD) at Marx House during her lunch break.

She gave two further interviews and told ASIO officers that she had also typed up her own summaries of documents and accounts of conversations, and sometimes made an extra carbon copy if she thought what she was typing would be of interest to Clayton. She put her actions down to youthful idealism, and explained that she had not seen Wally Clayton since marrying and moving to the outer suburbs of Sydney in 1945.

Independently of VENONA, Bernie's admission gave ASIO confirmation of public service leaks to the Soviet Union through the Communist Party of Australia.

It also offered a reason to approach Wally Clayton for questioning— but he was proving hard to find.

38

ANOTHER RAID

The security services seemed to believe the CPA was planning on removing documents and records from each of its state headquarters to safe places over the weekend of 18–19 July. They applied for search warrants to raid various premises in and around Sydney associated with the CPA and certain members. Ray Whitrod, now head of the Commonwealth Investigation Service, travelled to Sydney on 15 July.

On the morning of Friday 17 July 1953, ASIO and the CIS raided eight locations in the city and suburbs, including CPA headquarters and the *Tribune* at 40 Market Street, and the homes of more individuals: the *Communist Review* publisher, the *Communist Review* printer, a member of the CPA Central Committee, and again, Rex and Vivienne's home.

Rex may have been tipped off about the raids. The CIS went to the Ryde address they had for Rex, seemingly unaware that he and Vivienne had moved into their new home at Gymea Bay the weekend before. This mix-up would delay the search of Rex's home for three hours as a new warrant with the correct address was issued.

At the new address, officers tried to get Rex to admit authorship of a disparaging article against the monarchy in the *Communist Review* in June, as the Queen's coronation approached. Having already experienced a security raid, Rex did not answer their questions.

Apart from some articles at the home of the Central Committee member—including an extract from Richard Casey's confidential diary—nothing else of significance was found at the other properties.

The Communist press condemned the raids as the work of a Fascist government.

Ten days after the raid, a secret report reached ASIO of a meeting between Rex Chiplin and solicitor Harold Rich. Rex was requesting legal advice on a person's standing if they were being interrogated by the security police. Could he refuse to answer questions, and demand to see a warrant if there was a threat of being 'locked up'?

Mr Rich advised that Rex would not be obliged to give any information except his name and address, and that he could refuse to answer any other questions unless it applied to taxation, in which case he would have to supply information. Rex could also be arrested and taken to a lock-up and charged without a specific document with them to enable his arrest then and there, but he couldn't be held without charge.

Rex asked, 'Can't you sort of stand on your rights and say, "I will do nothing until a solicitor comes?"'

Harold Rich replied, 'You can do nothing, but they could take you by force.'

In Melbourne, after hearing about the raids, Russell Grant told Mercia that Rex had informed him in Canberra, back in 1949, that Rex was the liaison man between the Soviet Embassy and the Communist Party of Australia.

This information was duly passed on to ASIO.

When the Prime Minister returned from the new Queen's coronation, he was briefed by the head of ASIO about the extract they'd found from Casey's diary, and that several officers from the Department of External Affairs were under suspicion of passing information to the Soviet Embassy.

The following week, Fergan O'Sullivan, now working as Doc Evatt's press secretary, was seen travelling on the same plane from Canberra to Sydney as Vladimir Petrov. At the airport, the pair were seen entering the passenger terminal and the refreshment room together, before boarding a Commonwealth car that had been organised for Fergan, and driving to an address in Dulwich Hill, which would later prove to be Fergan's Sydney residence. Fergan got out with an overnight bag, checked the mailbox and then entered the premises. He returned to the car, which was then driven to Elizabeth Street in the city near Central Station, where Petrov alighted.

Two days before Christmas 1953, Vladimir Petrov's boss—the Soviet First Deputy Premier and Head of State Security, Lavrentiy Beria—was shot dead in the Soviet Union, as part of an ongoing power struggle in the Soviet Union after Joseph Stalin's death.

PART
2

EXPOSURE

39

DEFECTION

In January 1954, Petrov met Rex in Sydney's Kings Cross, acting on the request from Moscow for information on the previous External Affairs employee, Ian Milner. They were to meet there twice, but Rex was unable to help with the information Petrov sought.

MI5 had suggested to ASIO that getting a Soviet agent to defect would be the best way to source Soviet espionage information. The opportunity came as the time approached for Third Secretary Vladimir Petrov to leave Australia. Things had been going downhill for Mr and Mrs Petrov since the arrival in October of the new Russian ambassador, who was more critical of Petrov than his predecessor.

On the morning of 24 December 1953, Petrov had been in a car accident. He told Michael Bialoguski, the Russian doctor and security agent with whom he'd formed a friendship, that he had been driving to Cooma to meet a French diplomat when he had been forced off the road by a large vehicle. His car rolled several times and was burnt out. Petrov was not badly hurt, but still carried a limp when he was in Sydney on 29 December.

Petrov had been shocked by the accident, and told Bialoguski he was annoyed at the lack of sympathy from his colleagues. He was further upset that, because he'd let the insurance lapse on the vehicle, the ambassador was making him cover the costs of a new car. He told Bialoguski that he wanted to stay in Australia—even without his wife, who still had family in Russia.

Bialoguski met Petrov again in January and reported to ASIO about a frank discussion he and Petrov had about a possible defection. 'Look how they killed that bastard Baria,' Petrov is reported as saying. 'And how many people did Beria kill? I will stay here. I will tell the whole truth. I will write a true story. I will fix those bastards.'

Petrov knew his life would be in danger; his decision to defect would not have been made lightly.

On 19 February, Petrov told Bialoguski he had been ordered to return to Russia in two months' time, but he thought his wife had definitely decided against staying because of her family in Russia.

ASIO officer Ron Richards met Petrov eight days later at Bialoguski's flat to discuss the possibility of Petrov's defection. Petrov asked for a guarantee of physical protection and material assistance to establish himself in Australia. He was promised £5000, with six months' holiday to write his book.

On 17 March 1954, another article written by Rex caught ASIO's attention. His story, 'Dragnet Clause in Crimes Act', stated that Menzies would announce in his upcoming policy speech that the *Crimes Act*'s industrial and political sections would be amended to deal with Communists. The previous raids on Rex's premises had relied on the *Crimes Act* to obtain search warrants; the proposed amendments would be retrospective.

Rex also stated in the article that he had been told that in mid-1953, the Australian Attorney-General had met with US lawyer Richard W. Byrd, then a counsellor at the American Embassy in Canberra, to discuss how the US Attorney-General had got around the US Constitution, which specifically pledges freedom of speech, both written and assembly.

ASIO scrambled. On the same day that this article appeared, ASIO sent a secret memo from its regional director in Canberra, stating that, if the contents of Rex's article were correct, there could be another leak—this time in the Attorney-General's department.

The day of Vladimir Petrov's defection was decided: 3 April 1954. Petrov would be visiting Sydney to meet his replacement, Mr E.V. Kovalenok, who would be arriving from the Soviet Union. After meeting him, Petrov would not return to Canberra; making an excuse, he would stay in Sydney, where he would sign the application for political asylum.

On the day of his defection, Petrov was under ASIO surveillance the entire time, and was observed stopping for a beer at four different hotels. That afternoon Petrov met once again with Ron Richards, showing him all the documents he'd brought with him from the Soviet Embassy.

That evening, the head of ASIO, Colonel Spry, arrived at Bialoguski's flat and was introduced to Petrov.

Petrov signed the document seeking political asylum, and admitted being a Russian spy.

ASIO had their defector.

40

PETROV TALKS

Ron Richards started interviewing Petrov from the day he defected. Petrov talked, and Rex Chiplin was implicated from the start.

Petrov confirmed a lot of what the VENONA intercepts had shown—that documents on Australian foreign policy from the Department of External Affairs had been given to a member of the Soviet Embassy between 1945 and 1948. Petrov was also able to confirm the identities of Australians who helped or were of interest to the Soviets, and their relevant code names in the enciphered messages from Moscow Central.

Petrov told Richards that Rex Chiplin's code name was CHARLIE, and that in 1952, Rex had warned Pakhomov that the security services were interested in two women working at the embassy: a Miss Koslova and Mrs Petrov. This leak, Petrov later found, had apparently been passed on to Rex through a CPA Central Committee member, and had come inadvertently from a female secretary in the security services who was in love with a Communist.

Further, Petrov told Richards that CHARLIE said he had a few friends in the Department of External Affairs, a 'couple of chaps'.

Richards asked Petrov: 'Chiplin's code name is CHARLIE, that right?'

'CHARLIE, yes,' Petrov replied.

'Is Chiplin still active as an agent?' Richards asked.

'Yes,' Petrov replied.

Finally, after years of ASIO surveillance, here was proof that Rex was a Soviet agent.

'Does he still operate a group in External Affairs?'

'He told me one month ago,' Petrov replied.

'One month ago. In Sydney?'

'In Sydney.'

'He did not say who?' Richards asked. 'He didn't mention anybody?'

'No,' Petrov replied, 'I did not ask him about the names.'

When Petrov defected, he passed to ASIO several intelligence documents that he had taken or copied from the embassy safe. Only two of the documents were in English. One was a typed description of the habits of the Canberra press gallery. Document H, as it would become known, was written by Fergan O'Sullivan—Mercia and Rex's friend and fellow journalist, who at the time of the defection was the press secretary to Doc Evatt, Australia's Opposition leader.

Mercia had reported Rex talking about Fergan. Rex and Fergan had been seen together outside Bruce Yuill's flat in Canberra. Fergan was also known to have travelled to Sydney in the same plane as Petrov, then given the Soviet a lift in his Commonwealth-supplied car. Petrov also confirmed meeting Fergan for lunch the day after their shared flight. Fergan's move to the Opposition leader's office would have been of interest to not only the Soviets.

Petrov told ASIO that he met Rex on three occasions: once at the Soviet Embassy, and then twice in Kings Cross a month or so before his defection. Rex was also mentioned in the 'Moscow Letters'—cables from Moscow Central.

On 13 April, 10 days after Petrov's defection, the Department of External Affairs formally notified the Soviet Embassy of the event. Menzies told his Cabinet colleagues of the defection earlier that day, and waited until the Soviets had been informed before announcing it in parliament. In this stunning announcement, Menzies also stated that, in view of the evidence brought across by Vladimir Petrov, the government would be establishing a Royal Commission on Espionage in Australia.

The Soviet Government announced that it would recall its ambassador and staff from Canberra. Six days later, the embassy closed, and all its members departed.

On the day of the Soviet Government's announcement, Petrov asked if he could clarify the previous comments he had made about Rex Chiplin.

Petrov explained that, when Mr Richards had asked, 'Is Chiplin still active as an agent?' and Petrov had replied 'Yes', Petrov feared that his blunt reply had been misconstrued.

Petrov went on to clarify that in his opinion, if Chiplin had been asked for information by a Soviet official, Chiplin would have been prepared to supply the information if it was within his knowledge, otherwise he would try to obtain the required information. It was for that reason that Petrov considered Rex still active as an agent.

Petrov then added that Rex had never been paid for any information, and was not given any presents from the embassy, as far as he knew.

And at no time did he discuss with Rex the issue of the female secretary who had informed a Communist that the security services were interested in Mrs Petrov and Miss Koslova.

On 19 April, Mrs Petrov would also defect in dramatic fashion.

It had been organised that she would fly back to Russia via Darwin, accompanied by two armed Russian couriers, who linked their arms through hers and directed her onto the plane at Sydney's Mascot airport. But at Darwin airport, when the plane stopped to refuel, her two escorts were disarmed by Northern Territory Police. Evdokia was then formally asked by the Northern Territory's Acting Administrator if she wished to seek political asylum.

She said yes, but only after talking with her husband on the phone and ascertaining that he was in fact still alive.

Ron Richards flew to Darwin the following day and brought her back to her husband, where she then made a formal written application for political asylum.

Evdokia Petrov was as big a coup for ASIO as her husband; she was aware of and had handled many ciphered messages at the Soviet Embassy.

Evdokia too started to give ASIO information.

In the next edition of the *Tribune*, a scathing article accused Vladimir Petrov of being a traitor to his country and his class.

The article reported that Menzies had quoted Petrov as saying he was deserting Communism because he had seen the Australian way of life and wanted to live comfortably in Australia. The *Tribune*, which repeatedly ran articles applauding the utopian lifestyle in Communist countries, was full of scorn. The same edition also ran an article asking how much money Menzies had promised to give Petrov so he would be comfortable. The £5000 that was to be given to the Petrovs was not public knowledge at that stage.

The following week, once the terms of reference had been finalised, a Royal Commission on Espionage was announced. The Commission was to inquire into, and report on, four matters:

1. The information from Vladimir Petrov about espionage and related activities in Australia.

2. Whether espionage had been conducted or attempted by Soviet representatives or agents in Australia and, if so, by whom and by what methods.

3. Whether any people or organisations in Australia had communicated information or documents to any such Soviet representative that might prejudice the security of Australia.

4. Whether any people or organisations in Australia might have aided or abetted such espionage.

Three Supreme Court judges from across Australia were chosen as Justices for the Royal Commission: William Francis Langer Owen, who would also be the Chairman, from New South Wales; Roslyn Foster Bowie Philp, from Queensland; and George Coutts Ligertwood, from South Australia.

The Justices would be assisted by three lawyers acting as Counsel before the commission: Victor Windeyer, the Senior Counsel Assisting, George Pape and Bernard Riley. Major General Sir William John Victor Windeyer QC had commanded an infantry battalion during World War II and, upon returning to civilian life, had returned to the law, becoming a King's Counsel in 1949. Windeyer had been the first choice to run ASIO when it was first formed in that same year, but had decided against taking the position.

The Communist press questioned the fact that the Royal Commission would hold its first sitting just a few days before the upcoming federal election, with the *Tribune* calling it 'a continuation of Menzies' vicious attacks on the democratic rights of the people'.

41

ALBERT HALL

Victor Windeyer was keen to call before the Royal Commission witnesses based on Petrov's documents from the Soviet Embassy. But ASIO wanted to delve deeper into the papers, concentrate on the spy ring shown in them, and interview Petrov before he appeared at the Commission. Windeyer's counter-argument was that the terms of reference meant a report was required as soon as possible.

With the volume of work involved, ASIO started up a Royal Commission Section.

On 7 May, at his home in Sydney, Victor Windeyer interviewed both Mr and Mrs Petrov, accompanied by Ron Richards. Several witnesses were issued with subpoenas—including the elusive Wally Clayton, who had now been identified as KLOD by both VENONA and Petrov. But despite calls through the papers for information on him from the general public, Wally Clayton had disappeared. They did receive one letter from an optometrist, who said a man matching Wally's description had visited him recently, and investigations were ongoing.

The first hearing began on 17 May 1954 in Canberra, at the neo-classic Albert Hall near Parliament House. A ball was booked for the premises the following night, so the Commission had use of the hall for just two days.

A coat of arms had been placed over the entrance; inside, a plywood table was set up for the three Justices, with a small microphone in front of each. Gilded green and gold curtains hung behind the Judges with another small coat of arms pinned onto them, giving a faint air of formality. Two large plywood tables sat on a red-carpeted dais in front of the Judges, one for Counsel Assisting, and the second for witness Counsel.

Glistening diplomatic cars arrived outside, bearing ambassadors from the United States, China, Japan, Thailand, New Zealand, Canada and India; an officer from the Swedish Legation was watching Soviet interests in Canberra now the embassy was closed. The foreign representatives made their way into the hall to the click of press cameras. Their reserved seats were at the front of the court. Humorously, one of the journalists noted that an inevitable dog was present and had to be chased away from the entrance, twice.

A huge press and radio contingent were in attendance, including Rex, as the three Commissioners arrived, not in judicial robes and wigs, but in morning-dress attire—striped pants, black jackets and sporting Homburg hats, as worn by Winston Churchill.

Two barristers, Fred Paterson, the only CPA member elected to an Australian parliament, and Max Julius, were in attendance 'under a watching brief', a brief held by a barrister to follow a case on behalf of a client, who is not directly involved. It is assumed that this client was the CPA.

The three Judges made their way into the hall, to their plywood table; in front of them sat Mr Herde, the commission secretary. Counsel Assisting, Messrs Windeyer, Pape and Riley, were at one of the tables on the dais; behind them sat the head of ASIO, Colonel Spry, and seven ASIO staff. The second table sat empty.

Mr Windeyer was described as a tall, broad-shouldered, white-haired man, with 'deep rocking-horse eye sockets', who had one repeated gesture of quickly removing his horn-rimmed glasses and then immediately putting them back on. His opening address started by emphasising that the name of persons mentioned in the Petrov documents would not be revealed lightly as the Commission was not engaged in a 'witch hunt'.

The morning dragged on as he told how Vladimir Petrov came to Australia to spy on this country and on his own colleagues, documenting the diplomat's humble beginnings through to his position as Third Secretary at the Soviet Embassy in Australia. Windeyer described to the court Mr Petrov's and Mrs Petrov's Soviet Intelligence roles, their defection and the documents Vladimir Petrov had brought with him. These included letters sent from Moscow Centre to the Soviet Embassy (the Moscow Letters); Russian language documents from the embassy (the G Series documents); and the two documents written in English, Documents H and J.

Windeyer told the court that he would produce all of the documents Petrov brought with him, but they would not be available for publication, only what was read out in court. 'Some of them [the documents] relate to grave matters concerning widespread investigations which are still in progress,' Windeyer stated, also explaining that some of the people mentioned may have unwittingly passed on information, or were not aware of the Soviets' interest in them, and he asked that their privacy be respected.

When Windeyer explained the communication between Moscow Centre and the Soviet Embassy, and that there were code names for each—OLYMPIA for Moscow, and VILLAGE for Canberra—a ripple of chuckles came from the crowd. One of the police in attendance immediately stood and commanded silence. A bit of action in an otherwise dull morning. At the adjournment a man was seen sleeping in the crowd, with tiny snores coming from his half-opened mouth.

To the disappointment of many in the crowd, neither Vladimir Petrov nor his glamorous wife made an appearance. No politicians were in attendance, busy campaigning for the upcoming general election, twelve short days away.

After the Canberra sessions, the General Secretary of the CPA Lance Sharkey stated to the press that the Communist Party was not concerned with the Commission and would not be represented.

The Royal Commission sat in Canberra for two days, before moving to Melbourne the following month, from 30 June until 23 July 1954. A permanent court was eventually secured in New South Wales, with sittings resuming on 16 August 1954, and eventually concluding on 31 March 1955.

Over the next ten months, the Commission would sit for 126 days, the majority of them in Sydney. They would examine 119 witnesses and produce nearly 3000 pages of transcripts. The Commission received over 500 exhibits, including the documents Vladimir Petrov had handed to the Australian authorities.

42

LIAR

The federal election was held on 29 May 1954. The threat of Communism was again a major election topic, with both major parties denouncing the CPA in the run-up to election day. The Labor Party gained more votes than the Coalition, but the Coalition held the majority of seats and was returned to government.

The Leader of the Opposition, Doc Evatt was furious at the loss. Evatt's claim that Menzies had manipulated the timing of Petrov's defection to his own electoral advantage has been examined, re-examined and heavily debated ever since. The counter-argument is that Menzies had no say in when Petrov was to return to Moscow, and that its timing was coincidental. The timing of the Royal Commission itself was perhaps not so coincidental.

Doc Evatt would have been further dismayed when, five days after the election, on 3 June, his press secretary Fergan O'Sullivan finally admitted to being the author of Document H.

Later, when asked by Justice Philp why he had not confessed sooner, Fergan said confessing to a man like Evatt was not an easy matter. Evatt's reaction to Fergan's news was apparently explosive, and he dismissed Fergan from his service immediately.

In the interviews following her defection, Mrs Petrov, on 24 May 1954, just days before the federal election, gave a statement to one of the ASIO officers saying that the day after her husband had defected—but before it was known that he *had* defected—she'd had a discussion with Kovalenok, who was replacing her husband.

Kovalenok told her that he had been instructed to cultivate Fergan O'Sullivan, with the possibility that his boss Doc Evatt might become the next Australian Prime Minister—which meant Fergan would then be in a very important position for them.

The Russians had a saying, to be 'on the small hook', and they considered that Fergan had placed himself in this position. To be on the small hook meant Fergan had taken the first compromising step, by writing Document H; this made him vulnerable to future pressure.

The Commission reconvened in Melbourne on 30 June. Vladimir Petrov appeared and recounted his time working for Soviet Intelligence. Rex was sitting in the middle of the court room, reporting his version of events for the *Tribune*, in what would become his customary seat each day the Commission was in session.

Mercia was continuing to report to ASIO on her social contacts and people of interest. When the Royal Commission was based in Melbourne, she and Rex met. Rex told her he was reporting the Royal Commission not only for the *Tribune*, but for other Communist newspapers around the world, together with the TASS agency.

The order for Mercia to not be involved with the CPA was either lifted, or she was defiantly ignoring it. She was even hosting some of the CPA's St Kilda Branch meetings at her home on St Kilda Road. When Rex attended one of these meetings on 10 July 1954, ASIO was sitting outside Mercia's home, obtaining photographic evidence. His further movements were observed.

Neither Rex nor the CPA members were suspicious of Mercia. She was still completely undercover—and, if her past reports are an example, she would have been delivering information about what her Communist contacts thought about the Petrovs and the Royal Commission.

Wednesday 14 July 1954 would prove to be a turbulent day for the *Tribune* reporter. Rex arrived at the Commission anticipating that Fergan O'Sullivan would be called as a witness for the first time.

At the beginning of proceedings, Vladimir Petrov was questioned by both the Communist barrister Ted Hill and Counsel Assisting about his meetings and discussions with ASIO officer Ron Richards in the days after his defection. Petrov spoke of how the Soviets would destroy correspondence, his thoughts of suicide rather than returning to Russia, the payment of the £5000 to himself and his wife, denials of drunkenness, and the two documents written in English—H and J— that he had brought from the Soviet Embassy.

Mr Windeyer addressed the witness: 'Mr Petrov, in exhibits which have been tendered, you have stated that Mr Fergan O'Sullivan had a Moscow code name ZEMLYAK. What did Pakhomov tell you?'

'He said that Fergan O'Sullivan, according to his personal record, and according to the words of Rex Chiplin . . .'

At this mention of his name, Rex jumped up and shouted from the body of the court room, 'That is a lie, Your Honour.'

The Chairman, Justice Owen, looked over and told him to sit down.

'It is a lie,' Rex insisted. 'He is lying, and I demand the right to be heard here.'

'I expect you will be heard,' he told Rex before turning to a Peace Officer: 'Put that man outside court, Officer.'

'Liar!' Rex yelled at Petrov as he was escorted out of the court, yielding some dramatic photos for the press photographers positioned outside.

43

FERGAN

After Rex was removed from the court, Petrov continued: 'According to the words of Rex Chiplin he said he (Fergan) was a "Progressive", according to his personal record.'

'What is a Progressive?' Windeyer asked.

'Loyal to the Communist cause,' Petrov replied.

'Is this Mr Rex Chiplin of whom you speak—a man whom you know?' Windeyer asked.

'Yes,' Petrov replied.

'Did he have a Moscow code name?'

'Yes. CHARLIE.'

'Is he a member of the Communist Party?'

'Yes.'

Petrov went on to explain that Pakhomov had given him a personality record of Fergan, and he had received via an enciphered message from Moscow that 'ZEMLYAK is of interest and must be studied'.

Pakhomov continued to meet with O'Sullivan, and then this responsibility was handed to Antonov when Pakhomov returned to Russia in June 1952.

Petrov said he had seen Document H when Pakhomov brought it back to the Soviet Embassy. It had been photographed, and the undeveloped film sent to Moscow via the diplomatic pouch.

✽

Fergan O'Sullivan appeared as a witness. At first, he denied being the author of Document H, but eventually admitted it after his lawyer read the document and told him it contained nothing that was criminal or disloyal.

Fergan said Pakhomov had given him an official list of members issued by the Canberra press gallery, and he had then given information on each of the members. This information included, if he knew it, the person's religion—Catholic or Protestant—whether he was a radical or conservative, left- or right-wing in political thinking, whether he drank or was talkative, his financial position, marital status and number of children, and even claiming that one of them was promiscuous. Fergan also included himself on this list. He said he gave the list to Pakhomov so the TASS representative could ascertain if any of them would be interested in printing articles on Soviet activities, similar to those they gave to Rex Chiplin.

When asked about the mention of Fergan and his father in the Moscow Letters, he put it down to the obtuseness of the Russian sense of humour.

'I told Pakhomov,' he explained, 'about my father's news gathering methods in Dublin during the "Troubles", when the British considered him an Irish spy.'

'You told that as an anecdote?' Mr Windeyer asked.

'Yes, to Pakhomov.' Fergan said the Soviets had thought there was a real possibility that Fergan's father had been a spy, and they'd wanted to verify if this was true or not.

Fergan and two other members of Doc Evatt's staff had been named as sources of material in Document J, the other English-language document Petrov had taken from the Soviet Embassy.

Mercia's father William Masson was a journalist, and in 1923 he was on his way to Melbourne to cover a story when an accident happened, and he became a quadriplegic. Mercia was ten years of age. He spent many years in a wheelchair, and later in life was bedbound, residing in a hospital in Sydney's Eastern Suburbs.

Mercia's mother Lucy Masson nee Protti, sitting, with her friend Lorna, who lived with her, standing behind.

Mercia walking up the hill to 'Catherine'. The view is over Brisbane Waters, with the old Killcare wharf and baths at the bottom of the dirt road *(main photo)*.
Looking up the hill to the Killcare house 'Catherine', on Masson Lane, which has since been demolished *(inset)*.

A young Mercia enjoying the surf at Killcare Beach.

Mercia at Killcare.
The photos above and below were probably all taken on the same day in the 1940s after the war, possibly by a newspaper cameraman.

Mercia in the bush surrounding Killcare.

Two of the many photos Cindy discovered of her mother after Mercia died. She has no idea when they were taken or what the occasions were.

One of a series of three photographs taken on the same day, Rex Chiplin is in the centre of both. Mercia is wearing a white dress and hat and is walking to the right of Rex. The photo would have been taken between 1950 and 1955.

Another in the series of three, this photo shows Rex with three of the same women plus another man. Mercia had the third image in the series framed and hung on her wall, and Cindy took it to ASIO to try to identify who was with her mother. ASIO informed Cindy that of the four people they could only identify Rex from their files.

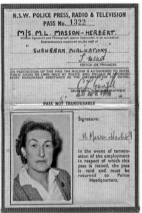

One of Mercia's press passes that Cindy kept after her mother passed away, and a photo of Mercia at work wearing the same suit.

Mercia socialising, probably in the 1960s. Along with many other areas of her life, Mercia didn't share these photos or the identity of the people in them with Cindy.

Mercia on a trip interstate, probably late 1960s, wearing her stole, which was fashionable at the time.

Mercia (*centre*), fashionably dressed as always, with yet more unknown people.

Another social gathering, possibly early 1970s, before Mercia (*centre right*) lost her hair.

Mercia in a wig (*bottom right*), 1970s, after cancer treatment.

(Left) Cindy when she lived with her grandmother in Newcastle.
(Right) Cindy standing in the garden of the Great Northern Hotel with a clocktower in the background. Mercia never went to Cindy's grandmother's house but always stayed at the Great Northern, and Cindy was taken to visit her there.

Cindy's school photo, Newcastle. Cindy is seated in the bottom row, second from the right.

This is the only photo Cindy has of her father, Harry Pearce. He poses here with his twin sister Iris.

Sister Perry, at her home in St Kilda, pictured with her pet sheep that she used as a lawnmower and her chickens. Cindy would regularly meet her after school in Fawkner Park, where they would walk their Irish Terriers. The unlikely pair became great friends.

Cindy with suitcase leaving a flat in Toronto, Canada, on her way to Alaska for a holiday.

Cindy on holiday in Queensland.

Cindy and two Irish Terriers, taken in Sydney, Kogarah Bay.

Cindy at Clovelly in one of her homemade dresses.

A modelling photo of Cindy. Portfolio shot.

RED REMOVED FROM COURT

Rex Chiplin was a reporter for the Communist Party paper *Tribune*. Mercia had a close friendship with Rex while behind his back reporting on his activities to ASIO.

IMAGE COURTESY OF ASIO.

Chiplin being thrown out of court at the Royal Commission on Espionage after objecting to being named by defected KGB officer Vladimir Petrov.

A crowd gathers outside the Royal Commission in Darlinghurst, Sydney, on 16 August 1954. FRANK BURKE.

Doc Evatt arriving at the Royal Commission in Darlinghurst, Sydney, on 16 August 1954. COURTESY STATE LIBRARY OF NSW.

Ernie Redford delivers Vladimir Petrov to the Royal Commission backdoor in Darlinghurst, Sydney, on 16 September 1954. COURTESY STATE LIBRARY OF NSW.

No. 785.   THURS., NOVEMBER 24, 1955   6d.

unmasks a Menzies'
secret police spy

THIS is the story of a spy—not a poker-faced Comic Cuts figure invented by Petrov —but a plain, middle-aged, native-born Australian woman worth

noticing for only one reason. She is a professional informer.

Her name is Mrs. Mercia Masson, of 549 St. Kilda Rd., Melbourne, "public relations" consultant.

She is the type of person Menzies is turning loose on the community in an effort to

disrupt and smash public opposition to his pro-American war policies.

A lot of folk from high-placed government servants to humble housewives know Mercia Masson, and she has made it her business to know them. Many are the doors of decent, honest, good Australians which have been opened hospitably to her in Mel-

bourne, Sydney and Canberra in the past six years.

All those doors have a number on them, listed now in the secret files of Mr. Menzies "thought control" police. Mercia Masson has been for many years closely connected with Mr. Whitrod who is well-known as a senior Security man.

This florid, gushing, gossipy, neurotic woman has played many roles, worked in many jobs, but the one role she has played faithfully is pimping on those she deliberately befriended.

For a handful of silver

For a handful of silver this woman posed, provoked and

Labelled her acquaintances

Part of the article that exposed Mercia Masson as an ASIO agent.

Mercia, again wearing her stole. Probably taken when Mercia first moved to Melbourne, before the Second World War.

Document J comprised thirty-seven pages of tightly typed material under several headings and subheadings. It covered Japanese interest in Australia, American espionage in Australia, war contracts in Australia, notes about the Australian Workers' Union and Doc Evatt. Victor Windeyer would later describe it as a 'farrago of fact, falsity and filth', stating that it would not be published or available to the public.

The original copy of Document J had been typed at the Soviet Embassy in Canberra on 23–25 May 1953 and given to Antonov. It and a carbon copy had then been handed to Petrov, who sent the original by courier to Moscow Centre. The carbon copy became Document J, and was brought out of the Soviet Embassy by Petrov when he defected and was now evidence before the Royal Commission.

Mrs Petrov told the Commission that journalist Rupert Lockwood had typed Document J at the embassy. Lockwood had been given the code name VORON (raven or crow in Russian) by the Soviets, but at the Commission's proceedings in Melbourne, he denied being the author of Document J, though he claimed authorship of a pamphlet called 'What is in Document J?', which offered a condensed version of Document J; this had been published just weeks before he appeared before the Commission as a witness.

Evatt became involved with the Commission on 16 August, appearing for the other two staff members he hadn't fired, who were implicated in Document J as sources of information. The Commission became bogged down over the question of authenticity of Document J. This discussion became complicated because Doc Evatt was not only being a leading counsel and an advocate for two members of his staff, but at times he was speaking as the Leader of the Opposition and making claims of there being a conspiracy to discredit himself.

On 7 September the Commissioners stated that Evatt's abuse of them in the media was grounds to withdraw his permission to represent himself, or his staff. After a day of heated argument, Evatt left the court.

Rex's expulsion from the Royal Commission had been published in major newspapers. In the *Tribune* the following week, at the end of an article about the Royal Commission, it was stated that the *Tribune* journalist Mr Rex Chiplin, who 'refuted an allegation made about him by Petrov and was forcibly removed from the Commission and warned not to return, will not be forbidden re-entry to the Commission sittings'.

Rex had also been given another reprieve, this time in Canberra. After being reviewed by the Speaker of the House of Representatives, W.C. Wentworth's action to remove Rex Chiplin from Parliament House had been thwarted. The Speaker decided that Chiplin, as the representative of a registered newspaper, was entitled to the facilities of the press gallery, provided he obeyed the rules of the House.

Rex couldn't help himself. He proceeded to bait the red-baiter, starting his column the following week with the question: 'So, we're an enemy agent, eh, W.C.? From your warped point of view we certainly are.'

Rex was once again reporting in Canberra, when he wasn't reporting on the Royal Commission.

44

MENTORS

Mercia's father died at the age of sixty-five on 11 October 1954. He had been a quadriplegic for thirty-one years.

Bill Masson had been a strong influence on his daughter's life. It would have been a tumultuous time for Mercia: her father gone, her daughter living with her in Melbourne, and the Royal Commission on Espionage in full swing. Her mother, Lucy, was still living at 254 Carrington Road, Coogee, with another woman—which Cindy never thought much about until later in life, even though the two women shared a bed.

All the time she had been in Melbourne, Cindy would be shipped off to various people and places for her school holidays, often to Lucy's home in Sydney. Mercia would take Cindy to the airport and hand her daughter over to an airline hostess. Cindy thinks they were probably DC3s that she flew in; she remembers thinking as a child that the trip always took forever.

Cindy would stay at Coogee with her grandmother, but they would often travel north to Killcare, taking a whole day to get there. They would rise early, catch the tram to Central Station, then the steam train to Gosford, with a brief stop at Woy Woy Railway Station, where an old man would run up and down the platform, trying to sell bottled oysters before the train left the station. At Gosford Railway Station they'd wait at the bus stop, eating the sandwiches they'd made before they left. The bus would take them along the dirt Scenic Road—a long and rough trip, passing through orchards and a few houses before reaching the top of the hill at Killcare.

Lucy suffered badly from arthritis, so taking the trip on the little launch boat from Woy Woy to Killcare would have been too difficult. Besides, she would never go near the water; she joked that the only way a shark could attack her was if it came up to her home in Carrington Road and knocked on her door.

Killcare was a lovely sanctuary for them. No electricity, and in winter a woodfire kept the worst of the chills out of the old house. Cindy's relationship with her grandmother lacked any show of emotion, but it was not as distant as the relationship between Lucy and Mercia. Lucy cared for her granddaughter in her own way.

Cindy and her mother travelled up to Sydney from Melbourne for Bill Masson's funeral, which was held two days after he passed, and was large. Bill had been a Mason, and most of his siblings were still alive and attended with their families and friends, as well as his former work colleagues. After a morning service at the Presbyterian Church in Randwick, Bill was buried close to his parents in the Presbyterian section of Botany Cemetery. His grave overlooks Botany Bay.

Mercia and Cindy returned to Melbourne after the funeral, to get on with their lives. Mercia was then employed as the public relations officer for a company, British Nylon Spinners, giving her access to fashionable bright nylon outfits, which Mercia wore with aplomb. After Mercia's death, one of the women who had asked for something of Mercia's to remember her by took some of these outfits and later donated them to the Powerhouse Museum in Sydney.

Mercia was always busy with work. Cindy was allowed a puppy, an Irish Terrier she called Tammy. Cindy would race home from school and take Tammy for a long walk at nearby Fawkner Park—where she met an older lady who owned two Irish Terriers. Sister Anne Perry was a baby health nurse and they'd often meet up, walking and talking together. Cindy always looked forward to seeing Anne Perry and her dogs.

Anne was a semi-retired spinster and lived in nearby Punt Road. In the middle of suburban Melbourne she bred budgerigars, kept chickens for their eggs and had a pet sheep to keep the grass down. She couldn't afford to pay someone to mow her lawn and preferred paying someone to shear her one sheep once a year. Cindy loved visiting Anne's home. She still thinks it funny that, even though her mother knew she was regularly going to Anne's house, she never bothered to meet her, if only to check that everything was okay.

Anne explained to Cindy the changes that were happening to her body, from being a girl to becoming a woman. Cindy matured early, menstruating at just eleven years. She had woken up in shock. Her mother told her to stay at home in bed and she'd bring her something home for her to use so she could go to school the next day. No explanation as to what was happening to her little girl's body. It was Anne who explained it all.

This unlikely pair became firm friends and Cindy kept in touch with Anne for many years, until the old lady passed away. Cindy found she could easily talk with her about anything that was worrying her, which she still appreciates, and Anne told her a great deal about her own life—in marked contrast with Cindy's experience of her own mother.

45

BEHIND THE SCENES

ASIO's own Royal Commission Section had been busy working behind the scenes, including trying to verify the information Mercia had given about the typewriter Rex Chiplin received from a 'grateful government'. When Rex's house had been searched on 17 July 1953, a Commodore portable typewriter was observed in the premises.

Initial inquiries showed that the machine originated in Germany, but no outlets sold them in Sydney. Mercia had mentioned in her report that the typewriter she saw had a German name on it. Some Commodore typewriters were assembled using German arms manufacturer Rheinmetall's parts.

Mr and Mrs Petrov had been questioned about the typewriter, and both stated they had no knowledge of it, and that during their time at the Soviet Embassy, no typewriter was received from Europe for any purpose. Mr Petrov suggested that Chiplin may have received it from the Czechoslovak Consulate General, who Rex knew well.

Ric Oke was in for a shock. On 25 November 1954 at 8.30 p.m., two officers, one from ASIO and the other from the Commonwealth Investigation Service, knocked on the door of his home at 13 Bayview Street, East Melbourne. They were admitted into the house by an unidentified woman, who informed them Ric was in bed.

She showed them the way into his bedroom.

One of the officers asked him, 'Are you Mr George Richard Oke?'

'Yes,' replied Ric. 'Who are you?'

'We are officers of the Commonwealth Attorney-General's Department,' the ASIO officer replied, producing a Certificate of Authority, which Ric took and read through. 'We have called to see you concerning matters under investigation by the Royal Commission on Espionage,' the officer continued, 'and we would like to know whether you are willing to cooperate with us in the matters which we wish to discuss with you.'

'I have nothing to say,' Ric replied.

'Do you wish to assist the Royal Commission in certain matters?'

'I will not assist the Commission in any way,' Ric stated.

'Those are rather strong terms,' said the ASIO officer. 'I think you might like to reconsider that statement.'

'I am not prepared to assist this Commission in any way,' Ric replied.

'You probably know, Mr Oke, that during the recent sitting of the Royal Commission in Sydney, you were referred to by a witness when giving evidence,' the officer said. 'It is possible that you may be called before the Royal Commission and be asked certain questions to explain these matters.'

'I have nothing to say,' Ric replied. 'I have never been mixed up in espionage.'

'We did not suggest that you were. We have merely requested your help in certain matters.'

'I have nothing to say,' Ric again stated, giving the same answer to any further questions.

Ric had been named by a Department of External Affairs employee who had been questioned about her past membership of the Communist

Party. She informed the Commission that she had resigned when she obtained her job with the department, giving her resignation to Ric Oke, a Communist Party functionary.

If ASIO had been trying to get Ric to 'turn' on the CPA, they had underestimated his resolve—but he, in turn, was still unaware that ASIO knew of his involvement in Mercia's CPA membership.

46

ALLAYING FEAR

Early in January 1955, straight after the holiday period, Mercia met Rex at the Repin's Café. The cloak and dagger meeting arrangements, with an initial phone call and then meeting at the entrance of St James Station, were seemingly now a thing of the past.

Rex had reportedly told Mercia that the Communist Party expected that the Petrov Commission would become 'dirty' when it resumed after the Christmas recess—and that they were 'flat out getting information' to try to discredit Mr Herde.

Mr K.H. Herde, the Royal Commission Secretary, had inadvertently made himself a focus of those opposed to the Commission, by inviting the Petrovs, all the Commissioners and Mr Windeyer to his home for a Christmas party in December. Many regarded the presence of the Judges, the Counsel Assisting and the principal Royal Commission witnesses together at a social event as an inappropriate folly, damaging its credibility for those critical of the Commission.

Rex told Mercia the many avenues they were investigating and the information they were hoping to publicise. He was trying to find out the names of all the Judges who attended Mr Herde's Christmas party, and all the solicitors and barristers who received and accepted invitations. Though Rex said some of the names were already known, it was not recorded in Mercia's statement how Rex had obtained that information.

Trying to discredit Herde and the Royal Commission further, Rex was asking how the Commission Secretary had received preferential housing on arrival in Canberra over other public servants, and why he was then allowed to sublet the property when he was away. Herde and his family had also been interviewed by various Australian magazines, and Rex questioned if this was appropriate as a public servant employee.

Rex was also delving into a business transaction, in which Herde had owned and sold a timber mill in Canberra, and whether he had received government contracts for timber from the mill prior to the sale. He was even trying to find out what purchase price had been paid by the 'New Australian' when the sale went through. This was all duly passed on to ASIO.

In further conversation, the subject of Fergan O'Sullivan and his father came up. Rex said he hadn't seen Fergan after he appeared before the Royal Commission, and warned Mercia to be careful of him as the Party was suspicious of him. Rex said the Party considered that his father, Chris O'Sullivan, was okay.

Rex had already mentioned the Christmas Party in his *Tribune* column of 21 December, filled with satirical references to those involved in the Commission:

We're told that the floor show at the Petrov Family Xmas Party was a wow.

Hit of the evening was Security walloper Richards who, as Mandrake [the magician], won ring applause with his most difficult trick—he produced a genuine document from a brief case he was carrying.

Petrov and his wife sang a parody Pennies from Menzies, and as an encore Petrov yodelled It Ain't What you Do, It's the Way That You Do It.

The rooms were tastefully decorated with tape recorders and from the ceiling hung garlands made from forged documents.

Novel table napkins were in the shape of pages marked Document J.

Guests were fingerprinted and sworn in and Bells whisky flowed.

A novel touch was that each guest was given a code name; some were Ananias, Lucretia Borgia and Humphrey Bogart. But there was a slight hitch at supper time when the walloper doubling as butler got his code names mixed and everyone was directed to the one seat.

Absent friends Joe McCarthy and Igor Gouzenko were toasted.

All-in-all she was a wonderful evening; justice and everyone else was blind at the end.

Rex's biting humour was in top form.

On 31 January 1955, Mercia and Cindy visited Rex's home at Gymea Bay. Cindy remembers nothing of the visit.

In her report, Mercia noted that Vivienne Chiplin was worried to the point of nervous collapse about the ongoing Royal Commission. With the threat of Rex being called to give evidence, they had decided to take a week's holiday. Worried about Vivienne's emotional and mental state, Mercia offered them her holiday house at Killcare, which the Chiplin family accepted—but, with the Commission about to start up again, they decided to wait until it was all over.

Rex, trying to allay any fears, said he doubted he would even be called. Unfortunately for him, he was subpoenaed not long afterwards.

He wasn't the only one. In February 1955, Mercia received a letter from the Deputy Crown Solicitor indicating she might be required to appear before the Royal Commission as a witness.

When the head of ASIO, Colonel Spry, heard about this, he travelled to Sydney and asked Windeyer not to call Mercia as a witness; the protection of undercover agents was paramount to his organisation.

On 23 February 1955, Jack Davis, Deputy Director of the Commonwealth Investigation Service, who was assisting Ron Richards' ASIO Royal Commission Section, arrived in Melbourne to take a statement from Mercia.

In early 1952, Mercia had already given a statement to Ray Whitrod and another unnamed security officer. That statement was lengthy and had drawn upon her reports on Rex Chiplin, Ric Oke and her work with the Democratic Rights Council and the Peace Council. This second document was an expansion of the first, and included her latest meeting with Ric, and further meetings with Rex from February 1952.

When her statement was finished, it was typed up and given to Mercia for correction. It was then sent to ASIO and Windeyer in Sydney.

47

BUILD UP

On the same day that Mercia was giving her statement in Melbourne, Rex Chiplin was due to give evidence at the Royal Commission in Sydney for the first time. Appearing for Rex was barrister Ted Hill who sought leave from Max Julius who was still on a briefing watch to the Royal Commission. Ted Hill knew Rex through the Communist Party, and his own brother Jim Hill had been named in VENONA as TURIST ('Tourist').

James Frederick Hill (TURIST) was thick-set like his brother and had been an Officer in the Department of External Affairs with Ian Milner, who had been identified as BUR. When interviewed in 1950 about leaks in the department, Jim Hill had denied any involvement. When interviewed again by the security services in London for the Royal Commissioners, he said he had never known or met Wally Clayton (KLOD), and had never improperly disclosed, to anyone, information or documents acquired in the course of his duties with the Department of External Affairs.

Victor Windeyer had been building up to the moment when Rex Chiplin would finally appear as a witness. On 23 February, he started the proceedings by reminding the Commissioners of the references to Rex throughout the hearings to date, and the four mentions of Rex in the Moscow Letters.

The previous mentions of Rex at the Commission had often arisen from Windeyer's own questioning of witnesses. The first was on 14 July 1954, when Windeyer was questioning Vladimir Petrov and Rex had to be removed from the court; Petrov had then gone on to identify Rex as the contact the Soviets code-named CHARLIE. Over the following two days, Windeyer was questioning Fergan about the document he'd created for the Soviet Embassy. Rex wasn't listed among the parliamentary correspondents described in that document, but Fergan explained to Windeyer that, at that time, Rex was attending parliamentary sessions, but wasn't an authorised member of the press gallery.

Then, in November 1954, the Commission had heard from witnesses attached to the Department of External Affairs. One of these witnesses had been earmarked by Moscow as a target for their operatives in Canberra, and had been code-named GOST (Russian for 'Guest'). Mrs Petrov told the Commission that GOST was being no longer pursued because of his guarded attitude to Soviet approaches, and because of the conditions that had arisen in the Department of External Affairs. Mrs Petrov added that the Soviets were aware investigations were being made within the department to find out where a report had come from after Rex Chiplin's *Tribune* article about the American Friendship Treaty had appeared in the press.

Mr Windeyer read from one of the Moscow Letters dated 25 November 1952: 'In connection with the measures which you know to have been taken by counter-intelligence against Rex Chiplin, we request you to exercise maximum caution in further work with him.' The first ASIO raids, including on Rex and Vivienne's home, had occurred just two months previously.

The same letter dealt with a public servant, F.J. McLean, who Moscow had noticed was no longer working in External Affairs. Moscow wanted to know if this was 'connected with measures taken in the Department of External Affairs' after Rex Chiplin's Treaty article had appeared. McLean was thought by the Soviets to be a possible source of information.

Frederick John McLean had been a journalist in Sydney and then a member of Canberra's press gallery. He had been suffering from tuberculosis for some time and was excused from appearing as a witness, instead giving an interview to two security service officers at his home. He told them he had left the press gallery after being convinced by Doc Evatt to start up a public relations section in the Department of External Affairs.

During their two-and-a-half-hour interview, McLean told the officers he was a firm supporter of the ALP, but had also been a member of the Communist Party for a few months in about 1942–43, when he was stationed in Hay during the war. He had been asked to join, and his main objective in joining the Party was to help the Russians defeat the Nazis. But, after reading a Communist Party pamphlet and not agreeing with its contents, he had dropped out of the CPA, never having been to a meeting.

McLean stated that he had met Russian TASS correspondents at cocktail parties, and had even been to TASS journalist Fedor Nosov's flat in Kings Cross while working as a journalist—but said he was cautious when dealing with them, as he didn't trust them. When shown the references to him in the Moscow Letters, he stated that it was 'wishful thinking on their part' and he would not have given them any information.

Asked by the officers if he knew Rex Chiplin, McLean said he'd met him in the press gallery. He couldn't remember who had introduced them, but he added that he avoided Rex because of his foul-smelling pipe. He knew Rex was a Communist.

※

On 23 February, Petrov was the first to give evidence. Victor Windeyer began by asking him about the Moscow Letters seeking information about Fergan's father. Petrov said he suggested to Antonov that he seek the information through Chiplin. Petrov was unsure if Antonov received any information but knew that he had been in touch with him about it.

Windeyer then asked about the meeting Pakhomov had with Chiplin in a park in Kingston, where Moscow was informed that Pakhomov thought they were photographed, and the request that Petrov 'should ascertain and inform us about the source from which CHIPLIN receives information, and not merely its contents, as you did when dealing with the question of exchange of ciphers between the governments of Australia and America'. Petrov explained that it actually referred to two events where Rex had supplied information to TASS agents—once when Rex met Pakhomov in a park in Kingston and told him about Miss Koslova and Mrs Petrov being of interest to Australia's security services, and the second when CHARLIE had passed information to either Pakhomov or Antonov—Petrov couldn't recall which—that the American and Australian governments had exchanged enciphered telegrams or cables. What had been in these had not been indicated, nor was CHARLIE's source revealed. Moscow wanted to know who had given Rex these bits of information; they wanted his sources.

After lunch Windeyer then asked about the reference to McLean in the Moscow Letters. Petrov told Windeyer that, upon making inquiries, he found that McLean was ill and was in a sanatorium, which was why McLean was no longer working at External Affairs, and that he had never spoken to Rex Chiplin about this man.

Windeyer then asked Petrov about his interviews with ASIO officer Ron Richards just after he defected, when he said Rex had told him Rex had two friends—'two chaps'—in External Affairs. Petrov had already confirmed to ASIO what they had suspected: that Fedor Nosov, when in Australia, was a Soviet agent who had obtained information primarily from one man, KLOD, who operated a group of agents who reported information to him.

Petrov explained to the Commission that he had never met Nosov, but that Nosov had been close to Rex Chiplin of the *Tribune*. Petrov admitted he had never seen any of this information, but had learnt of it through Pakhomov.

When Windeyer asked about the raids on the *Tribune* and Rex's home, Petrov replied that he had informed Moscow of these events.

The Counsel Assisting was steadily building his case against Rex.

Windeyer then asked Petrov what he meant when he said Rex was still active as an agent. 'We had the possibility of asking him at any time for information, and he would have given it to us,' Petrov replied.

When Windeyer asked about Petrov's two meetings with Chiplin in Kings Cross the previous January to seek information, Max Julius interjected, trying to clarify some details about each of the two meetings. Julius questioned Petrov's order of events, and why he, rather than Antonov, had met Chiplin—and even whether Petrov actually understood how the cipher system worked.

Petrov told the court that his first meeting with Chiplin in Kings Cross had been arranged by a woman in the Australian–Russian Friendship Society in Sydney, who had already appeared as a witness to the Commission; his second meeting occurred when they met unexpectedly on a tram before their arranged meeting. Petrov explained that he had asked Rex about a former employee of the Department of External Affairs, Ian Milner; he had asked if Rex could get the opinion he sought, and Rex replied that he would try. At the second meeting, the only new information Rex gave him was that Ian Milner's father was a clergyman; the rest Petrov already knew.

48

CHOICE OF WORDS

Midway through the afternoon, Rex Chiplin was called into the court and affirmed.

Rex clarified that he was a journalist who wrote for the *Tribune* and that his articles were picked up by other papers both in Australia and overseas. He lived at 80 Ellesmere Road, Gymea Bay, and had been there for three or four years. He had previously lived at 68 Clissold Parade, Campsie, for two years.

Next followed a curt exchange between the QC and his somewhat evasive witness.

'Did you know Pakhomov?' Windeyer asked.

'I did,' Rex replied.

'Did you know Fergan O'Sullivan?'

'Yes.'

'Did you ever discuss O'Sullivan with Pakhomov?'

'Not that I remember,' Rex replied.

Windeyer tried again. 'Did you ever mention O'Sullivan to Pakhomov?'

'I could have,' said Rex. 'I am not quite sure.'

'Did you by any chance introduce them?'

'No. I could not say,' Rex replied, his answers brief. If Windeyer had expected a cooperative witness after the string of evidence already produced, he was going to be disappointed.

Windeyer asked if Rex had been to the Soviet Embassy, or taken Fergan to the Soviet Embassy. Rex stated that he had been to the embassy twice for functions, but had not taken Fergan. He admitted having seen him there at one of these functions.

'Did you know Fergan O'Sullivan fairly well?' Windeyer asked.

'As well as journalists working together know one another,' Rex replied.

Windeyer asked Rex about meeting Fergan at his flat in Canberra, which Fergan had shared with Bruce Yuill—an event that had been noted in an ASIO report and witnessed by an agent. Rex denied the meeting.

'Never?' Windeyer asked.

'Never,' Rex stated.

'You were not in his house on the 19th November 1952?'

'No.'

Perhaps if Windeyer's choice of words had been 'at' rather than 'in' the flat, Rex's answer might have been different. As well as being brief, Rex showed astuteness in his replies.

The QC then changed tack, asking Rex about the two meetings in Kings Cross with Petrov, and Rex turned Petrov's order of events around. He told Windeyer that his first meeting with Petrov was a chance meeting in a tram as he went to Kings Cross to buy cigarettes for his wife. Petrov had suggested a coffee in a café; they then had a couple of beers, and it was Petrov's suggestion that they meet again. Chiplin agreed and met him at 4 p.m. the following week at another café.

Rex then told the Commission that Petrov had mentioned the Department of External Affairs employee's name to him out of the blue, calling him Yan Milner, and that he did not offer any help to Petrov, nor make any subsequent inquiries.

Windeyer asked about Rex meeting Pakhomov in Kingston Park. Rex replied that there were a lot of parks in Kingston, and that he had met Pakhomov in Canberra many times. On further questioning, Rex said they had never discussed the two women working at the Soviet Embassy.

'You never said anything to Pakhomov about it?' Windeyer asked.

'No,' Rex replied.

'You have heard the evidence given about it?'

'Yes.'

'As far as you are concerned it means nothing to you?'

'It means nothing at all,' Rex replied.

It was Rex's word against Petrov's.

The Commission was adjourned at 4 p.m.

Windeyer would have to continue with Rex the following day.

49

NEVER

On 24 February, Windeyer again quizzed Rex about the meetings with Petrov in Kings Cross, but Rex answered these questions with denials. When asked whether he had told Petrov about having 'two chaps' in External Affairs, the emphatic reply was 'Never'.

Windeyer then asked about Rex's work at the *Tribune*. 'I suppose as far as you are personally concerned, you do not put anything in the *Tribune* which you know to be untrue?'

'No,' Rex replied.

Windeyer's next set of questions would have made both Rex and Ted Hill, start to wonder.

With knowledge of Mercia's statement to the Commission, as well as her reports to ASIO, Windeyer asked: 'You are a member of the propaganda committee of the Party, aren't you?'

'No,' Rex replied.

'Have you never been a member of the propaganda committee?'

'Never.'

'Do you know of a propaganda committee?'

'No.'

'Have you never heard of one?'

'Never.'

'I ask this specifically,' Windeyer paused. 'Did you go to a meeting connected with propaganda—a committee meeting—in Melbourne in May 1952?'

'No,' Rex replied.

'On the thirtieth of May 1952?'

'No.'

'Did you ever travel to Melbourne as "J. Matthews"?' Windeyer asked.

'Never.'

Ted Hill, who had coincidentally also been observed by ASIO at Sydney airport and on the same flight Rex undertook in May 1952, interjected: 'I don't know about this, Your Honours. I don't know if my friend is cross-examining from instructions, but that is a very serious question to put to a man, and in other cases those instructions have turned out to be completely inaccurate. I ask that Your Honours ask my friend to exercise very great care in putting a matter like that to him.'

'Mr Windeyer does,' the Chairman replied.

This would have been frustrating for Ted Hill and Max Julius. They were not privy to the security files that Windeyer and the Justices had seen, and were using—and, as the Chairman had repeatedly told Mr Hill, the Royal Commission was not the same as a criminal or civil court. There was much in the security files that ASIO did not want leaked, especially to anyone affiliated with the Communist Party.

Ted Hill tried again. 'Well, it is not the first time it has happened. He has got a direct denial now, and I suppose that is all that can be done about it. But it is not very nice to have a question put to you, "Did you travel as so-and-so?", when apparently it is quite inaccurate.'

Ted Hill's words were left hanging as Windeyer continued his questioning.

'You say you never travelled by air to Melbourne under the name of "J. Matthews"?'

'Yes,' Rex replied.

'Did you ever know of a "Mr. Matthews: living at 68 Clissold Parade, Campsie?'

'No.'

Windeyer then asked if he knew Mr Richards, the now Deputy Director of Operations at ASIO, by sight.

'No,' Rex replied.

'What I am suggesting to you is that you travelled in the same aeroplane as Mr Richards coming back from Melbourne in May 1952.'

'I would not deny that I travelled in a plane with Mr Richards,' Rex replied. 'But I certainly deny that I travelled under the name of Matthews.'

Unfortunately for Rex, the day he flew into Sydney, an ASIO agent had checked the passenger list, and noted the seat that Rex had occupied next to Richards was in the name of J. Matthews of 68 Clissold Parade, Campsie—Rex's address at the time. Windeyer knew of this, but Rex was unaware of the intense security surveillance on him that day.

'You are a member of the Communist Party?' Windeyer asked.

'I am,' Rex replied.

'And you have never used any other name?'

'Never.'

'You write a column in the *Tribune*, I suppose, which is under your name?'

'I do.'

The Chairman then asked Rex which international papers he also wrote for.

'And of course, you have taken a considerable interest in the proceedings of this Commission?'

'Yes,' Rex replied.

Windeyer reached down for a paper in front of him and looked at Rex. 'I just want you to tell me what is the reason for this paragraph, which appears in the issue of the *Tribune* of 25 August 1954, under the heading "Rex Chiplin Says".'

Windeyer started reading from the paper in front of him:

'A tardy report from one of our contacts is that on the Friday before the current sitting of the Petrov Commission opened in Sydney he saw W.J.V. Windeyer come down the steps of the C.I.B.(Criminal Investigation Bureau), followed five seconds later by Justice Owen.'

Ted Hill interjected, submitting that as a journalist Rex should not be cross-examined about a matter unless it is directly relevant to the inquiry's terms of reference.

Justice Philp replied that it was directly relevant to Rex's credit, if he said such a thing and it was a lie. Justice Ligertwood also interjected, saying that Rex had been in conflict with Petrov's evidence, and the Chair let the question be asked.

Rex's antagonism to the Justices and the Royal Commission in the *Tribune* was backfiring on him, and Ted Hill was unable to stop it.

50

A TARDY REPORT

'I was asking you, what was the point of your saying that?' Windeyer said to Rex.

'Point of interest,' Rex stated.

The Chairman, Justice Owen, then asked Rex where the Criminal Investigation Bureau building actually was, and the court established that it was in Police Headquarters on the corner of Phillip and Hunter streets in Sydney.

'You did not realise that the next-door building, where the Arbitration Court sits, was at that period the headquarters of the Commission?' the Chairman asked Rex.

'No, I certainly did not know that,' Rex replied, going on to explain under questioning that he received literally hundreds of messages, communications and letters from people with information.

'Do you put in any bits of gossip you hear, without caring whether they are true or false?' Windeyer demanded.

'I do not put in any gossip at all, but what I do put in, I take responsibility for.'

'Yes, but let us assume for the moment that it were true...' Windeyer continued, before Ted Hill interjected.

'If this is directed to his credit, he is now being asked to assume something,' Hill stated. 'And you have his answer. Apparently, there was some substance in it.'

'Some substance in it?' the Chairman asked.

'There was an error made as to the building,' Hill replied.

'Are you saying there is some substance in it?' the Chairman demanded.

'All I said was that there was an error made as to the building,' Hill replied. The Chairman repeated the question to Mr Hill. 'I accept what Your Honour says unreservedly, of course,' Hill replied.

Windeyer clarified that it was the building with the TAA airline on the bottom floor, and that for some weeks it had been the Commission headquarters, and that he personally went in there and came out every day.

'What I wanted to ask the witness was this, Your Honours,' Windeyer said, turning to Rex: 'If you will pardon me putting it this way, you got that information, but so what? What is the purpose of publishing it?'

'It is a matter of public interest,' Rex replied.

'It is a matter of public interest that I have been—assuming it were true, which it is not—in the office of police headquarters?' Windeyer asked.

'In the contemporary setting,' Rex replied, 'yes.'

'What—this was a conspiracy between His Honour, myself, and the State Police: is that it?' Windeyer asked.

'No suggestion of that at all,' Rex replied.

'What is the suggestion?' Windeyer demanded.

'The suggestion is that it was a matter of news interest.'

'But you have not worried to report that His Honour and I have been seen in Phillip Street together, and at this court at Darlinghurst?'

'No; I think that would be general knowledge and of no news interest to anybody in that sense.'

'In fact, it was intended to be in some sense or another a smear?' Windeyer accused.

'No,' Rex replied, 'I do not see it that way at all.'

Windeyer then stated there had been allegations in the *Tribune* of evidence and material having been fabricated at the Royal Commission.

Rex replied that the *Tribune* reports had been based on Commission proceedings.

Changing tack, Windeyer again questioned Rex about his work with the propaganda committee, and the production of pamphlets, leaflets and satirical verse thought to have been written by Rex—all of which Rex denied.

Windeyer asked Rex about his dealings with TASS men, and the fact that Antonov was a frequent visitor to the *Tribune* offices, and that Rex was on friendly terms with the two previous TASS men, Nosov and Pakhomov. Rex explained that they were his source of Russian news.

Windeyer then asked about his dealings with the Soviet Embassy, the Australian–Russian Friendship Society and Wally Clayton, and the fact that Wally seemed to have disappeared.

'Did you ever by way of interest make any inquiries as to what had happened to him?' Windeyer asked.

'No, none at all,' Rex replied.

'None at all?'

'None.'

'Not a news item?' Justice Ligertwood asked.

'No,' Rex replied.

The Commission adjourned briefly at 11.14 a.m., in what would turn out to be a big day for Rex as a witness, and a frustrating one for Mr Windeyer.

51

THREE NAMES

When the Commission reconvened at 11.33 a.m., Windeyer continued querying Rex on a list of names he had before him, with Rex replying with short sharp answers, admitting he knew some and not others. Then Windeyer brought up Rex's article in the *Tribune* about the Friendship Treaty, and the booklet 'Where is the Nest of Traitors?'.

'I take it that you are aware that this material which you have published is based upon a draft of a proposed treaty?' Windeyer asked.

'Yes,' Rex replied

'You say this was based upon a draft. You say in your article: "A highly placed government official revealed the existence of the Treaty to me ..." Do you remember saying that?'

'I do.'

'And that, I suppose, is true?'

'It is.'

'Who was it?'

'That ...'

'I object to that,' Mr Hill cut in. 'This man has given evidence that he is a journalist, and I submit that the normal practice is that a jour-nalist should not be asked to disclose his source of information.'

Mr Hill then argued that the Chairman had tried a case on this subject involving *The Sydney Morning Herald*.

'We think the question is admissible and relevant,' the Chairman stated.

'If Your Honours please,' Windeyer replied, turning to Rex, 'my question to you, Mr Chiplin, was: Who is he?'

'The information was given to me in my profession as a journalist,' Rex replied. 'It was given to me in confidence, and I respect that confi-dence. I refuse to answer.'

Despite Windeyer's ongoing attempts, Rex would not disclose the name of the man who had given him the information on the Friend-ship Treaty, only calling the public servant official who gave him the information a 'real patriot'.

Under continued questioning, Rex admitted writing the article, specifying that he would not have accepted information on something like a secret armament as suggested. But then he had to admit that he did accept a Cabinet secret, claiming that this was similar to the annual budget leaks to the press that happened in parliament. Rex further admitted in one-word replies that the man was a senior government official; that he was given the information in Canberra; that there were other papers; and that it was given to him in the reading room at the library in Parliament House.

Rex then said, under further questioning, that the official was not connected to either the Department of External Affairs or Treasury. He was not naming his source, but each piece of information drawn out of him, however reluctantly, was a small win for the Counsel Assisting the Commission.

Nonetheless, Windeyer wanted the name.

Making a show of it, Windeyer took three small pieces of thin bluey-grey note paper and wrote on them in pencil. Windeyer handed Rex the first piece of paper and said: 'Look at the name I have written on this piece of paper and tell me if that is the name of the man.'

Rex looked at the paper, then at Windeyer as he handed it back.

'No,' he stated. 'It was Mr McLean whose name you wrote and, for Mr McLean's own benefit, it was not Mr McLean.'

'All right,' Windeyer said, getting the second piece of paper. 'Well, look at this name.'

Ted Hill stood up. 'I object to this, Your Honours. The witness has said he refuses to answer.'

'You are a little premature,' the Chair replied. 'He is merely being asked at the moment to look at a name.'

Hill again tried in vain to stop the process, but was overruled.

'I am putting this to the witness in writing, and for the sake of the names I write down, I suggest to the witness that his proper course is not to do more than look at the name and answer.' Windeyer turned to Rex: 'You see the name I show you on the piece of paper?'

'I do.'

'Was that the man?' Windeyer asked.

'I am not answering any more questions on names,' Rex stated. 'I merely mentioned Mr McLean's name to defend Mr McLean, who is sick.'

The Justices tried to get more information as to the identity of the official responsible for the leak, but Rex refused to answer.

'I want to show him another one,' Windeyer explained to the court.

Showing the third piece of paper to Rex, Windeyer asked, 'Do you know the person whose name is on that piece of paper?'

'I am not answering any more questions relative to names,' Rex stated.

'I am simply asking you: do you know that person?'

'Yes, I know that person.'

'And you have been associated with that person?'

'Socially, yes.'

'Socially—in various activities?' Windeyer asked.

'Yes.'

'Did that person have anything to do with this matter?'

'I am not answering any more questions about that particular matter.'

Mr Windeyer had written three separate names, one on each piece of paper. The first had been F.J. McLean, whose evidence had already been given to the Commission—the interview given to ASIO back in November.

The name on the second piece of paper was J. McGregor Dickens, a man known and recorded by ASIO as having been seen with Rex at another Communist Party member's home in Canberra.

The name on the third piece of paper was M. Masson.

52

FRIENDSHIP TREATY

Rex had no choice but to continue on as Windeyer turned his attention to the draft treaty. If Windeyer had planned to unsettle Rex with his list of names, it appeared to have worked, as his answers now seemed less defiant.

Windeyer showed Rex a typed document and asked if it had been gained from the Commonwealth Investigation Service raid on the *Tribune* office on 29 August 1952. Rex remarked that it could have been; it had similar wording to his article on the treaty. Pushed further, Rex explained that he had been shown the treaty document, and that he'd made handwritten notes from it before typing his notes up on his return to the office.

Windeyer then produced a copy of a two-page document, which he showed to the court.

'That document does not set out the draft treaty,' the Chairman noted. 'That appears, from my hurried glance of it, to be a series of comments on various provisions in the treaty.'

'If I gave the impression that I had the actual draft of the treaty . . .' Rex started. 'What I had in my possession was an explanation of various clauses of the treaty.'

'And a copy of the treaty?' the Chair asked.

'No,' Rex replied. 'I am sorry if I have given the wrong impression. I had a copy of this document in a different form. I wrote it out in pencil and then typed it out as it appears here.'

Windeyer then showed the court another document, this time of a two-page minute with a Commonwealth Department letterhead, dated 2 June 1950. It contained comments on certain aspects of the draft Friendship Treaty. Rex said he had never seen it; the document he saw did not have a departmental letterhead. Although the contents were, in general, the same. He had seen a separate typed document; it had taken him between twenty minutes to half an hour to copy, and then he'd handed it back to the man who had given it to him. This had taken place in the reading room, also known as the newspaper room, at the library in Parliament House.

Windeyer questioned him further. 'Was the officer who gave you the document the same officer with whom you had the discussion, and who, in the words of your article, told you about the matter?'

'Yes,' Rex admitted.

'If you look ... you will see that the departmental minute is addressed to someone by name. Do you notice that?' Windeyer asked.

'I notice that, yes,' Rex replied.

'Did you meet that man?'

'I am not answering any questions about names.'

Rex then refused to answer any further questions put to him by Windeyer, or any of the three Justices, regarding names and the treaty document.

'In the circumstances, Your Honours,' Windeyer stated, 'I do not think I can usefully ask this witness any further questions.'

Justice Owen then asked Max Julius if he had any questions for this witness.

Mr Julius rose and started to ask Rex questions regarding his evidence. Rex repeated that he had never travelled under the name of J. Matthews. Julius gave Rex the opportunity to point out that there had been a considerable amount of time—nine months—between the publication of his Friendship Treaty article and the raids on the *Tribune* and his home.

'Personally, I think that what he has done is completely lawful,' Max Julius said to the three Judges, 'but apparently the Government did not think so, and Your Honours apparently are of the opinion that the *publication* of it was not lawful.'

'What we are concerned about,' Justice Owen replied, 'is the fact that the information was given to *anyone*—not that it was published.'

'The public servant, if it be a public servant, who gave it, I should think certainly comes under the *Crimes Act*,' Justice Philp added, 'and of course if Mr Chiplin kept his mouth shut, as he has here, and refused to divulge the source, how could anyone prove who was the source?'

Rex further explained, under questioning by Max Julius, that he had not communicated to any Soviet person about ciphers or enciphered communications between Australia and America, and that as a journalist it was his job to seek out and investigate information for publication, other than just the scripted information that was handed out by different government departments or politicians.

Rex then stated that he had accidentally met Petrov the first time in Kings Cross while getting cigarettes for his wife, and that he had not said that he would obtain information for the Soviet.

After Mr Julius sat down, Windeyer started on Rex again.

'What you got were comments on a proposed draft treaty,' Windeyer stated.

'Yes.'

'Why did you speak of a treaty which had been made?' he asked.

'Well,' replied Rex, 'it had been made. It had been drawn up; it had been initialled.'

'Who told you it had been initialled?' Windeyer demanded.

'I was told it had been initialled,' Rex replied.

'By whom?'

'That I refuse to say.'

'By the same man?' the Chairman asked.

'Yes, Your Honour,' Rex admitted.

'But did you not change the words which appeared in the document which you saw, and the document which you typed and had in your office?' Windeyer asked. 'Did you not change the wording?'

Rex asked if he could have a look at the document.

'Yes—read it,' Windeyer said passing it to Rex. 'What I am putting to you, so that there will be no doubt about it, is that you were seeking to convey the impression by your article, that the treaty had already been made, whereas the document you got speaks of it as a draft treaty which may or may not be accepted in its then form.'

'Would you mind again—the question?' Rex asked.

'Didn't you make it appear in your article that the treaty had been concluded?' the Chairman asked.

'No, Your Honour.'

Windeyer stated, 'You changed the word "accepted" to "applied", I notice, in more than one place.'

'You refer to it as "the Treaty" right through, don't you?' Justice Ligertwood asked.

'Yes,' Rex replied.

'Doesn't that mean it was a completed treaty?' Justice Ligertwood asked.

'Well, in one sense of the word I suppose you would be right, but in the loose sense of journalism, a treaty just meant to me, a treaty, whether it was applied or not,' Rex said.

'It was a mere chance that you changed the wording in the type-written material you had made—you changed the word "accepted" to "applied"?'

'I should say,' Rex pointed out, 'it may not even have been me who changed it. I am not saying I did or did not.'

Windeyer wasn't getting anywhere. He needed to call his next witness.

'Your Honours, there is nothing further I want to ask Mr Chiplin at the moment in view of the attitude he has taken,' he said. 'For the purpose of further investigation of this matter there will be other evidence that I wish to call this afternoon.'

He halted for a moment: 'At least, I think not,' he said turning back to the Judges. 'I would ask that Your Honours should adjourn until tomorrow.'

The Commission adjourned at 1 p.m.

It is not known who Windeyer silently communicated with during that pause. He resolutely wanted Mercia to take the stand, despite Colonel Spry's previous intervention seeking to protect his undercover agent.

But it was not going to happen that afternoon.

53

MRS A

Mercia was in Sydney, having been called to attend as a witness; her second statement hadn't been enough to avoid fronting the Commission.

However, when Windeyer had wanted her to appear on the afternoon of 24 February, she had refused. And because there was no sitting the following day, Friday 25 February, despite Windeyer suggesting there would be, the next sitting date would be Monday 28 February—with or without Mercia.

Mercia's case officer, Stan Roper, called Ray Whitrod in Canberra, telling him Mercia was distraught and wouldn't go into the witness box. She had broken down emotionally and was refusing to testify. He asked Whitrod to come to Sydney urgently and give his former agent some support so she would testify.

Ray Whitrod flew to Sydney and spent time with Mercia, finally getting her to agree.

Cindy and Kieron were told by ASIO at the end of their first meeting that Mercia had agreed to testify at the Royal Commission because she felt it was the right thing to do—not just for herself, but for her country. Mercia, they said, was a woman with high morals, and she wanted Rex to know where the information about him was coming from.

※

On Monday 28 February, the court started half an hour late, after being cleared of the press and the public. Mercia's evidence would be given 'in camera', with no press or public present, to help protect her identity—but not from Rex.

Mercia Masson was called to the witness stand. There in the empty court room, sitting in front of the Justices and the witness box, were Ted Hill, Max Julius and a stunned Rex Chiplin.

Mercia was sworn in, and the Commission directed that her name and address not be published, giving her some anonymity. She would be known in the transcripts—and eventually to the public, if the transcripts were released—as 'Mrs A'.

Windeyer took her gently through her general situation as he knew it. She was a widow, living in Melbourne; she had worked with Naval Intelligence, the Commonwealth Investigation Service and then ASIO. She had worked in the Department of Post-War Reconstruction and had met Chiplin in about 1950 in Canberra and continued to meet him socially at various functions. She was connected with the Democratic Rights Council in Sydney, attending functions and helping them prepare literature for distribution, while working at *The Daily Telegraph*.

'Can you tell us how you came to become connected with the Democratic Rights Council?' Windeyer asked Mrs A. 'What happened? I would like you to tell us in your own words, if you could.'

'Well, I had first come across this particular section a few years before in Melbourne, and therefore I knew of its activities, and I thought that I would like to—I cannot recall the particular public thing that was happening at the time which created or re-created my interest,' Mercia began, pausing to compose herself. 'I asked Mr Chiplin how I

202

would go about joining the Democratic Rights Council in Sydney. He referred me to Mr Harold Rich, and Mr Harold Rich referred me to the office of the DRC in Daking House.'

'At that time,' Windeyer began, 'was it the Democratic Rights Council, or the Communist Party that you were concerned to join?'

'Well, I knew that the Democratic Rights Council had an affiliation with the Communist Party,' she explained. 'That is not strictly right,' she corrected herself, 'I did not know that precisely. I knew that a lot of people were associated with the same bodies.'

'You knew a lot of people were associated both with the Communist Party and with the Democratic Rights Council,' Windeyer said. 'Is that what you mean?'

'Yes,' Mercia replied. 'And equally so, there were a lot of people who were not connected,' she added.

Mercia was trying, somewhat belatedly, to protect those she felt were not directly involved. The facelessness of her reports to the security service had provided a buffer between herself and those she was reporting on. Now her face was being shown, her anonymity gone. She was exposed—exactly what Colonel Spry had tried to stop.

The whole time Rex would have been in front of her, watching her, knowing that his friend, in all the years that he had known her, had been an ASIO agent.

In Mercia's second statement, given in Melbourne two weeks previously, when describing Rex's trip to Warrandyte, when they had been drinking rum by the fire at her home on that cold, late autumn day, the word *anxious* had been crossed out and replaced with *amorous* before Mercia had signed the retyped document. The sentence then read, 'He became somewhat ~~anxious~~ amorous and said, "Don't you worry . . .""

In Cindy and Kieron's second ASIO meeting, the possibility that Mercia and Rex could have been lovers was briefly discussed, and they all concluded that the pair were really just good friends. But reading reports from an old file can only reveal so much; Ray Whitrod, for one, believed there was something more. In his interview with author

David McKnight in the early 1990s, he said when Mercia had moved from Sydney to Melbourne, she didn't know anybody; her only contacts were those ASIO pushed onto her. Whitrod said, 'She was looking around for, God help me, some male company.' He had been Mercia's case officer, and they only met once a week. He felt he should have seen that she was looked after—but he didn't. 'She got involved with Chiplin,' he told McKnight.

54

OVERWROUGHT

'Can you tell us, what was your conversation with Mr Chiplin which led to this joining of the Democratic Rights Council?' Windeyer asked.

'As far as I can remember,' she started, then stopped. 'And after all, it is some years ago . . .'

'Yes,' Windeyer said, 'I am only asking you to give us the words, or the substance of them, as nearly as you can remember.'

Mercia collected herself and began recounting how she had told Rex that she wanted to do something, and she was referred to the Democratic Rights Council.

'When you say you felt you wanted to do something,' Justice Philp asked, veering her attention away from Windeyer, 'for whom?'

'I wanted to find out really what was happening,' she explained. 'At this stage it is a little hard for me to explain, but I like to know what is going on, and I like to know what all people are thinking and doing and acting. I did want to know more about it, and I can only explain it as that.'

Windeyer then asked if she knew Mr Chiplin was connected with the *Tribune* newspaper.

'Oh, of course,' she replied.

'At this time, when you made this suggestion to him that you would like to be doing more, you had already had many meetings with him?' Windeyer asked.

'Yes, that is so.'

'Can you remember what he told you when you made that suggestion?' Windeyer probed. 'What did he say, as far as you remember?'

'If I remember rightly,' Mercia began, 'I was told to see Mr Harold Rich, and to tell Mr Rich Mr Chiplin had sent me to him.'

'Did you see Mr Rich?'

'Yes.'

'Where did you see him?'

'I saw him in his rooms,' Mercia replied, 'I think it is the building next to Daking House at the railway; I do not precisely know the name of it.'

'Can you remember what you said to him?'

'Yes, I told him precisely what I had been told to tell him, and he told me to go across . . .' She stopped.

'What was that about you wanting to do something?' Windeyer asked, trying to get her back on track.

'Your Honours,' Mr Hill interjected, 'I do not know where this is going to. It seems a long way removed from any matters in dispute here.'

'Mr Hill, I am not clear myself where this is going,' Justice Owen replied. 'We will just have to wait for a while.'

'Your Honours,' Hill replied, 'the matter has been debated many times. But I submit that, if my friend has something that is relevant to the matter in issue, it should be brought forward.'

'Mr Windeyer, I think, is trying to get material from the witness without asking her leading questions,' the Chair stated.

'I am sorry, Your Honours,' Hill replied.

'Yes, Your Honour: I could make it much shorter,' Windeyer said.

Justice Owen turned to Mercia, who was looking unsteady on her feet. 'Are you sure you do not want to sit down?' he asked. 'You may, if you want to.'

'I apologise for being so slow,' she replied.

'That is all right,' the Chairman told her.

Windeyer questioned her carefully, asking about the events at the Democratic Rights Council in Sydney, assuring her that no names would be unnecessarily published.

Mercia briefly explained her work both in Sydney and Melbourne, the film evenings and how they were organised. Then, under further questioning, she described the events that took place at the Ironworkers' Club at the party for the war correspondent Wilfred Burchett, where Rex asked her to drop her work with the Democratic Rights Council. She kept apologising for not recalling it all in more detail.

'Did he tell you why he wanted you to drop your association with the Democratic Rights Council?' Windeyer asked.

'Yes. He did not want me to be publicly associated with these activities,' she replied.

'Did he tell you why?'

'I think he felt he had other things—there were other things I could do,' she replied. 'I cannot recall it. I am sorry. You are asking me to go back over things that happened years ago that I have no . . .'

'I quite appreciate the difficulty about it,' Windeyer said. 'I am only asking you as far as you can . . .'

'I will do my best,' Mercia replied.

'At all events, he asked you to drop your association with the Democratic Rights Council. Did you say anything about it?' Windeyer asked.

'I did not want to do it,' Mercia stated.

'You told him that?'

'Yes.'

'And do you remember what you said, in any sense? Did you say . . .' Windeyer looked down at a paper in front of him: '"I cannot do that, I could not let people down, what would they think?", or something to that effect?'

'That is so,' Mercia replied. 'That is true.'

'And do you remember what he said?'

'No,' Mercia again halted. 'I think he said leave it to him.' She stopped. 'I am not sure about that.'

'You did give an account of this about two years ago, did you not?' Windeyer asked.

'Yes. I cannot remember it. I am sorry,' Mercia added, before breaking down completely.

We don't know if Mercia was apologising to Mr Windeyer, the court, or Rex.

The morning's proceedings were suspended at 11.02 a.m.

When that day's proceedings resumed at 2.30 p.m., Windeyer explained that the witness was in an overwrought and emotional state as a result of 'the stress of having to give evidence about a long and extraordinary course of events' and was not fit to give further evidence that afternoon.

It was suggested that for the following day's hearings, if Mercia was unable to be questioned, they would instead move on to Windeyer's next witness, Ric Oke.

After the court was adjourned, Rex Chiplin had a long conversation with his counsel.

55

TRUE AND CORRECT

Mercia did manage to gather herself together overnight, and she appeared again the following morning to continue her evidence.

Ric Oke had been summoned to the Commission, and Ted Hill asked to appear for him, which was granted, the result being that Mercia now had Ric, as well as Rex, Max Julius and Ted Hill watching her as she continued to give evidence.

The proceedings opened on time at 10 a.m., with the Chair asking Mercia if she was feeling all right.

'Thank you,' she replied, 'I apologise.'

Windeyer started by asking Mercia if she had written reports and was in regular contact with security officials at the time of the events. She said she had.

'And what you wrote in those reports at the time were true and correct?' he asked.

'Yes,' Mercia replied.

'That may help us,' Windeyer explained, 'and make it easier to ask you about matters.'

Mercia had brought along her diaries, referring to them for more accurate dates as the day went on. After a shaky start, her answers became more confident as Mr Windeyer led her through her work with the Department of National Development and her involvement with the Democratic Rights Council in Sydney, and with the Peace Council in Melbourne.

She was shown the handwritten note Rex had left for her at the Hotel Kingston when she was working in Canberra for Commander Jackson in September 1951, after the failed referendum on Communism—the same note she had handed on to ASIO. It read, in full:

```
Mercia -
    Called tonight—have also left message with F.
    I will ring you in the morning about 9-9.30 a.m.—
particularly want to see you honey.
    I am going back tomorrow afternoon train.
    Love etc R.C.
```

When questioned about the identity of 'F', she told the Commission she assumed it to be Fergan O'Sullivan, who she had introduced to Rex, and who she herself sometimes saw when back in Canberra.

Mercia explained that she and Rex did meet the following morning, and this was when he asked her for information about Commander Jackson—anything to do with defence, commerce, and the agriculture section of a pact with America that was in the news at the time, and any information she could get on American investments in Australia.

'Was anything said about defence matters?' Mr Windeyer asked.

'The only reference I can remember at the moment is defence in relation to food production,' Mercia replied. 'At the time it was a very top secret plan—am I permitted to tell you?' she asked the Chairman.

'Yes,' he replied.

Mercia explained that Australia would become the food 'arsenal' of the Pacific in the event of another war. The different divisions within the Department of National Development were handling this matter through their regional surveys. She also mentioned that the Industrial Development Division's job was to know precisely what every industry in Australia consisted of and to what extent—together with how much could be switched to war production if needed. This provided an assessment of Australia's industrial potential.

Under further questioning from Windeyer, she said Industrial Development was a division that she did not have access to, as she had explained to Rex.

'Had you had any conversation with Mr Chiplin or anybody about what I might describe as Communist Party associations in Melbourne?' Windeyer asked her.

'Yes, I did,' she replied. 'I was anxious to carry on my work down there.'

Mercia recalled that Rex had told her not to 'take any public association', and that there were quite a lot of people like her.

Mercia faltered, paused, and then continued. Rex had told her there were a lot of people who could not be involved in public activities. 'I cannot remember the precise words,' she said, 'I am sorry. I can only give you my memory of the impression of that.'

'Well, give us that,' Windeyer said.

'That is,' she replied, 'that I was in a position to give valuable information to the Party, therefore I was to be protected.'

Windeyer then questioned her about another meeting with Rex the following November at the TAA lounge in Sydney—the same building the Commissioners had spoken about earlier, when Rex had given evidence, as being near the Commission office.

She told the court that she handed to Rex documents that had been vetted by ASIO: a graph on coal production, and documents about American investment in Australia, all approved by her case manager. She had then apologised to Rex for not having anything further, but Rex had told her not to worry, that he had fallen on 'something', he had come across a 'bundle' the previous week, though she was uncertain about the wording he had used at the time.

They then talked about the meeting where she handed Rex surveys of the Channel, Kimberley and Gulf countries, as these were the particular areas that her division was surveying.

'There was nothing confidential about them?' Windeyer asked. 'A person who had a legitimate reason could have got them?'

'Provided the reason was very legitimate,' Mercia replied. 'They were certainly restricted, but they were surveys that any team of experts could have made themselves, I should think.'

'In any event, did Mr Whitrod know about giving this to Mr Chiplin?' Windeyer asked.

'Yes,' Mercia replied. She started to falter again when Windeyer clarified that she had handed these to Rex at a further meeting.

'Did he ask you what you were going to do when Jackson left Australia?' Windeyer asked.

'Yes,' Mercia replied.

'Would you like to rest for a minute?' Justice Owen asked.

'It is all right,' Mercia replied.

She paused again before explaining to Windeyer that she told Rex, who was still sitting there watching her in the court room, about the possibility of going to the ministerial staff of External Affairs or Defence. She told the court that Rex thought that move would be good; she would have access to various important channels of information. She spoke again about Rex telling her to steer clear of her left-wing associations.

'Did he say this, or something like this: "We have lots of people like you whom it is sometimes better to accept as members in name only?"'

'Yes, that is so,' Mercia replied.

'And did he say, "Not that we don't trust you, but there is a group or panel of special workers too valuable to risk as open members?"'

'That is so, Mr Windeyer,' she replied before pausing. 'Could I rest for a moment?'

'Would it be a good thing if we adjourned at this stage, Your Honour?'

'Yes, we will adjourn,' Justice Owen agreed.

The sitting was adjourned at 10.43 a.m.

56

FRIENDS AND ENEMIES

When proceedings recommenced at 11.08 a.m., Mercia interrupted Mr Windeyer's questioning to ask the Chairman if she could say something first, and Justice Owen agreed. She needed to explain her behaviour.

'It is not easy for me to state this,' she began, 'because during my long association with these people, I met a lot of people I didn't like and a lot of people I came to like very well, apart from their ideals. It is not easy at the moment. So I apologise for my slowness about this.'

'I haven't asked you the names of any officials,' Windeyer stated.

'No,' Mercia replied, 'but you are going to, and I am going to have to say it, Mr Windeyer.'

'I would not if I could avoid it,' Windeyer replied.

'The human factor does come into it,' Mercia stated, 'and you cannot avoid it.'

'Perhaps it is easiest to mention the name,' Windeyer suggested. 'What you want to say is that a lady, Miss Cohen, was a friend of yours?'

'Yes,' Mercia replied.

'Genuinely a friend of yours?'

'Yes.'

'And that in your friendly associations with her, on the basis of friendship, there was no pretence on your part?'

'No, definitely not.'

Mercia then confirmed that Leila helped introduce her to a lot of people, and confirmed Leila had never sought or received any information which would be improper to receive.

'So far as I understand it, her name comes into the matter only incidentally, as a person through whom you apparently met other people,' Windeyer reassured her, before leading Mercia into the various appointments they had together in connection with joining the Communist Party, and Ric Oke's role in securing these.

Mercia was struggling to remember exact details, consulting her diary from the time, confirming different meetings, when, where and who she was with. Mr Windeyer helped her, reading from her past reports the specific details of conversations. Her answers were short, but she did explain in more detail about Ric going to enrol her into the CPA and the fee structure as he had explained it to her, together with his desire to set up a secure system of communication between Mercia and Rex.

Windeyer then asked if Rex had said anything about her joining the Communist Party, but Mercia could not recall.

'When you came to Sydney you usually saw Chiplin: is that so?' Windeyer asked.

'I never failed to see him,' she stated.

Windeyer asked her about the GAPS document she was working on for Commander Jackson, and Rex's desire to see it, together with other meetings with Rex and Ric, which Mercia verified with her diaries.

He then asked, 'Did he say anything about the Russian Embassy?'

'What?' Justice Philp asked. 'In connection with meetings?'

'Yes,' Windeyer replied.

'Do you remember?' Justice Owen asked Mercia.

'I can remember things about the Russian Embassy,' Mercia replied, 'but I cannot remember them precisely. Some things I can. As I have said, again it is very difficult.'

'Was anything said about meeting anyone connected with the Russian Embassy?' Justice Philp asked.

'Mr Chiplin, I think,' she said, pausing, 'was going to discuss with somebody at the Embassy—my position.'

'Did he say that to you?' Windeyer asked.

'I have the impression at the moment,' Mercia replied. 'But I cannot remember very precisely.'

'I want you to remember all you can about this,' Windeyer said to her. 'A few minutes ago you said it was very difficult, and I realise that it is difficult.'

'It is difficult,' Mercia said again. 'You cannot become so close to people without . . .'

Mercia couldn't continue and again broke down.

'We shall adjourn for a few minutes,' the Chairman stated.

The sitting was again suspended at 11.53 a.m.

When the sitting resumed at midday, Mercia was gently questioned about Rex's mention of a man called Ivan at the Russian Embassy. She agreed that she had met the TASS correspondent, a Mr Pakhomov, at an event in Sydney at the Russian Social Club, but had never known his first name was Ivan. She had never been inside the Russian Embassy, she added.

When asked whether she'd had any other conversation with Rex about persons at the Russian Embassy, she explained that Rex was upset with Fergan O'Sullivan's behaviour, as he had 'OK'd Mr O'Sullivan to the Embassy'.

'Was anything said by Mr Chiplin or Mr Oke about contact with the Embassy by them or any other Australian?' Windeyer asked.

'I cannot get the impression . . . I was under the impression that . . .' Mercia hesitated. 'I could have only known from circumstances which happened at the time.'

'Your Honours, I object to the impression,' Ted Hill interjected.

215

Mercia turned on him. 'You will not get any misimpressions, though, Mr Hill,' she stated, before turning back to Windeyer. 'I do not remember, Mr Windeyer. At this stage I do not remember, but I do remember that there was a typewriter there which had been a gift from a government—from "a grateful government"—and that came through the Embassy.'

'A typewriter?' Windeyer asked. 'You mean . . .?'

'In Mr Chiplin's home,' Mercia stated.

'You mean it came from the Russian Embassy?' Justice Philp asked.

'He did not say directly it was from the Russian Embassy,' Mercia replied, 'but it was a gift from "a grateful government".'

Windeyer didn't dwell on the typewriter, as ASIO's investigation showed him that they couldn't directly link Mercia's report to the Soviets.

He asked Mercia about starting with the Department of National Development, and whether Rex asked her to get any information she could for him about a Friendship Treaty, or a proposed Friendship Treaty, with the United States.

'Yes,' Mercia replied. 'That at the time was also in the public news.'

'You remember, do you not, that there was a publication in the *Tribune*?'

'Yes.'

Mercia then went on to recount how she had been interviewed by Mr Wilks, and her fears of being under suspicion for giving the treaty document to Rex.

'Did you in fact give it?' Windeyer asked.

'No,' she replied, 'anything I gave Mr Chiplin I have already told you about.'

57

THE MISSING CABINET

Mrs A's long day of giving evidence continued. Windeyer tendered a two-page undated letter from Rex to Mercia that she had handed over to ASIO after receiving it. In the letter Rex asked, 'You mentioned certain things in your last letter, have you anything further on friendship etc?'

Windeyer asked Mercia, 'Do you yourself know anything about the way in which Mr Chiplin got to know of a Departmental comment on the draft Treaty of Friendship, Commerce and Navigation?'

'No, but Mr Chiplin had contacts in External Affairs,' she replied.

Windeyer asked about her meeting with Rex on 10 March 1952, where Rex spoke of atomic testing, and about the additional security precautions to be taken before they next met. He asked about their meeting on 19 March, where Rex had requested any information about uranium and 'the Yanks' that she could get him, and then her dealings with Ric Oke, right up to the failed meeting on 26 March.

Windeyer ran through the various meetings she'd had with Rex that she had reported on, including the one after she'd been interrogated by Mr Wilks, when she reprimanded Rex for drawing her into it.

While speaking about her research work with the Department of Post-War Reconstruction, Mercia suddenly went off on a tangent that Mr Windeyer hadn't asked for.

'I had been doing some special research work for Commander Jackson,' she said. 'And I discovered that a whole cabinet connected with that division had disappeared—a complete cabinet of documents,' she explained. 'I discovered that during my research in Canberra and it was thought that it may have disappeared during that switch over, but it was a whole cabinet containing the assessments that had been made of Australian industry during the war, and it had complete records in it of every firm in every industry which existed in Australia. As far as I know, it is still missing.'

The Chair asked which department, and Mercia gave a brief history of the merger of sections of Post-War Reconstruction into the Department of National Development. When asked by the Justices about a departmental minute on the treaty, which she was then shown, she paused and replied, 'I have never seen this minute. That would not be in the file that I had access to.'

Windeyer ran her through her phone call to Rex from Melbourne, which she had been instructed to make, and Rex's subsequent trip down to Melbourne and Warrandyte, using a false name.

Windeyer then handed the file containing all of her reports to the Justices to review, with Mr Hill objecting on the same basis as he had previously—that he was not able to access them.

The court was adjourned at 3.15 p.m., giving Ted Hill enough time to get instructions.

He and Rex had a lot to discuss. Hill was set to cross-examine Mrs A the following day.

58

UNDERLINES

Among her mother's belongings that Cindy had kept, one item puzzled her: the dog-eared copy of the Official Transcript of Proceedings of the Royal Commission into Espionage, from 28 February to 8 March 1955.

When Cindy first read through it, she couldn't see her mother's name anywhere, but she put the pages in a storage box, which she wouldn't open again until she moved to Killcare after her divorce. It was only after her first visit to ASIO, as pieces of her mother's puzzle started falling into place, that she dug the transcripts out again—but they still didn't make sense.

The transcripts show the seemingly haphazard way the questions by counsel could lead to other questions and answers, jumping back and forth in time, and were difficult to put into context without knowledge of the time and the events leading up to this interrogation. Cindy's confusion on re-reading them was compounded by the fact that several pages were missing. Had they been lost in the move? Cindy didn't think so. Had her mother lost them? Possibly. Or had she simply disposed of them?

Some sections of the transcripts had been underlined. At times her mother had used a thin black felt-tip pen; a few were in wobbly blue biro, the lines sometimes ragged and unsteady; others had been made with the help of a ruler to form a hard straight edge. Sometimes certain words were underlined, sometimes sentences or complete paragraphs.

Was Mercia remembering parts of her testimony she deemed important? Was she trying to justify something to herself? Or was she perhaps leaving a message, explaining her actions, to a daughter she couldn't talk to.

On the first difficult day that Mercia had appeared and eventually collapsed, there is nothing noted, nothing underlined, and all the pages are present.

On 1 March, the first half of the day's transcript is unmarked, but an unsteady black line underscores the section where she answered Mr Windeyer's questions about Mr Oke and the possibility of working for the Department of Defence:

'There was another discussion,' she interjected, 'I think we discussed the coming atomic experiments, the British atomic experiments in the West.'

'What did he say?' Mr Windeyer then asked.

'Mr Oke wanted to know, or asked me did I know, who might be on that as far as—what Division would be handling—I am not clear about this; I think it was the Press people who would be permitted to attend, and what Division would be handling it. I said that I would be in Defence, but I had no idea of the Division that would be particularly concerned in those sections.'

The shaky black underlines again appear when Mr Windeyer asked Mercia about her meetings with Rex—specifically the meeting she had reported at his home on 11 March 1952. She was explaining to the Commission that public meetings were ruled out, and then a more clandestine approach to their meetings was arranged:

'... if I rang Mr Chiplin to make an appointment I was not to say who was speaking, and we would meet at the Market Street entrance of St James station, and I would not mention the place, but simply say the time.'

Rex was taking measures not to be observed. The transcript continued:

'And did he say something to you about the delay in your appointment?' Windeyer then asked.

'Yes,' she replied.

'What did he say about that; do you remember?'

'Yes,' Mercia replied. 'He asked me, did I know why, and I said that I did not—and I really did not; and the Security matter came up again. He said not to worry, that he thought it was just a normal check.'

'The security "what" came up?' Windeyer asked.

'A normal security check.'

'And did he say anything to you about these missile experiments?' Windeyer continued.

'We did discuss that, but Mr Chiplin said that it was only missile experiments at Woomera, that the other tests were taking place at Christmas Island.'

As mentioned previously, the first test occurred in the Montebello Islands off the Australian mainland in October 1952, with limited knowledge of it in the public domain from February 1952. The subject of atomic testing and weapons was of huge interest to the Australian Government and public—as well as the Soviets. In 1953, two more atomic explosions occurred at the isolated Emu Field in the South Australian outback, 510 kilometres north-west of Woomera.

In Mercia's writing at the top of the next page is an asterisk and the date 'March 1952', the corresponding asterisk to the doubly emphasised following exchange between Mr Windeyer and Mercia about Rex:

'Do you remember his saying anything in particular about
'uranium' and the 'Yanks'?' he asked.

'Yes,' Mercia had replied. 'Anything you can get
on uranium and the Yanks at this stage would be very
welcome.'

Shaky blue biro underlines further comments about Christmas
Island, when Mrs A was cross-examined by Mr Hill on 2 March:

'Now, I just want to put to you a couple of matters about
Mr Oke. Yesterday did you give some evidence about
Christmas Island?'

'About which?' Mercia replied.

'Christmas Island,' Mr Hill repeated.

'I mentioned it,' she replied, 'yes.'

'Where did you mention it?' he asked.

'I mentioned it in a discussion with Mr Chiplin about
atomic experiments which were to be held in Australia,'
she replied.

'What she said,' the Chairman interjected, 'was that
guided missile experiments would take place at Woomera
and the atomic explosion would take place at Christmas
Island. That is the substance of what she said yesterday.'

'And that is why they were bringing landing barges
with them,' Mercia added, 'because of Christmas Island.'

'Yes,' Windeyer commented, 'that is what Chiplin said.'

'That is what Chiplin said to you?' Mr Hill asked
Mercia. 'Was it?'

'Yes,' she replied.

By underlining these sections, Mercia emphasised the discussions
around the nuclear tests. She had been working for the good of the
country—fear that atomic secrets would be shared with foreign powers
was a clear and present danger.

In the highly charged atmosphere during the Cold War years in Australia, the double fears of Communism and atomic weapons were a powerful motivating force for those who felt the need to help their country.

Even if it meant betraying friendships, Mercia's loyalty to her country came first.

59

BATTLELINES

On 2 March, proceedings started at 10.05 a.m. Mercia once again stood in the witness box, ready to be cross-examined. Mr Windeyer told the court that he had completed his examination of the witness.

Mr Hill began questioning Mercia, an exchange that was far from cordial. He asked about Rex Chiplin, how long they had known each other and the fact that, as journalists, they would exchange information of a general character. In Mercia's personal copy of the transcript, her intermittent underlining continued:

'You know Mr Chiplin's family quite well, do you not?'
    'I am very fond of Mr Chiplin's family,' Mercia stated.
'I still regard Mr Chiplin as he was, a friend. I think I have been doing the right thing by saving the people I like, from thinking the wrong way.'

Mercia explained that she had even offered her holiday house in Killcare to the Chiplin family to use, as she was concerned about Vivienne's health with the Royal Commission underway. And then she emphasised that the offer was still open.

Hill continued to ask her about her friendship with Chiplin, and the fact that he had assisted her with her troubles. He was someone to talk to about her family problems, and about looking after Russell Grant.

'You found Mr Chiplin a very sympathetic person?' he asked.

'He has always been a most sympathetic person. Mr Chiplin has been a very honest person to deal with. I have no wish to do Mr Chiplin any harm. I think I told you that yesterday. This is not easy for me, Mr Hill, none of it,' Mercia stated. 'I have lost everything in coming here—everything that I had up until Monday. I have lost my friends—my close friends over the years—and my association with the left wing; I have now lost my left-wing friends. I have probably lost my position. I shall probably have to remove my child from the school, and my mother from the house in which she lives. I do not think there is anything else I can possibly lose.'

Mr Hill prodded her repeatedly, about reporting on people she knew so well.

Mercia underlined her reply:

'It is not easy to do this sort of thing; you have to have something very much bigger and stronger and see what actually will come out of it ultimately not only for yourself but for the people you like, and this is the only way I can look at this. I have not done anything to hurt anybody individually.'

And when asked by Hill, 'Did it ever cross your mind that you might be better off if you were not doing it?', she answered:

'I think the first thing you have to do is to set out quite clearly what you want in life and what you believe in; and once you have that, and if it is strong enough,

225

then you take the course. You do not jump into it before
you make your decision.'

Hill then changed tack, and this exchange is to be found in two pages
missing from Mercia's copies of the transcript.

'I do not want to pry into your private affairs, but that diary you
have got . . .'

'You may have a look at them if you like,' Mercia replied to Mr Hill.
'I have told you that they are the ones I keep in my purse.'

'I want these documents tendered, Your Honour,' Hill stated.

'These are my personal property,' Mercia objected. 'They have
personal notes in them.'

Justice Owen asked to look through the diary, which Mercia
handed to him.

'I ask that before they are taken,' Mercia requested, 'I'm allowed
to copy certain telephone numbers.' The Chairman reassured her that
they would not be taken from her.

'Do you mind if I have a look at the one for November 1951?' Hill
asked.

'Certainly,' Mercia replied.

'What date?' the Chair asked.

'All of November 1951,' Hill replied. 'May I have a look at them?'

'Yes,' the Chairman said, handing the diary over to Mr Hill.

'May Mr Julius look through it for a moment—for November?'

'Yes,' Justice Owen replied, 'you can look through the November
entries.'

Mr Hill then handed the diary to Max Julius for him to scrutinise
as he went on to question Mercia further. They could not have access
to her reports, but they could look through her diaries.

60

ANOTHER LOOK

Among the missing pages of Mercia's transcript, Hill asked her, 'Did you report to the security officer that you had failed to join the Party?'

'I think you will find all that in those reports. As I told you, they were fully covered.' Mercia explained that she had been told that she was to be an undercover member, though not by who, with Hill replying, 'You know a little more about it than I do!'

'I wouldn't say that Mr Hill,' Mercia replied.

'We don't want to debate it on a personal basis,' Hill stated.

'No,' Mercia replied, 'I don't intend to.'

He started asking if she had an interest in the *Tribune* and Rex.

'I do not think I had any more special interest in Mr Chiplin's column than I had in any other column,' she replied. 'I am very interested in topical events, and that is the only place usually in a newspaper where there is a chance to express any individuality about a topical event,' she said. She added that when living in another city, she had found it difficult to keep abreast of what was published in the *Tribune*; that was the job of others in security, not hers.

Hill showed her a *Tribune* article published on 10 October 1951, titled 'War Cabinet formed in Canberra; Secret Reports from America', and Rex's column on 9 January 1952, which reported that Commander Jackson was sailing back to England with the finished GAPS report.

Hill then made his first accusation: that Mercia had given Rex the information contained in those articles.

Mercia admitted that she had been seeing Rex around those dates but, so far as the first article was concerned, she stated: 'I was not in possession of secret reports from America. It is quite possible, you know, for a journalist to write this sort of thing from a collection of conversations with various people. I do not think it would even be possible for Mr Chiplin to have got this information from one person. It traverses about, from my brief glance at it, at least four Government Departments; and, as I have said, a lot of what is in it is news to me, even at this late date.'

When pushed further by Mr Hill about the article, she said, 'I cannot recall ever giving Mr Chiplin any information like that.' She went on to say that she and Rex naturally talked about many personalities and topical events. 'I discussed all of this sort of thing,' Mercia stated. 'I had to do it, and a lot of it was part of the pattern,' she explained. 'A lot of my colleagues talked and exchanged gossip.'

'All I am asking you is: did you give, in any form, that information to Mr Chiplin?' Hill asked.

'One of the things I was engaged to do,' she explained, 'to make this particular position look right, was a gathering of certain information. I could have told Mr Chiplin, and that story could have been based on that.'

'You did?'

'It could have been, but I did not write this story, and I did not give him any of this precise information.'

Mr Hill said he had not accused her of writing it. He continued on, going through various articles Rex had written and then accused her of giving additional information to Rex about Commander Jackson and his wife, and of sharing information other than what she had been instructed to.

'Once the lead was given by Mr Chiplin about what he was interested in, of course that in itself . . .' Mercia started to explain, but was interrupted by Justice Philp.

'You mean you had no personal interest either way?'

'You cannot,' Mercia stated. 'You have to remove yourself right away from personal interests,' she said addressing Rex's counsel rather than Justice Philp. 'I think what you do not realise is that a good deal of these things Mr Chiplin did know were happening, because he then mentioned them to me; he did not have to learn from me what was happening precisely.'

Hill kept questioning her on her meetings with Rex and information passed on before Mr Windeyer interjected, 'Your Honours, the witness said yesterday that these documents were available to anybody who had any legitimate reason for asking for them. She also said that, in response to requests by Chiplin, she gave him certain documents, getting approval for doing so from Mr Whitrod.'

'Yes,' the Chairman agreed.

'There was never any suggestion, as I understand it, that the documents that she gave him were of any confidential character or secret character,' Windeyer continued, coming to Mercia's aid. 'Merely that she got permission, being under Mr Whitrod's direction in this operation, to respond to Mr Chiplin's request by the production of certain matters which, obviously, it was innocuous and harmless to let him have.'

Mr Hill then asked Mercia to look at the copy of the two-page typed minute concerning the draft treaty that had been tabled the previous day by Mr Windeyer.

'I told you about this yesterday, Mr Hill,' she stated.

'Yes, but did you read it yesterday?'

'I did.'

'Now I want you to just have another look at it.'

'Will you tell me why you want me to have a look at it?' she asked.

'You see there is no heading on it?'

'Mr Hill, I have told you all about this document yesterday. There is nothing more I can tell you about it. With the permission of the court . . .' Mercia implored.

'Ask the question, Mr Hill,' the Chairman replied.

'This would not be even in the files of the department I was in,' Mercia objected.

'Would you ever have seen a document with the same contents, but without that heading?' Mr Hill asked.

'I do not quite understand what you mean, Mr Hill,' Mercia replied. 'You asked me if I had seen this document; I told you that I had. But this document did not belong to us; it belonged to Industrial Development.'

'What I understand you are being asked is this,' Justice Philp suggested, 'have you ever seen the matter contained in this document— the same matter?'

Ignoring Justice Philp, Mercia stated, 'Mr Hill, I have told you, I have told everything about it.'

'Well, what is the answer to that question?' Hill demanded. 'It is very simple.'

'No, I haven't seen it,' Mercia stated.

Windeyer again tried to come to Mercia's aid, stating that the draft treaty had been circulated to several departments for comment.

'I suppose you do not know the newspaper room in the Canberra Parliamentary Library?' Hill asked her, ignoring Windeyer's comments.

'Yes, I do,' Mercia replied. 'There are a number of rooms, of course, used by journalists.'

'A newspaper room annexed to the Parliamentary Library, Canberra.'

'I have not been in that since 1949. I have had no reason to be there. I have had no reason to be in Parliament House,' Mercia stressed, explaining that the only time she had been into Parliament House since she had left Post-War Reconstruction was on one occasion, to see some fellow journalists.

'I suggest to you that you in fact gave Chiplin that document?' Hill accused.

'I did not give it to him,' she shot back.

'That she gave it to him?' Justice Ligertwood asked.

'That she gave it to him?' Justice Philp repeated.

The atmosphere in the court was about to turn against Mrs A.

61

FIGHTING BACK

'I have given my evidence on this,' Mercia stated. 'I am asking now that I not be questioned any more about it.'

When no response to her request was forthcoming from the Justices, she turned back to Mr Hill.

'I have been waiting for this. Mr Hill, I have been waiting for so much from you this morning.'

At this point, Justice Ligertwood interjected, asking Mr Hill: '<u>You are not suggesting she gave it to him, that your client committed perjury?</u>' (This comment by Justice Ligertwood was underlined in Mercia's copy of the official transcript.)

'Well, Your Honour . . .' Mr Hill started.

'In Canberra?' the Chairman asked.

'Yes, Your Honour,' Hill replied.

'I did not give it to him,' Mercia interrupted. 'I have never been in the Canberra Library.'

'Madam,' Mr Windeyer exclaimed, 'His Honour is not talking about you.'

'I am not addressing you, Madam,' the Chairman stated, before turning back to Mr Hill. 'Are you suggesting, Mr Hill, in the face of the evidence which has been given by him, that this woman gave your client this document in Canberra in the first week in November?'

'Your Honour, my instructions now are that this lady . . . I cannot identify it to the first week in November . . .'

'No, but Chiplin identified it,' the Chairman stated.

'I say, Your Honour,' Hill continued, 'that my instructions are that this lady handed him a document which is, in this correspondence, the substance of this document, in Canberra.' Hill then asked that Mr Chiplin again come to the witness box to explain.

'I shall certainly ask that he be called again,' Windeyer replied.

Ted Hill turned to Mercia, 'I want to suggest to you that that is the explanation for you being upset.'

'You are wrong,' Mercia stated. 'My upset was that direction I have told you that I have given it over and over again. Apparently now I am also to have the usual run of ruthlessness and persecution which I have known about. I have been pretty gentle about this too, but I can stop being gentle at any moment, and if I start talking, I just will not stop talking about what has been going on in the last twelve-and-a-half years.'

'What—in the way of espionage, people giving information?' Justice Philp asked.

'About people in this . . .'

'I think you should give it to us if you know about it,' Justice Philp stated.

They all waited for Mercia to respond, but she stood mute in the witness box.

'Go on, Mr Hill,' Justice Owen finally said.

'Did you say, "I am amazed and disgusted to think that the Government would sign away the independence of Australia"?' Hill asked Mercia.

'I do not recall having said that,' she replied. 'I might have said that in the course of my duty. I have said many things such as that.'

'Did you ever say anything like that to Chiplin?'

232

'It is quite possible I may have said that,' she stated, 'and I may have said a lot of things worse than that about this Government, considerably stronger than that. I have been saying it for so long that it is easy to say.'

'Did you ever discuss the treaty with him at all?' Hill asked.

'Yes; I think you will find that in my notes,' she stated. Notes in her reports, which Mr Hill was unable to see.

'You never said about this document, "It ought to be published", or about the contents of it?'

'I do not think so.'

'Could you have said that? Did you ever suggest that the proposed treaty should be published?'

'I have given a report about the proposed treaty,' Mercia replied. 'I have nothing further to say about it.'

'I put this conversation to you,' Hill continued, 'that you said, "This should be published" and Chiplin said "It certainly should".'

'I do not remember that at all.'

'Did you say: "You can make a copy of it. I will pick it up later"?'

'Oh no, definitely not,' Mercia replied. 'Look; I have been pretty gentle and upset about this whole thing, but you are certainly making me fight now, Mr Hill, and I will fight. I never said that at all to Mr Chiplin.'

'Did you say: "This has been kept a secret. I came across it in the file"?' Hill continued.

'I did not.'

'Did you say you would leave it with him and come back in half an hour?'

'I did not. That is an absolute lie,' Mercia replied. 'I have not been in the library in Canberra, as I have told you, since 1949. I can almost tell you word for word about the research that I did, the exact *Hansard* that I obtained on that occasion. I have not been in there since, and what is more, I think that any of the journalists in the gallery at Canberra will verify that too.'

'When Mr Wilks interviewed you, you knew that you had nothing to fear. Is that so?'

'That is so.'

62

MR OKE

Ted Hill, having raised doubt as to which side Mrs A was on, started to question Mercia about Leila and the 'special' method of communication that the Communist Party was said to have, and that implicated Rex. He asked about the information she had shared with Rex about an ALP sympathiser, before moving on to Rex's visit to Warrandyte and her evidence against Ric Oke.

'I want to turn to Mr Oke for a moment. You had told Mrs Mullett, as you know her, that you were anxious to join the Communist Party?' he asked.

Mercia agreed that she had discussed with Leila Cohen/Mullett her desire to join the Communist Party, and Leila had said she would talk to a friend about it.

'When you saw Mr Oke in the Peace Council,' Mr Hill continued, 'did he say to you, "Well, I am pretty busy, and it would be better if we met at some later time"?'

'No, I cannot recall that. We had quite a discussion at the Peace Council room.'

'When you saw him at the first full discussion, did Mr Oke say to you that Miss Cohen had informed him that you were anxious to work for the Party and join the Party?'

'That is a possibility. I cannot recall that precisely.'

'Do you recall that he explained to you the nature of the Party, its aims and constitution?'

'No.'

'The rate of dues payment?'

'I told you that I asked him how much my fees would be. I think Mr Oke realised or thought that I knew the aims and objects of the Party. Anyway, nothing could be done any further until another meeting. There was no suggestion at that first meeting, and I knew that he would have to make investigations about my work in Sydney.'

'You would have said something like this, would you, that you "wanted to assist in the movement to preserve peace"?'

'Definitely, yes; not those precise words, but I would have given that impression.'

'And that you had known Rex Chiplin in Sydney and had been influenced by him?'

'I cannot recall the influence by him; I know I used Mr Chiplin's name. Mr Chiplin had considerable standing with people.'

'That you had assisted Mr Chiplin in his position as journalist on the *Tribune*?'

'No, I cannot recall that. I do not think I did say that.'

'Did Mr Oke suggest that you should perhaps think over what he had told you about the Party and see him again in about a month's time?'

'No, the arrangement was that he would let Miss Cohen know when I was to meet him again, and she would let me know.'

'Yes, we agree on that; but do you not recall that he said to you, "Now, you think it over and I will see you again and make an appointment through Leila Cohen"?'

'Part of what you say, yes; but I cannot recall about thinking it over. I think there was possibly more to it on the other side about me.'

'That is what you thought?'

'Yes. It is not easy to become a member of the Communist Party.'

Mr Hill went on to suggest that Rex had urged her not to apply for the position in the Department of External Affairs, because she would have to assist in administrating a policy of the government that she hated.

Mercia denied this. 'That is not so,' she replied.

Mr Hill turned his cross-examination to the typewriter that Mercia had mentioned in evidence the previous day. 'All right. Just about this typewriter, about which you told us yesterday. I want to put this to you: that typewriter was a typewriter of West German make.'

'She said East German, Mr Hill,' Windeyer interjected.

'Did Mr Chiplin say to you that it came from the Russian zone?' Hill asked.

'He said it was a German typewriter.'

'Did he tell you that it had come from the *Tribune* office?'

'No, he did not. He said it was his own. He said he would not part with it for the world.'

'Did you report that it was an East German typewriter?'

'No.'

'Did you make any report about this typewriter?'

'Yes.'

'And did you suggest in that report that he had got that from "a grateful government"?'

'Those were the words that were said to me, Mr Hill,' Mercia stated. 'I do not suggest it.'

'Your Honour,' Mr Windeyer interrupted. 'May I just read on the notes what the witness did say in a report dated 14 February 1952? It refers to events on Thursday 7 February. She says: "On Thursday February 7 I went to Campsie as arranged with Chiplin." Then it speaks of other matters, and in the reference to this it said:

'Chippo had a typewriter and files on the table and a mass of written copy which he said was copy from the Builders' Union paper, which he edits. I said, "Is that a new typewriter?" He said, "Have a look at it. I wouldn't part with it for the world." On inspection it proved to be a portable, but with German writing on it. I said to him, "It is a beauty, but I don't know the make." He said, "That's a gift from a grateful government, and I'm very proud of it. It comes from East Germany and was given to me here through the Embassy—It's a bloody beauty."'

Windeyer turned to Mercia: 'Do you remember writing that report?'

'Whatever I put in that report would be correct, Mr Windeyer. I cannot recall precisely these things.'

Mr Hill then asked to look at Mercia's diary again, specifically November 1951, and it was handed to him.

Rex had told his counsel that he had received the draft treaty comments up to ten days before publication, in the reading room at Parliament House. As he usually travelled to Canberra on Tuesdays, returning on Thursdays, the only dates that matched for a meeting with Mercia in Canberra before the article was published on 14 November would have been from 6–8 November; this is the link that both Hill and Julius had looked for in Mercia's diary. According to Mercia's reports, she was in Newcastle with Commander Jackson over that time.

'According to the diary,' Justice Philp read his notes as he tried to place Mercia's movements, 'on 5 November 1951 the witness has marked "Sydney 2 p.m., 4.30".' Turning to Mercia, he asked, 'Does that mean you left Melbourne at 2 and got to Sydney at 4.30?'

'Yes.'

'And the next day, the 6th, is marked, "5.50pm 7.40". Does that mean you got to Newcastle at 7.40?'

'Yes, that is so.'

'How did you travel—by train?'

'By the Newcastle Flyer,' Mercia agreed.

'So, she was in Sydney until 5.50 on the 6th,' Justice Philp stated

'And the report dated the 6th shows,' the Chairman added, 'that it is written the day after the events which are reported in it, because she speaks of having spent a sleepless night.'

'Yes,' Windeyer replied. 'And she said that she met Chiplin on the 5th; on arrival in Sydney, she met him in the TAA lounge in Phillip Street.'

The Chairman said, 'I think it might be as well, for the sake of convenience, if some of these dates were read on to the transcript. I am looking through these,' the Chairman added. 'There is a report made in Melbourne on Friday 2 November. There is a report made on Tuesday 6 November of events which had taken place the preceding day, and a statement in that report that the witness was going to Newcastle on the day on which she was reporting, namely the 6th, and that Chiplin had said he "was not going to Canberra until tomorrow". There is a report of 7 November from Newcastle. There is a report of 12 November from Sydney stating "came down last night" to do certain business, and in the course of that report there are passages which show that on the preceding day she had been in Newcastle.'

The Chairman added, 'There is a further report from Sydney of 13 November. Then there is a report which appears to have been made from Melbourne on 15 November [a Thursday] in which there is a reference to these terms: "I am booked for Canberra Wednesday and Melbourne Friday". So, in Melbourne on Thursday 15 November she was speaking of being booked for Canberra for the following Wednesday. Is that right?'

'The witness is asking you to look at her diary, Your Honour,' Mr Windeyer suggested. The diary was handed to the Commissioners.

'Yes,' the Chair said, 'the diary shows that she went to Canberra on Wednesday 21 November, that she was in Canberra on 22 November, and that she left Canberra for Melbourne on 23 November.'

'May the witness be excused, Your Honour?' Mr Windeyer asked. 'No doubt she is entitled to remain, if she wishes to, during the examination of other witnesses, but she may prefer to leave.'

'Yes,' Justice Owen replied.

'And will Your Honours excuse her if she wishes to leave?' Windeyer asked.

'Yes,' the Chairman replied. 'Thank you, Madam.'

'I am not suggesting that she be released altogether at the moment,' Windeyer added.

'No. She may leave the court room.'

Mercia left the witness box and the court room.

'Call Mr Oke,' Windeyer announced, before suggesting that, as it was a private hearing, Rex should also be ordered to leave the court room, which he duly did.

It would have been an uncomfortable meeting if Rex had bumped into Mercia in the corridor outside.

❧

Mercia was not called again as a witness, and she was released from attendance the following day. We don't know if she went straight back to Melbourne, or whether she stayed to hear the rest of the sessions that related to her, finishing with Mr Julius's summation on 8 March.

Cindy would have been waiting for her mother's return in Melbourne, being looked after by a housekeeper—always a different lady. It wasn't until she read it in the ASIO files that Cindy discovered that ASIO had organised and paid for a housekeeper whenever her mother was working. On one occasion, ASIO had not been happy with one of the housekeepers, so a different woman greeted her the following day after school. That memory only came back to Cindy on reading it in the file in Canberra.

The young Cindy certainly wasn't aware that her mother had been at the Royal Commission in Sydney. Cindy was attending school and involving herself in all the out-of-school activities that Mercia had organised for her. Each morning Cindy would get up, get ready and start her day; sometimes she saw her mother, sometimes not, as her mother would often go away with 'work'.

Mercia was not involved in her schooling, nor did she ever attend Cindy's piano or elocution lessons. Cindy doesn't remember anything special or unusual about this time, when her mother would have been going through emotional turmoil.

Mercia could hide things well.

63

RIC AND REX

After Mercia left the court room, George Richard Oke was affirmed and gave evidence. He admitted joining the Communist Party, and that he had been a full-time paid official of the Communist Party up until returning to work as a fitter and turner in August 1953. His role was to maintain a proper relationship between members, if there was a question of any dispute between them, he explained—but he was not solely responsible for vetting prospective members. He did, however, meet with Mercia at the request of his old friend Leila Cohen, but in his opinion she was unstable.

Ric also denied speaking with Rex about Mercia, only hearing of Mercia's friendship with him at their second meeting at Gibby's Coffee Shop. He said it was usual for people who wanted to gain membership to put it in writing, but that he told Mrs A to think carefully about joining the Party. He told her they would have a further conversation after she had given it consideration, and that they would arrange another meeting through Leila.

At the third meeting, which Ric agreed he could have instigated, he denied saying that he would put her membership forward to the proper authorities.

He explained that after their first discussion, he formed the opinion that Mrs A was a verbose, neurotic and erratic person, and it would be undesirable for her to join the Party. Mercia's emotional breakdowns and angry exchanges with Mr Hill in court hadn't defended her well against Ric Oke's characterisation.

Ric told the court that his opinion of her unsuitability was confirmed after their second meeting, when she explained that she would possibly be working for Mr Casey in External Affairs. Firstly, he did not believe that such an erratic and unstable person would be appointed to such an important position. Secondly, it could lead to the Party being attacked if a member in such a position secured information to which they weren't entitled.

When asked by the Chairman if that had always been the CPA's attitude, Ric replied it was, as far as he knew.

He denied knowing a long list of people that Mr Pape read out to him; but he did admit knowing Ian Milner through the Left Wing Book Club. In Mercia's copy of the transcript, she had underlined just about all of these people's names—perhaps suggesting that Ric did in fact know them, and Mercia knew it.

Ric then told the court that he had suffered a breakdown in 1953 and acute iritis of his right eye as the result of a work injury, so he was no longer able to attend branch meetings or any other CPA meetings.

Finally, he said he hadn't seen Rex Chiplin since he became ill.

It is probably a good thing Mercia wasn't in court to hear Ric Oke's evidence. She would have been infuriated.

The following day, Rex Chiplin was again in court. This is a day where all of the pages are missing from Mercia's transcript. Mercia must have had them at some stage, as she had the front cover, but the contents were gone.

Rex was about to turn his evidence around, and Windeyer was going to exploit the opportunity to show Rex as being in contempt of court.

'Do you put yourself forward as a truthful witness?' Windeyer asked.

'I do,' Rex replied.

'And on the last occasion on which you gave evidence, you had undertaken to tell the truth, the whole truth, and nothing but the truth?'

'I did.'

'I want to ask you about an answer you gave when you gave evidence last Thursday,' Windeyer began. 'His Honour the Chairman said to you—"Did this man, whoever he was, give you a copy of the treaty?" and you answered, "Yes, Your Honour." Do you remember that?'

'Yes,' Rex replied.

When asked if he had a complete copy of the treaty or a copy of a departmental minute, Rex explained that he was confused at the time, saying he did correct himself later, explaining that it was a departmental minute of comments, rather than a completed draft, and admitted that he gave the wrong impression in the article.

When asked did he have any information about it other than the document, the departmental minute, Rex replied, 'I was told it was made.'

'I see,' Windeyer said. 'Who told you that?'

'Mrs A.'

'Where did she tell you that?'

'In Canberra.'

'When?' Justice Philp asked.

'I do not know the precise time, Your Honour.'

Rex went on to say that he first heard about the treaty from Mercia; he didn't mention it to her first. When asked to remember about changing the wording in his article from 'would' to 'will'—making it seem that the treaty had already been made—Rex said that he couldn't remember.

He told the court that he met Mercia in the library at Parliament House. He said he had a clear recollection of it, up until he heard Mrs A's evidence around her diary entries, which showed she was not in Canberra in the ten days before the article came out. Then an element of doubt had crept in.

'Do you realise now that if, as you said on the last occasion, it was given to you in Canberra within ten days of publication of the *Tribune*, it was certainly not given to you by Mrs A?' Windeyer asked. 'Do you realise that now?'

'No,' Rex replied. 'Not exactly, not in as rigid terms as that. I have tried to put it as best I can.'

When asked whether the 'highly placed Government official' he had mentioned in his article was in fact only a temporary female clerk, Rex replied, 'I meant the personal assistant to Commander Jackson.'

'Why did you say it was a man?' Windeyer asked.

'I don't think I did,' Rex replied.

Windeyer then read to him from his article in the *Tribune*— 'A highly placed government official revealed the existence of the Treaty to me because he was disgusted'—and then asked again why he said it was a man.

Rex replied that he used the term 'he' as a neutral gender term.

He said he tried to use the word 'person' when questioned at the Commission, and when he had used the term 'he' or 'man', he had fallen into the terminology adopted by the Commission. He saw it as a neutral term. He was trying to protect the identity of his informant, and in no way meant to mislead the Commission. He had not lied in his evidence, Rex professed; he had been confused.

'You know of course that Mrs A was the secretary of a government official?'

'Yes,' Rex replied.

'And you know that this document, this information that she handed to you, was top secret?'

'She told me so,' he replied.

'And you so published in the *Tribune*?'

'Yes.'

They again ran through the dates in November. Rex asserted that he had made a copy of the document, in the reading room at Parliament House, in pencil, on the side of one of the wide-armed leather armchairs, and that his informant had left the room while he made the copy. Slipping back into his 'neutral gender' description, he said, 'That is my memory of it as it was the other day—that he went away and came back.'

Windeyer continued to question Rex about his use of 'he' when describing the person who gave him the document.

'In your article you said it was a masculine person and, in your [previous] evidence, you said it was not Mrs A. Now you never suggested to anybody that it was Mrs A until Mrs A came and gave evidence which you regarded as hurtful to you?'

'I have never told anybody until I told my counsel on Monday morning,' Rex replied.

'And that was after Mrs A had given evidence?' Windeyer asked.

'After Mrs A had revealed she was working for the Security,' Rex said, 'I went out and told my counsel at the first adjournment.'

'So, you were anxious, to protect her identity—until you found that she worked for the counter-intelligence, the Security?' Windeyer prodded.

'I considered Mrs A had breached my hospitality and that she had forfeited all rights to protection as a working journalist who was bound by the same rules as I was.'

64

KEEP YOUR MOUTH SHUT

The day of the missing transcripts continued. The Commission was trying to pinpoint the movements of both Rex and Mrs A. They established that Rex had been in Canberra from 6 to 9 November, when parliament was sitting. Mrs A said she had been in Newcastle from 6 to 12 November; the Commissioners said hotel and travel records should be checked to ascertain this. ASIO's Royal Commission Section were already calling up Mrs A's expense claims and gaining a copy of the hotel register for the Great Northern in Newcastle.

Under questioning by Max Julius, Rex also stated that Mrs A was the source of his article about a War Cabinet being formed in Canberra, as previously mentioned to the court. When asked by the Chairman where she gave him the information for that particular article, Rex explained that it was at various places, various meetings in Sydney, Melbourne and Canberra—not from documents, but from conversations between the two of them.

When Windeyer demanded to know the truth about the treaty document, Rex replied, 'The truth of it is that I got the information from Mrs A. My firm impression last Thursday was that I got it in the reading room, the newspaper room, in Parliament House, Canberra. That she came up and gave it to me, that we had no previous discussion about it whatever.

'Then, when Mrs A gave her evidence and read out certain statements or remarks from diaries, or what I think were Security reports, an element of doubt then crept into my recollection of the whole thing. But in spite of that I have a very firm belief that I still got it in the newspaper room in Canberra within ten days of publication.'

When asked about Mercia's desire to join the Communist Party, Rex said she had requested to join numerous times, and indeed met many members of the Party at his home over the time he had known her. But he had not spoken with Ric Oke about her joining; in fact it had been a surprise to him that the two of them had even met, before coming to the Commission.

Rex told the court that he had not spoken to Ric Oke about Mercia's membership. He had not suggested to her that she should not be associated with any left-wing activities; that she should stay away from the Peace Festival; that she should give up her work at the Democratic Rights Council; that she should not join the Party.

He too explained that he felt she was not emotionally equipped to be a Communist, being a highly strung, emotional type.

Rex agreed that he saw a good deal of Ivan Pakhomov and Victor Antonov. It was his duty, as a journalist with the *Tribune*, to be in contact with the TASS men; they were the only source of information of Soviet news and feature articles in the country. He would visit them, or they would bring items that they thought would be of interest to the *Tribune* office for publication.

Rex denied owning a portable typewriter, saying he hadn't owned one since 1944, and that he would bring a typewriter home from the *Tribune* office. The *Tribune* owned two portable typewriters, one a Consul and the other a Commodore, which did have German writing on it.

Max Julius then questioned Rex further about the treaty.

'Did you discuss this Friendship Treaty with Mrs A after November 1951?'

'Oh yes,' Rex replied.

'The article in the *Tribune* refers to it. May I have the article?' Mr Julius asked the Commission Secretary, who handed the volume marked *Tribune* to him. 'The article is in the *Tribune* of 14 November 1951 and states that this Friendship Treaty is entitled, "Treaty of Friendship, Commerce and Immigration with the USA"?'

'Yes,' Rex replied.

'The word "Immigration" is . . .?'

'Is wrong,' Rex replied.

'Is wrong?' Justice Ligertwood asked.

'Yes,' Rex replied.

'How did you find out that the word "Immigration" was wrong and that it should have been "Navigation"?' Julius continued.

'Mrs A told me, after Inspector Wilks had interrogated her,' Rex explained. 'That by a typing error, the wrong title had been put on the document and they were able to go direct to the Department concerned for the source of the informant.'

Julius continued, 'You told us of this trip to Warrandyte in 1952. You said that Mrs A rang you?'

'Yes,' Rex replied, going on to explain Mercia's phone call.

'Did you go down?'

'I did.'

'First of all, was she worried?' Julius asked.

'Yes, she was worried.'

'Did she say about whom she was worried? Did she say she was worried about you?'

'Both of us,' Rex replied. 'She said she was worried about both herself and myself. I told her, as I had told her before, that I would not disclose her name in any circumstances, that, so far as I was concerned, she was quite safe, that it depended upon herself, and if she kept her mouth shut, she would be safe.'

65

AN EXTRAORDINARY RELATIONSHIP

There were yet more pages missing from Mercia's transcripts of the Royal Commission hearings, including where Max Julius suggested to the three Justices that they should 'take into consideration that one is in a very unfamiliar and strange field when accounting for what appears, on the face of it, an unfamiliar and strange incident, and certainly an extraordinary relationship between Mrs A and Mr Chiplin'.

Julius continued, 'Without wishing at all to be offensive to Mrs A, I may be excused for remarking that she was obviously emotionally upset; she was highly nervous; she broke down several times and was unable to continue her evidence; and from Your Honours' observation of her, you could readily agree with Mr Oke's and Mr Chiplin's assessment of her being emotionally unstable.'

It was true that Mercia had been emotional giving evidence, and had broken down in court. Julius, as Rex's counsel, was using this to portray Mercia as an emotionally unstable woman—an assessment easily given and accepted in its day.

'She was unhappy and she emphasised many times her loneliness,' Mr Julius said, arguing that despite this she had connections with the Democratic Rights Council, connections as a journalist and was employed as the personal assistant to Commander Jackson, with all the opportunities for social engagement that would bring. That she was a person who did not cut herself off from the Democratic Rights Council but continued, who went along to film evenings and even held film evenings at her own place, who went along to the Peace Council and did not cut herself off from the Peace Council. 'There was a burden of her complaint at one stage, as I understand it, that she was cut off—or she was saying Mr Chiplin and Mr Oke wanted to cut her off—from left-wing friends; whereas in fact it would seem she was in no way cut off from friends of the Left, the Centre, or the Right.'

Mr Julius was suggesting that Mercia's breakdowns in the court room could have been due to more than not wanting to give evidence against her friends, as she claimed. Her fear of being revealed, as having passed over a document she shouldn't have, might have caused anxiety in a woman normally able to hide her emotions well—even from her own daughter.

'She lived a double life politically, an extraordinary life. I think Mr Windeyer himself described it as an extraordinary story that she was to tell. It was extraordinary not because of what Mr Chiplin was supposed to have done—because when one calmly examines her evidence,' Julius stated, 'what she says Mr Chiplin is supposed to have done really boils right away to nothing from the point of view of anything unlawful, leaving out of account at the moment the question of accepting information which was published in the newspaper.

'I submit, with respect, that Your Honours should take into consideration that she had a particular assignment to, shall I say, get close to Mr Chiplin,' Mr Julius continued, 'and to remain close to him; and inevitably her assignment, her objective, must colour her reports.'

He then started on the subject of the draft treaty, and Mrs A's behaviour while giving evidence. 'First of all, there was a serious attempt on her part to make it quite clear to everybody that there was no secrecy about the treaty.' He went on, 'When Mr Hill first attempted to question her about the treaty, she was in an emotional state, and

MY MOTHER, THE SPY

approached the Commission for protection so that she would not have to answer any further questions about it. I am asking you to deduce that she was anxious to make it quite clear that there was no secrecy about the treaty.'

Julius read to the Commission Mrs A's transcripts, highlighting her emotional state at various times.

Philp interrupted when Julius spoke about Wilks interviewing Mercia. 'Wilks could not have suspected her, or would not have suspected her, if he had known she was working for Security.'

'As a matter of fact,' Philp continued, 'I think I agree with you to some extent, Mr Julius, that her manner was unusual, emotional, and she was upset. It may have been caused by the fact that she may have thought *we* may have thought *she* was the person.'

'I hope to convince you so,' Mr Julius replied.

'You will have to put your best foot forward,' Justice Philp stated, 'because of the change of evidence we have had from your client, comparing last Thursday with today.'

'Here is a human story,' Max Julius returned, 'a story of Chiplin being placed in the ironical position, the extraordinary position, that on Thursday he was, in his mind at any rate, prepared to go to jail, if need be, if he was prosecuted for the offence, rather than give the name of the person. On one account of it, perhaps of His Honour Mr Justice Ligertwood's account, he was prepared to commit perjury. Then on Monday he was faced with the ironical position of being prepared to go to jail for a person who was not a friend, but an enemy.

'An easy way out for Chiplin was not to come along and give evidence—and stand up to a most rigorous cross-examination—but to say to Your Honours, "Yes, I used the word 'he'; it is misleading". There are deep emotional factors in this matter to be taken into consideration.'

※

Mr Cedric Ralph, the Melbourne solicitor who had appeared before the Commission for journalist Rupert Lockwood, turned up in newspaper reports on 4 March, saying that Wally Clayton had instructed him to make an application to appear before the Royal Commission. 'Mr Clayton is moved to do this because he considers there have been published about him a number of highly defamatory and slanderous allegations and he wishes to answer them,' Mr Ralph was reported as saying.

Wally Clayton was going to appear at the Royal Commission on Espionage, nearly nine months after being subpoenaed to appear, and right near the end of the Commission sittings.

66

DIFFERING ACCOUNTS

On 8 March Rex reappeared, answering further questions by Mr Windeyer about a government department source for the information used in another article Rex had published in the *Tribune*, but Rex wasn't of any help. Rex stated that the source had been other articles in the national press. Mr Julius would go on to provide these to Windeyer.

The only other matter Windeyer wanted Rex to answer related to a report written by Mercia on 10 March 1953.

'I will read the relevant parts and then ask you about it,' Mr Windeyer said. 'The report states: "I met him at 5.00 p.m. at Market and Elizabeth Street. We went into the Elizabeth Hotel and had a beer. He told me they had moved to Ryde for three months and were building a prefabricated home at Gymea Bay. I asked him how much it was costing and how he had managed it. He said it was a three-bedroom home and was costing £2000."'

Mr Windeyer looked up at Rex and added, 'Then there is more about the house. I only mention that to bring the incident to your mind.'

'Yes,' Rex replied.

'Then she refers to a house where you were living: "It is 123 Princes Street Ryde. It took more than an hour in the bus to reach there and is a long walk from the main road. It is a small but comfortably furnished weatherboard cottage on the opposite bank of the river from Yaralla hospital." Now, stopping there, do you remember that occasion?'

'No, I'm afraid I do not.'

'She goes on in the report: "I told him in the Hotel how upset and worried I had been because Mr Wilks had been to see me. He said, 'Don't talk about it here, leave it until later.' After dinner and on the way from the bus, he asked me to tell him the whole story and not to leave anything out." Do you remember that?' Windeyer asked.

'No, I do not remember it,' Rex replied.

'The report goes on,' Windeyer remarked, again reading from the Security file: '"He said, he knew the investigations were proceeding and where, but he had no idea that I had been worried, and was most distressed. I repeated the story of the interview and said I had been threatened with imprisonment. I also told him that I thought he was a stinker not to have told me how close I was to such things or people in the Industrial Division. He said he was sorry but sometimes it was better for a person not to know—'If you don't know you can't tell, and you can say with all honesty you don't know'. He said it was not that he didn't trust me, but for my own sake and the future it was better that I only knew a little about things. He warned me that he had constantly advised me not to mix or be seen with Party and left-wing friends. I told him that Mr Wilks had known about my association with left-wingers in the department."'

At this point Windeyer stopped reading from the file and asked, 'Does that call the matter to your mind at all?'

'No, but I would say there is a lot of that letter that is not true,' Rex replied.

'Which part would you say is not true?'

'The alleged conversation I have with Mrs A in which she implies that there was some outside party connected with this raid and investigation.'

'You appreciate that this is why I am asking you about it, because her statement in the box about the conversation was less detailed than this report which she made in March 1953; but you say it is not true?' Windeyer asked.

'I say it is not true,' Rex replied. 'Her statement regarding the interview with Mr Wilks and the story she actually told me, both differ too.'

Nothing further was explained.

Max Julius rose to ask some final questions about the conversation Rex had with Mrs A regarding her interview with Mr Wilks, before the Chair reminded him that they had already heard the evidence.

Julius then turned to Rex and asked, 'There was some reference to a document called "The Movement of Ideas"?'

'Yes,' Rex replied.

'First of all, what is that document?'

'"The Movement of Ideas" is a speech by one Santamaria to a religious group in Melbourne—a trade union clerical . . .'

'Is that the origin of the word "Movement", Mr Chiplin?' Justice Philp interjected.

'I do not think so, Your Honour,' Rex replied.

Bartholomew Augustine 'Bob' Santamaria was an Australian Catholic anti-Communist political activist and journalist for *The Catholic Worker* and *News Weekly*—newspapers that were strongly anti-Communist. He had founded and was head of the Catholic Social Studies Movement, known as 'The Movement', in 1941, which opposed the spread of Communism, particularly in trade unions, with its members infiltrating both trade unions and the Labor Party.

The 'Movement of Ideas' pamphlet was a speech that Santamaria had delivered to a group of clerics and laymen in the Catholic Church. It criticised Chifley's policies, saying that the 'Chifley legend' needed to be destroyed.

'Did you have some discussions with Mrs A about that?' Julius asked Rex.

'Yes, we did.'

'Did you make a trip to Melbourne to see her in 1954 about that?'

'Yes.'

'Did you try to get some additional information about the Labor Party from Mrs A?'

'Yes.'

'Was that as a result of a discussion with Mr Hill?'

'Yes.'

'Did you endeavour to get the information from Mrs A?'

'I did.'

'Was any arrangement made about getting the information through Miss Cohen?'

'Yes.'

'If Mrs A could get it for you?'

'Yes.'

'That information was about those who were present at the meeting that Mr Santamaria addressed?'

'Yes.'

Even before ASIO was established, The Movement—or Catholic Action as ASIO referred to them—had been used by security force members to gain information about CPA members and their activities. This practice was discouraged by ASIO, though some security officers independently contacted Catholic Action members, and a liaison officer between ASIO and Catholic Action was appointed. Ray Whitrod had for a time been the acting liaison officer, and he would no doubt have been disturbed to find that Mercia had handed information regarding Mr Santamaria to Rex, unless he had sanctioned it.

Rex was thanked by the Chair and allowed to withdraw. This was his final appearance in the witness stand at the Royal Commission. The Commissioners would ultimately have to decide whether it was him or Mrs A telling the truth about who handed him the treaty document.

The hotel registers in Newcastle and Canberra, together with Mercia's travel and accommodation reimbursements, showed the Commissioners that she could not have met up with Rex in Canberra during the ten days prior to publication of his article. An accompanying memorandum, attached to the copy of the hotel register and sent to Counsel from ASIO officer Ron Richards, shows he had no explanation for the surname Pearce in brackets appearing after Mercia's surname on the first night she stayed at the hotel before Commander Jackson and his wife arrived.

It seems Mercia had managed to keep one secret of her own from ASIO, or at least from Ron Richards—the existence of Cindy's father, Harry Pearce, who was very much alive, despite Mercia claiming to be widowed.

❧

On 9 March 1955, the Solicitor-General, in consultation with the Department of External Affairs, answered questions from Mr Windeyer in a letter that set out the Solicitor-General's view on the Draft Treaty of Friendship, Commerce and Navigation with the United States.

They found that there never had been a treaty, as distinct from a draft.

No copy of the draft treaty could be found 'initialised' by Sir Percy Spender—either in February 1950, when it was first received, or at any other time. In their view, it was very unlikely that it had been initialised—but even if it had, that fact would not have been known outside his own department, the Ministry of External Affairs.

The treaty had first been proposed in 1947 and presented as a draft to serve as the basis for discussion. Mr Percy Spender, as he was at the time, issued a press statement on 3 January 1950 saying that proposals for such a treaty had lain dormant for many months, and that the new government proposed to give them active consideration. This gave some credence to Mercia's claim that Rex was already aware of the proposed treaty, and knowledge of it had been in the public domain.

Four copies of a fresh draft were presented to the Minister of External Affairs by the American ambassador on 28 February 1950. On 2 March, the minister sent a copy of the ambassador's letter and the draft treaty to his colleagues in the Treasury, to the Minister for Trade and Customs, and to the Minister for Commerce and Agriculture.

Three months later, Spender advised the American ambassador that the text of the draft was accepted as a basis for negotiation, without commitment.

Discussions followed among Australian officials, and between Australian and US officials, but the text of the 1950 draft had still not been concluded. The Solicitor-General's explanatory letter stated that, if a document had been initialised at that stage (which had not been found on any of the copies), it would have been merely to show he had seen, noted or considered it—not that it had been approved.

The acceptance of the draft treaty by Cabinet as a basis for negotiation was known to a large number of officers in a large number of departments: the Prime Minister's Department; External Affairs; Treasury; Trade and Customs; Attorney-General; Commerce and Agriculture; Territories and Immigration; and National Development.

An inter-departmental committee met from time to time, and numerous memoranda had been circulated among the departments.

If Rex had other informants in the Department of External Affairs, as Petrov stated, they could have given him the information about the 'Friendship Treaty'; it was clear that the comments on the draft that Rex had copied in his article had come from the Department of National Development.

The typing error of the title, where 'Navigation' had been replaced by 'Immigration', had occurred in the Department of National Development.

Rex had copied this error into his article, stating that it was a 'Treaty of Friendship, Commerce and Immigration'.

His leak had been from the department that Mercia was working for at the time.

PART
3

AFTERMATH

67

IN CAMERA

The six days during which the Commission heard Mrs A's evidence were held 'in camera', in private, meaning the press and public were not allowed to attend.

However, the transcripts of her evidence were released by the Commission to the public on 11 May 1955. While the pseudonym 'Mrs A' gave Mercia some protection, when the press released details of her testimony, they spelt out where and when she worked, and who she had reported on. She would have been identifiable to many journalists, to public servants, and to those in the left-wing groups she had penetrated.

The press loved the details in the transcripts: the Democratic Rights Council and the CPA, talk of war plans, missing documents in a filing cabinet, atomic testing, classified documents given to a known Communist.

Following the release of Mrs A's transcripts, the Solicitor-General, Sir Kenneth Bailey, received a phone call from the Deputy Leader of the Opposition, Arthur Calwell, saying one of his fellow party members, John Dedman, was annoyed. Dedman had been the Minister of Post-War Reconstruction in the Chifley government, and his local paper—the *Geelong Advertiser*—had featured the details of Mrs A's testimony in a way that he felt reflected badly on him. The newspaper had made it appear that, from the evidence given by Mrs A, secret information about atomic experiments and explosions had been given to Communists while she was an officer of his department.

Calwell was annoyed that the Commissioners appeared to have accepted this evidence without criticism, and without giving an opportunity to any of the people concerned to refute it. He told the Solicitor-General he wanted the Commission to reopen the inquiry to give the public servants in charge at the time an opportunity to give evidence.

The Solicitor-General, who was about to catch a plane to Melbourne, explained to Calwell that he thought Mrs A's evidence centred around giving information to Rex Chiplin while she was employed by the Department of National Development, and that everything she did was cleared not only by the department, but by security. He said he vaguely remembered a story about a filing cabinet of documents having disappeared, but he didn't think there was any accusation made against the Department of Post-War Reconstruction in Mr Dedman's time. Mr Bailey promised to check the transcript himself and to get back to Mr Dedman once he arrived in Melbourne.

Unfortunately for Mr Bailey, his plane was delayed due to bad weather. He arrived late in Melbourne and missed Mr Dedman when he tried to call him at his office, and he couldn't raise him on his home number in Geelong.

By the time Bailey phoned Arthur Calwell later that night, Calwell had already spoken to the press, saying he was trying to reopen the Royal Commission to deal with the matter. Bailey expressed regret, telling him he had read through the transcript of evidence on the plane and was satisfied that it didn't in any way reflect poorly on Mr Dedman, and promised to ring the aggrieved politician in the morning.

It took four or five phone calls the following morning before he reached the former Member for Corio, who was dodging calls from the press, and hadn't read the transcript. The Solicitor-General told him he would send over a copy, and pointed out that the Royal Commission could not be expected to make itself responsible for correcting inaccurate press reports. However, the newspaper concerned would have no protection in private proceedings if its report was unfair and inaccurate.

The Solicitor-General spoke with the Chair of the Royal Commission, Justice Owen, who told him that at no time did the Commissioners hear anything that reflected adversely on Mr Dedman or on the Department of Post-War Reconstruction. Furthermore, the Commissioners didn't want to make any statement or reopen the hearing because of misstatements in the press.

After reading the transcript, Mr Dedman rang the Solicitor-General and agreed that there was nothing in the evidence.

But the damage was done: an aggrieved former politician and a Royal Commission witness further exposed in the press reports ensued.

68

FINDINGS

On 22 August 1955, Justices Owen, Philp and Ligertwood signed the final report on the Royal Commission on Espionage, which was then presented to the Governor-General, Sir William Slim, and the government, with the Justices' findings and recommendations.

From the evidence received, the Commissioners established that from around 1943, the Soviets operated an espionage ring in Australia out of their embassy in Canberra. The full final report dealt with the workings of the Soviet's military intelligence section (the GRU) and internal affairs ministry (the MVD) in Australia, from information supplied by Vladimir and Evdokia Petrov. The Commissioners found that the Petrovs were truthful witnesses, and that the only known Soviet collaborators in Australia were Communists.

Wally Clayton, a CPA organiser, had appeared at the Royal Commission from 15 to 18 March 1955. For a person who wanted to clear his name, the report found that he wasn't very cooperative. Instead, the Commissioners found him to be evasive. He refused to answer questions, and when he did, he lied. Wally told them he had never met any member of the Soviet Embassy, despite Petrov saying otherwise.

The Commission found that he was KLOD in the VENONA files, and the principal channel through which material from the Department of External Affairs was passed to the Soviets.

The final report contained a separate chapter dealing with each of the MVD operations, with the chapter on journalists focusing on just two individuals, Fergan O'Sullivan and Rex Chiplin—both of whom had been mentioned in the Moscow Letters as sources of information.

The Commissioners accepted that Fergan knew Pakhomov was a TASS representative, but they were doubtful he had no knowledge that Pakhomov was also an MVD agent. Fergan had admitted writing and handing over what became known as Document H—the descriptive list of journalists in the Canberra press gallery—but said he thought it would only be used to assist Pakhomov with finding sympathetic journalists who might be interested in publishing Soviet news items. After receiving Document H, Moscow Centre took a keen interest in O'Sullivan and regarded him as a promising prospective agent—as a result of his secret meetings with Pakhomov and supplying Document H, he was already 'on the small hook'.

The Commission saw Fergan O'Sullivan as a foolish young man, rather than a journalist involved with espionage.

The Commissioners were not as gentle with Rex. They started by noting that, according to Petrov, it was Rex who first introduced O'Sullivan to Pakhomov—and Pakhomov had also told Petrov that it was Chiplin who recommended O'Sullivan as a progressive, which led to Pakhomov procuring Document H from O'Sullivan. Rex denied this.

According to Petrov, Rex also claimed to have contacts in government departments who might be potential information sources—that he had 'two chaps' in External Affairs. Rex also denied this.

The Commissioners accepted that Moscow regarded Rex as a person who was willing to give information to Soviet officials. He had been given the code name CHARLIE by the Soviets, and 'it had been earlier reported to Moscow that Chiplin had been acquiring information from government sources and passing it directly or indirectly to Soviet officials'.

The report then turned to Rex's newspaper article 'Secret Treaty Sells Us to the US', and his claim that his source was a 'highly placed government official'. The report labelled Rex's article as a piece of dishonest journalism, saying he well knew there was no concluded treaty, and that at the time of writing the Commission report, it was still under departmental consideration. When questioned about his source, Rex had refused to name 'him', and the Commissioners found that 'he gave a most circumstantial account of having been in the library at Parliament House at Canberra in a room set apart for the press on a day between 4th and 14th November 1951'.

On Mrs A's appearance as a witness, the report stated:

Chiplin had known her for many years and had regarded her as a pro-Communist friend and an undercover agent of the Communist Party. To his obvious surprise, it emerged that Mrs A had for many years been an agent for various Australian intelligence organisations. She was in June 1951 temporarily attached to the Department of National Development at the request of its permanent head for the purpose of detecting whether suspected leakages from the department were in fact occurring, and, if so, in what manner.

Rex had tried to use Mrs A to gain confidential information, and 'on all occasions, on instructions from a Security officer, she had passed on to Chiplin innocuous information'.

They found that Rex instructed his counsel to cross-examine Mrs A to suggest that she had in fact passed him the information, which Mrs A denied doing. The Commissioners didn't believe Rex's changed claim, given that departmental records, a hotel register and travel records showed Mercia had not been in Canberra in the period specified by Chiplin. Based on the evidence they had in front of them, Mrs A could not have given Rex the Friendship Treaty document in the ten days before publication.

The report noted that Rex then modified his second version of events by saying that his first impression had been that it was in Canberra, but that it could have occurred in Sydney. By changing his story, twice, the Commissioners deemed that Rex lied in 'one or other of his inconsistent stories, and we have no doubt that he lied in saying that he was shown the departmental minute by Mrs A'. They suggested that Rex had another source—someone 'in Departmental circles that provided him with the confidential information'.

They concluded that, while obtaining this particular confidential information was not directly connected with Soviet espionage, it showed that Rex was a person 'willing and able to obtain confidential information and shows that the Moscow Centre opinion of him—as disclosed in the Moscow Letters—was well founded'.

No prosecutions were recommended in the Royal Commission on Espionage's final report.

On 15 September 1955, the Royal Commission report was tabled in the House of Representatives, and on 28 September an article in the *Tribune* reiterated that 'the exclusive exposure of Menzies' Secret Treaty planning to betray Australian commercial interests to America had been in the public interest'.

Rex stated: 'The cold fact is that the misnamed Treaty of Friendship, Commerce and Navigation has been implemented piecemeal, as I told the Commissioners'. He went on to explain how 'British–Australian Government to Government buying contracts for our primary produce have since been abolished as demanded in the Treaty', and that 'the Government has legislated to abolish double taxation between Australia and the United States, giving US monopolies such as General Motors an open go to "plunder the country"'.

The article noted that there was no mention of evidence given by an anonymous security agent, Mrs A, before the Commission, and that Rex Chiplin had in an open session refused to name his informant—but later, when Mrs A appeared to give evidence for the security services, he considered she had betrayed his friendship, and that of his family, and therefore she had no further call on his protection.

The article finished with three questions.

The first was aimed at the Secretary of the Commission. Rex asked whether it was a fact that, since Mrs A had given evidence at the Royal Commission, the Department of National Development had written to the Commission stating that Mrs A's statements concerning the Department were not true, and pointing out that she was regarded as unreliable.

The second question was aimed at Brigadier Spry (who had been promoted from Colonel), asking whether security had written off Mrs A as a liability, and whether he did his best to keep her away from the Commission: 'And was it a fact that Mr Windeyer insisted that she appear, and over Spry's protests served a subpoena on her?'

The third question was directed at the Solicitor-General. In the Commonwealth Investigation Service investigation into what Rex still liked to refer to as the 'Traitor Treaty', whose name did that investigation give as the source of the file that was apparently in Rex's possession?

The first question could have been linked to the flurry in the press about Mr Dedman and Mrs A's evidence. The second poses a further question: was Rex speculating about Spry protesting about his agent appearing—or had such information actually been leaked from inside Mr Windeyer's office, or even from ASIO itself? His third question would remain unanswered: who did the CIS investigator, Inspector Wilks, name as the public servant who leaked the treaty document?

Mr Wilks's investigation into the leak pointed to the Department of National Development, because of the typing error in the title of the Treaty. The minute that had been shown to Rex was a series of comments on each section of the treaty. The main difference between the document he copied and what appeared in his article were his comments and the fact he changed the context, making it appear that the treaty was concluded. Rex at the Royal Commission stated he had been told by his source that the treaty had been initialised, that it 'had been made'.

Wilks also found that Mercia had accessed the file containing the minute that was shared with Rex; she had 'flagged' the file. Mrs A had claimed she could not recollect all of the files she had requested in her research. She denied giving the document to Rex Chiplin, but she did not deny knowing him and socialising with him.

If Wilks had found Mercia was the source, why wasn't she prosecuted under the *Official Secrets Act*?

It would have been a strange outcome if the only person recommended for prosecution by the Royal Commission on Espionage had been an ASIO agent under the *Official Secrets Act*.

69

OFFICIAL TRANSCRIPT

The Royal Commission's final report had appeared and there had been considerable commentary about it in the newspapers before Mercia ordered her copy of the Official Transcript of Proceedings.

The sections Mercia underlined show the toll on her emotional and mental health of giving evidence and being 'outed' at the Royal Commission. She underlined where she had spoken about how difficult it was to testify against her left-wing friends. Mr Ted Hill, a barrister representing Rex, had asked her whether or not she had welcomed the prospect of working in Melbourne; she underlined part of her reply, where she stated that she did not think about it, and that she had *been trained in Intelligence for twelve-and-a-half years*.

Strangely, she used a ruler to draw a box with straight black lines around a discussion between Communist barrister Max Julius and the Commissioners about a statement made by Vladimir Petrov on 3 April 1954. In the discussion, the Justices ran through the permanent and temporary heads of the MVD (Soviet internal affairs ministry) in Australia up until Petrov's appointment. There are no asterisks or notes alongside to explain why Mercia highlighted this section.

With so many different pens used for her highlighting, it can only be imagined how many times Mercia pored over these documents. The pages that are missing from her copy contain information that was perhaps too painful or uncomfortable for her to read.

On 2 March 1955, Mr Hill started his cross-examination of Mercia, and the day ended with Ric Oke giving evidence. Four pages are missing from that portion of the transcript.

These include where Mr Hill kept questioning Mercia, asking her whether their meetings were in public, and where Mrs A admitted there was nothing clandestine in her meetings with Rex. Mr Hill asked about Leila and Ric Oke, confirming that Mercia probably never officially joined the Communist Party as she never paid her dues.

Mr Hill then started questioning Mercia about her thoughts on Communism, and her work with left-wing organisations. When he asked whether she believed in the ideals of the Peace Council in the defence of peace, Mercia replied: 'No, I think it is futile. I think their whole way of doing it is futile.' She added, 'The climate was different. If you remember, we had Nazism.' And she then admitted she had joined the Peace Council under instruction from ASIO.

'Do I take it that you really wanted to join the Communist Party, or was that under direction too?' Mr Hill asked.

'That was under direction too,' Mercia replied. 'I had to realise this: that once I had a membership card I would lose even the few privileges that were left to me outside, but, because I believed I was doing the right thing I went ahead with the arrangements to join.'

'But when you had embarked upon it, you really genuinely, in your mind, became anxious to join the Communist Party, didn't you?' he prodded.

'No, Mr Hill. I did not want to belong to the Communist Party. I am a member of the Australian Labor Party. I am quite clear; it has taken me a long time to find where I stand on the political level.'

The exchanges between Mr Hill and Mercia appear abrupt. When he suggested she never actually joined the Communist Party, Mercia explained that she had been told she would be a 'special' member,

271

without a membership card, and that this was possible. Mr Hill commented that it appeared that she knew more about it than he did.

Were these pages disposed of in disgust by Mercia? Perhaps she was upset at the exchange with Mr Hill. Or that she had been a member of the ALP—the political party that in later life she found so abhorrent. Or perhaps that it had been spelt out to her that she had failed to officially join the CPA—as shown in Ric's evidence in the pages that follow—despite her telling ASIO she had.

The second set of missing pages relate to Ric Oke, where he declares that Mercia was too garrulous to be reliable, that she was unstable, firmly stating that she would never have been a member of the CPA. Their conversation had been quite innocuous as far as Ric was concerned; he was merely assessing her suitability as a Party member. He denied having asked her if there was a security reason why she was unsuccessful with the position at External Affairs, and that he said to her that in the cause of Peace they should know what was going on in Defence. He denied talking about atomic experiments, or that he had told her to stop her work with the Peace Council, or that he had spoken with Rex Chiplin about her membership.

All of Ric's evidence would have angered Mercia—whether because she thought him to be lying, or because it was so negative about her as a person, or that it made a falsehood of her reports.

The entire transcript for 3 March was also missing from Mercia's set. This was the day Rex appeared after she had given her evidence, saying she was the person who had given him the typed copy of the comments on the draft treaty.

The first few pages of 4 March are also missing. ASIO officer Ron Richards had been called to give evidence about the draft treaty leak, and then Max Julius gave his summing up of her and the evidence against Rex. Mr Julius's summation would not have been terribly flattering for Mercia to read.

When questioned by Mr Hill about the leaking of the draft treaty document, Ron Richards replied that he took an interest in the leak, but was not concerned with the investigation. (Having no access himself to the security files, Mr Hill was trying to ascertain more details of Mr Wilks's CIS investigation.) Ron Richards told Mr Hill that Ray Whitrod, up until he moved to the CIS, had been Mercia's controller, and that an officer of the security services had been present at Mrs A's interview with Mr Wilks.

After Ron Richards withdrew, Mr Julius reminded the Commissioners of Mrs A's behaviour in court, her hostility to Mr Hill upon his cross-examining her, that she had flagged the file in question containing the document with the comments on the draft treaty, and the near-hysterical nature of her denials that she had handed Rex a copy of a departmental minute.

Mr Julius then referred to the transcripts and to the moment when she had paused, after the exchange between herself and Justice Philp, where she stated: 'I have been pretty gentle about this, but I can stop being gentle at any moment, and if I start talking I just will not stop talking . . .' Justice Philp then asked her, 'What—in the way of espionage, people giving information?', and advised her to give such information to the court if she knew about it. Mr Julius reminded them that Mercia's pause had been long, before the Chair had told Rex's counsel, Mr Hill, to continue his cross-examination of her.

Julius told the Commissioners:

That did occur, and I put that only on the basis of showing her attitude, showing her preparedness to colour her evidence, to make wild accusations which apparently have no basis or fact, because when there is a close examination it really boils away to nothing so far as anything that Mr Chiplin is supposed to have done in the way of giving information to the Soviet Government or doing anything underhanded is concerned.

Mr Julius further debunked Petrov's claims about Rex as 'hearsay'.

Mercia had broken down and stopped giving evidence in court three times. Rex would have been watching her the entire time. On Rex's last day, he told Mr Windeyer that her reports differed from his recollections, that they were untrue.

Mercia's reports to ASIO were her record of what happened in each instance. The danger is that the reports are one-sided; they are one person's recollection of an event. Reading through the statements she made for the Royal Commission, drawn from her reports to ASIO, takes you back to a time and a place, recording what happened where and when and with whom; but sometimes the reader gets an inkling of what else was important to her, what other details she was including.

In her statement, on her last meeting with Ric Oke, she devotes one section to the sacrifices she was making by donating books to the Left Wing Book Club, and her explanation to Ric about her being able to arrange exclusive gatherings that wouldn't be boring. Ric Oke had been short with Mercia at their previous two meetings, so the thought of him listening to this conversation and agreeing with her seems a stretch.

In another part of one statement, about another meeting with Ric, Mercia stated that he had said to her that it would be 'criminally wrong to stand in your light'. This was from a man who was categorised by ASIO as being unable to express himself well.

CPA barrister Ted Hill told the Royal Commission that he viewed her reports as 'coloured'. These were the same ASIO reports he had been prevented from reading.

70

A MENZIES SPY

Mercia would have been through a tumultuous time with the Royal Commission and immediately afterwards. She had kept her double life a secret for so long, and continued to do so with her own daughter.

Mercia's hope that her identity would be kept secret was completely destroyed after the *Guardian* published a lengthy article, titled 'Guardian Unmasks a Menzies Spy', in December 1955, giving not only her name, but also her address in Melbourne. This article was then published in the *Tribune*.

Mercia was well and truly named and shamed. Both articles called her a 'plain, middle-aged native-born Australian', and rapidly went downhill from there. It went on to describe her as a 'florid, gushing, gossipy, neurotic woman' who 'pimped on those she deliberately befriended'. The entire article is dripping with contempt, accusing her of 'creeping' into the New Theatre and the Australian Labor Party, into organised discussion groups that took an interest in the union problems of journalists, and into work for the Australian Peace Council. 'She even went so far as to "join in the struggle" against the Industrial Groups in the ALP.' It continued:

In Melbourne in the past two years, she attempted to penetrate branches of the Labor Party, particularly in St Kilda, and offered to type out lists of persons to be circularised with material.

Mercia always portrayed herself as lefter than left, according to the article:

She was always being 'frank' about her Left-wing views and urging others to do the same. She had a smattering of Marx and less of Lenin, but enough to mouth socialist phrases when the occasion required it.

The article even outlined her work under Commander Jackson, accusing her of going through:

the elaborate pretence of smuggling out secret files of information on Australia's industrial development plans and problems. Nobody ever asked her to do it. She offered them to colleagues to read privately, then when they did so, reported them as spies attempting to obtain government secrets.

It added:

Mercia Masson was loyal to nobody. She publicly joked about the 'stupidity' of her employer Casey, and the personal foibles of Jackson and his wife Barbara Ward.

The disgraced journalist Fergan O'Sullivan, author of Document H, was identified as a friend of Mercia Masson's, who she introduced to friends at private parties in Melbourne as far back as 1951.

The article even goes on to accuse her of having contacts with a 'United States spy-ring' in Australia, through her work with an American advertising agency, J. Walter Thompson—where Mercia secured a job after the Royal Commission. The J. Walter Thompson promotions company had been mentioned in journalist Rupert Lockwood's Document J, together with its American managing director, Loyd Ring Coleman. Lockwood accused the American of acting as 'a semi-official spokesman for the US government, publicly defending its war policy in newspaper articles and [gave] speeches to business and reactionary political gatherings'. Document J also stated that the US advertising company had a large staff 'that does a tremendous amount of research into [the] Australian economy', with 'business surveys being a regular feature for the advertising agency'.

According to Document J, those companies receiving advertising contracts had to post copies of their local papers in which their advertisements appeared, allowing the research staff to keep a close watch on almost the entire press in Australia, with anything critical about the American Government receiving a letter to the editor against the criticism. With Mercia's experience in researching and compiling economic data, she would have fitted right into the advertising agency's research staff.

A faint, almost unreadable version of this same article was found among Mercia's belongings. It had been reproduced in a New Zealand journal, *People's Voice*, in January 1956. The only thing legible in her copy was the blurred title, 'Meet Mercia—police pimp'. The typeface was too small and the text too faded to read.

By the 1956 Melbourne Olympics, Mercia was again working as a journalist.

Cindy remembers going to watch the Opening Ceremony and being allowed to take time off school to attend different sporting events at the Olympics with her mother. They went several times to the swimming pavilion to watch the pool events, but it was the fencing competition that caught Cindy's eye—or perhaps a certain Hungarian fencer did, and she wanted to take up the sport. So, on top of her piano, ballet, ice skating, horse riding and elocution lessons, Mercia organised for Cindy to have fencing lessons at the YWCA. Another expense, with Mercia having to buy the protective outfit and fencing foil.

Having a mother as a journalist meant Cindy would sometimes accompany her on stories her mother was covering on weekends or after school. She remembers one Sunday morning they had to cover a big factory fire.

They met various celebrities. Cindy remembers going out to interview racing car drivers Stirling Moss and Sir Jack Brabham. In 1964, Mercia and Cindy were given front row seats to The Beatles concert in Sydney Stadium at Rushcutters Bay, the only venue able to hold 10,000 people at the time. The cacophony of screaming teenage girls around them meant they were unable to hear the music, even so close to the stage. Prim and proper Mercia hated it; Cindy, on the other hand, loved it. They then went backstage, where Mercia interviewed the four musicians and Cindy was introduced to the 'Fab Four'. There were at least some benefits to her mother being a journalist.

Fergan O'Sullivan continued working as a journalist. In January 1955 he was working on a regional newspaper in Bathurst, and he became a sub-editor of the *Bathurst National Advocate* the following year. Fergan's journalist father, Chris, had worked on the paper before moving to the United States in 1919, and then Ireland in 1920, where he had met and married Fergan's mother, and where Fergan and one older brother were born.

The lure of politics again beckoned the Irish-born journalist. In September 1961, the press were in an uproar when it discovered Fergan was now the public relations officer for the Labor politician for the state seat of Bathurst—Mr C.A. 'Gus' Kelly, the Chief Secretary and Minister for Tourism.

After the Royal Commission ended, a secret memorandum from ASIO's Director-General dated 2 March 1956 showed ASIO was still investigating Rex's possible sources or contacts in the Department of External Affairs. Of particular interest was Petrov's evidence at the Royal Commission, about CHARLIE's knowledge of enciphered telegrams between America and Australia, the knowledge of which he passed on to the TASS representative.

It seems unlikely that Mercia—who didn't appear to have contact with the Australian or US embassies, the General Post Office, or Department of External Affairs—would have been the source of this information. If Rex was gaining information from a Department of External Affairs employee, it appears from notes on the memo that it could have been someone from the Canberra office, as this was where enciphered telegrams were exchanged with the US Government.

According to Mercia's reports, Rex told her, when she was applying for the position with the Department of External Affairs or Defence, and when she was complaining of being lonely, that if her job took her to Canberra, he would put her in touch with some people like herself.

Vladimir Petrov stated that Rex told him, a month before Petrov defected, that he had 'two chaps' in External Affairs. That would have been in March 1954—a meeting that wasn't brought up at the Royal Commission. The other meeting that wasn't mentioned was in early 1952: following a telephone intercept, Petrov was followed to Manuka and was seen meeting Rex by two ASIO agents.

Rex applied for a visa to travel overseas in 1956. According to Czechoslovakian police files, he arrived in Czechoslovakia on 29 May 1956, and was expected to stay until 8–9 June. He was met by the editor of *Rude Pravo* (Czech for 'Red Justice' or the 'Red Right'), the official newspaper of the Communist Party of Czechoslovakia, together with a Mr Kralova from the International Organization of Journalists.

Rex was the first *Tribune* correspondent to be stationed in Moscow. An anecdote linked to Rupert Lockwood—who later took up the same position in 1965, as the third representative for the newspaper—tells that, when Rex returned to Australia, he:

got off the plane at Kingsford Smith Airport, took a taxi to
the Communist Party headquarters, then still in Market Street,
Sydney, and shouted at the Central Committee functionary, as
he flung his party membership card down on the table, 'If
that's Communism, you can shove it up your arse!'

Rupert's daughter Penny remembers Rex fondly, saying he was
'such a lovely man'. She remembers Rex's resignation from the CPA,
and how quite a few CPA members remarked what a shame it was that
he left the Party. Interestingly, her own father, Rupert, also resigned
from the Communist Party on his return to Australia from Moscow.
Her mother kept her membership and the couple ultimately divorced.

In 1974, Rex saw Mercia at the North Sydney Railway Station.
Rex was then working as a chief sub-editor at Cumberland Press, a
chain of Sydney suburban newspapers owned by Rupert Murdoch. It
is doubtful they spoke. Mercia would have been very ill at this stage
with cancer—on top of which, with a compromised immune system,
she had contracted shingles and would have been in a lot of pain.

In the papers of Professor K.H. Bailey, the Solicitor-General at the
time of the Royal Commission on Espionage, is a copy of Mercia's
first statement to Ray Whitrod. The subtitle on the file details a list
of people mentioned within, as well as 'the alleged attempted subver-
sion of Mercia Masson by Rex Chiplin, George Richard Oke and a
Cecilia Mullen'—with 'Mullen' being a misspelling of Leila's married
name: Mullett.

One typed paragraph, undated and unsigned, also sits in the same
file, and reads:

Cecilia Mullen, Rex Chiplin and George Richard, known
as Rick Oke, conspiring together and with other persons
unknown to induce persons having in their possession or

control information which has been entrusted to them in confidence by persons holding office under the King [sic] or Commonwealth, to communicate that information to persons other than the persons they were authorised to communicate it to in contravention of Section 79(1) of the Crimes Act, contrary to Section 86 of the Crimes Act.

If this paragraph is in relation to the documents vetted by ASIO that Mercia handed to Rex, the information contained in the documents does not seem to have been passed on to the Soviets as ASIO expected it would—but rather, it went only as far as a CPA journalist and was included in newspaper articles.

We don't know if Mercia ever saw Ric Oke or Leila Cohen ever again.

71

RUS

In February 1957, Mercia married for the second time. Cindy isn't sure how she met Mr Herbert, a recent divorcee with two sons, but she knows it was not a happy marriage. The marriage did, however, give Mercia the chance to change her name.

Mercia gave interesting details on her certificate of marriage. She stated that she was Mercia Leonora Zoe Masson-Geeves; that she'd been a widow since 1943; and that she'd been born in Rosebank in Scotland, not Sydney, Australia. She also stated that her mother's name was Leonora Irene McDonald, not Leonora Irene Protti; and that she was forty years of age, when she was actually forty-three.

Despite all of these little white lies, Mercia did at some stage tell Mr Herbert about her being Mrs A. After the wedding, Mercia and Cindy moved into Mr Herbert's home in the inner-city Melbourne suburb of Elwood, leaving St Kilda Road forever. As far as Cindy remembers, Russell Grant stayed with Mercia and Cindy at St Kilda Road right up to her mother's marriage. He had stayed in his room mostly, a loner, and after St Kilda Road, lived in a boarding house at 12 Parliament Place.

On Monday 29 September 1958, the boarding house proprietor called into Rus's room at seven in the morning and told him his rent was in arrears. Rus explained he would be seeing a friend that day who would give him the funds, and that he'd pay what was due the following day.

Just after midnight on 1 October, a waterside worker saw what he thought was a fully clothed body, floating in the Yarra River. He informed a policeman on patrol and returned to the scene with him; the body was recovered and sent to Prince Henry's hospital, where it was confirmed that the man had died.

Mercia told Cindy that she'd had to go and identify the body, but the Coroner's Court account differs, recording that James O'Connor, Secretary of the Australian Journalists Association, identified the body. He stated that he had known Rus for twenty years, and that twelve months before Rus's death, his friend's demeanour had changed. Rus was again consuming alcohol to excess and suffering from some ailment, but was not receiving medical attention and refused to do so.

When James saw him the week before his death, Rus had appeared nervous and agitated, explaining that he was experiencing financial difficulties. In the Coroner's Court, James told the coroner that Rus had indicated nine months previously that he would take his own life.

Rus's autopsy showed no disease and no injuries other than a small abrasion on his left cheek. There was a strong odour of alcohol, with water, alcohol and mucus found in his stomach and lungs—typical of someone who had drowned. The coroner found that Rus had entered the water and drowned on or around 30 September.

In a strange twist, James O'Connor received a letter from a previous lodger at the boarding house where Rus had been living. The woman was certain that Rus had been poisoned. When she lived there, she had found him in a bad state, she claimed; he had obviously been poisoned, and she had organised for an ambulance to take him to hospital to have his stomach pumped.

James handed the letter to the police. It had been written from the Larundel Mental Asylum; at the coronial inquest, its author was deemed to be 'completely mental and suffered from delusions'.

Mercia attended Russell Grant's funeral. Cindy remembers her mother saying to her that she'd had to tell his parents of their son's death.

Among Mercia's belongings was a ragged scrapbook containing his articles and a short story, published in various newspapers up until 1953.

Mercia had kept those items, together with his book on Leninism, all those years.

72

THE ROAD TO DOUBLE BAY

Cindy did not like, or get on with, Mr Herbert. It became so bad that she found herself living in Canberra with a journalist friend of her mother's and his wife. Their name and the fact that she was living with them were noted by ASIO, which reactivated Cindy's memories of abandonment when she read the reports. ASIO was still keeping an eye on Mercia and her family at this time.

Cindy can't remember how long she was in Canberra, possibly a few months, but she remembers getting sick and the doctors detecting an ovarian cyst. She was admitted to hospital to have the cyst removed and was unable to travel for a time after the surgery. Her mother and Mr Herbert came to pick her up, and Cindy returned with them to Sydney, where they were then living. She remembers little comfort being given to her, despite the fact that she was recovering from surgery.

Mr Herbert was certainly aware of his wife's previous work with ASIO, and their marriage was not going well. Mercia had been in and out of hospital with stomach ulcers, and the hospital bills were mounting. Her husband rang ASIO to ask for $750 to cover the bills;

ASIO said 'No', at a time when they were trying to distance themselves from the Petrov affair and the events surrounding it.

When Cindy first arrived in Sydney, they were living with one of Mercia's friends for a short time. Then they found a rental in Clovelly and Cindy loved that house. If her mother was not at home, she could walk around the cliff to her grandmother's house in Coogee. Cindy enjoyed a good relationship with her grandmother Lucy and her female friend.

Lucy suffered a massive heart attack and died in July 1965, just after Cindy's twenty-first birthday. Mercia decided to cremate her mother and place her ashes in a rose garden in a separate section of Botany Cemetery, even though her father was buried in the Presbyterian section of that same vast cemetery. The headstone on his grave had space for his wife; Lucy, when she had ordered this headstone, must have expected that she would be buried with her husband.

While researching her family's history, Cindy discovered that the ashes of Annie Protti, Lucy's mother, had never been collected, and had been distributed by the crematorium into an unknown resting place ten years after Annie passed away. Mother–daughter relationships didn't seem to be a strong point in the family.

Mercia and Cindy came home to the Clovelly house one afternoon to find that it had been stripped bare. Mr Herbert had left Mercia for another woman and cleaned them out of most of their furniture. Mercia collected anything of Mr Herbert's that he had left behind, and asked Cindy to drive her to his new house in Rose Bay, as Mercia didn't have a driver's licence. They arrived and dumped Mr Herbert's belongings unceremoniously on the front lawn and drove away. This was something Cindy repeated when her own marriage ended.

Mercia told Cindy there was nothing more they could do; they couldn't report him to the police. Mercia didn't explain anything further—but after reading the ASIO files, Cindy realised her mother was worried that Mr Herbert would tell everyone about her being Mrs A, when she was trying to get her life back on track.

Mother and daughter moved into a flat in fashionable Double Bay, where Mercia felt they were sure to mix in the right circles. Mercia knew how to fit in with the Eastern Suburbs ladies—what to say, how to act—just as she had with her previous left-wing friends while working for the security services.

Among her close friends at this time were Thelma Bate, Secretary and then President of the Country Women's Association, and the estranged wife of Liberal politician Jeff Bate (who later married Dame Zara, the widow of Harold Holt), and Lady Mary Fairfax, wife of Sir Warwick, who would give Mercia her old clothes, maintaining Mercia's love of expensive fashionable clothing. Mercia used her event-hosting skills and became well known in the well-heeled suburb; she went on to raise funds and support for the Sydney Opera House, and to attend its opening.

Cindy knows there were moments when her mother felt haunted by the Royal Commission. One time she found her at home upset; Mercia had tried to join a women's business group and had been rejected. She explained to Cindy it was because of her past, and there was nothing she could do about it. Mercia was accepted in some circles, but not in others.

Cindy tried to do all the things her mother wanted of her. She attended the June Dally-Watkins modelling and deportment school, and made her social debut at the Royal Motor Yacht Club at Port Hacking. She remembers her mother being particularly impressed and delighted by that event.

Cindy finished school in Sydney and started an Arts degree at the University of Sydney, majoring in psychology. She didn't enjoy it, so she started studying interior design at East Sydney Tech, at her mother's suggestion. Cindy withdrew from that course as well, and Mercia helped her get a job at the ABC office in Pitt Street, as one of two receptionists who sat outside the office of the general manager, Charles Moses, and would run messages around the multiple ABC buildings in the city. Cindy remembers hearing the Sydney Symphony playing in the Forbes Street recording studios and loved the work.

In December 1961, Mercia received a letter from Ray Whitrod. She must have been applying for another journalist position and had asked him to be a referee.

The letter read:

Dear Mrs Herbert,

I am happy to be of some small service to one who has done much for the public good, and you certainly may give my name at any time as a reference for a prospective employer.

Whilst I am not a journalist, and to that extent limited in my capacity to assess your worth in newspaper and public relations work, nevertheless, I am a trained investigator with experience both in the field and administratively. From this background I am able, I believe, to make some useful comments on your professional ability.

Whitrod went on to list the special qualifications she possessed that would be of value in the journalistic or public relations field:

- An above average ability to recognise the priorities in importance of matters you are dealing with, and of giving them your prime attention;

- A perceptual capacity to observe items of interest in unusual situations, and to discard irrelevancies;

- An intelligence which permits you to handle a large volume of work, and to analyse and correlate the significance of its content.

I have selected these three characteristics because they are aspects which may be overlooked by other referees not having had my somewhat unique opportunities. There should be no need for me to comment on the thoroughness and enthusiasm which you display in your attitude to your job as these ought to be well known.

The fact that I am writing this reference is proof also, if this is needed, of my confidence in your loyalty to the principles of democratic government.

I wish you the best of luck in your endeavours.

Yours sincerely,

RW Whitrod
Commissioner
Commonwealth Police

73

A TALE OR TWO

Mercia did not allow Cindy to wear jeans or thongs, and she could never listen to popular music at home. At the age of twenty-four, Cindy decided it was time to start a new life for herself, as far away from her mother as possible.

She worked a second job cleaning offices in Circular Quay at night to save up for her move. Mercia was not impressed with this second job; Cindy was mixing with common tradespeople. Mercia was once again trying to influence her daughter—a daughter who felt her freedom was being impinged.

In 1968 Cindy moved to Canada, enjoying some leisurely travel along the way. Before she left, Mercia handed her three books: a collection of Australian verse, *Catcher in the Rye* and *Animal Farm*. The verse might give her a sense of nostalgia for the country she was leaving, but the others—a book about a teenager railing against the phoniness of the adult world, and another about a group of animals hoping to create an equal, free and happy life through rebellion, often seen as a satire critiquing Stalin and life in the Soviet Union—were certainly interesting choices to give your daughter as she leaves you, possibly forever.

As well as the books, Mercia handed her a certificate signed by Liberal Prime Minister John Gorton, asking that 'Any facilities which may be accorded the bearer whilst absent from the Commonwealth will be greatly appreciated'. Mercia still had political connections.

Cindy didn't learn about something else she was supposed to have taken with her, until her second and final visit to ASIO. It was a letter of reference given to Mercia by Freda Brown, whose husband, Bill, had worked at the *Tribune* with Rex. It contained a list of people or places that Freda suggested Cindy visit if and when she went to travel in Communist countries while overseas.

Despite the Royal Commission, Freda Brown seemed to not only be seeing and talking with Mercia, but wanting to help her daughter. However, Mercia never handed the letter to her. Cindy thinks it was one of the documents that had been in the filing cabinet Mercia had in her garage, which was collected after her death.

After Cindy left Australia, Mercia obtained a job as an ABC journalist in Adelaide, apparently with the help of ASIO. She was being encouraged to go into TV journalism, but moved back to Sydney and took up a job in the newsroom in the ABC's Sydney office.

Mercia threw herself into her new job. Her rounds covered both the visual and performing arts, as well as general reporting. She was said to have had a 'mothered interest' in the new cadet journalists, helping them develop their skills.

It was here that she again contacted ASIO. Mercia was suspicious that a pro-Communist was doctoring—changing—international news reports coming in via cable from ABC offices overseas, before being relayed out across the ABC network. Mercia informed ASIO about her suspicions. Though the outcome of this was never recorded in the files that Cindy and Kieron saw, they could see that Mercia had met with ASIO officers in a car behind the Domain carpark. She was again a part of ASIO, and she apparently felt good about it.

Mercia also carried out large blocks of relief duty for the ABC in regional NSW offices. It was around this time that Mercia decided to finally get her driver's licence. Cindy wasn't aware of this until she arrived back from Canada and her mother picked her up from the airport. The relatively short drive back to Double Bay was horrifying; her mother sat so low that she had to look through the steering wheel to drive. Cindy says she was the worst driver in the world and should never have been allowed on the road.

Cindy thinks Mercia enjoyed working out in the regions, particularly on big social events such as the country races, where she could dress up and show a bit of style. And it may have been the alcohol talking, or wishful thinking, but she appears to have told some tall stories about herself.

While working in Albury in 1973, the local paper ran an article on 'Mrs Masson', who was working at the ABC office in the border town. Mercia was no longer hiding behind the Herbert surname.

The author of the article, known only as 'Judy', called Mercia one of the most fascinating and interesting women in Australia. Mrs Masson was apparently ranked 'at the top' in promoting and fostering the arts in Australia, having raised $18,000 in one night to send the Australian Ballet Company on a successful East European tour.

'Then there was the famous *Don Quixote* night,' Mercia told Judy, the 'first major social event to be held in the new Opera House last month. We charged $50 a ticket and could not meet the demand.' Mercia went on to describe the Governor arriving in an open carriage with a mounted police guard, and how she'd had to source 2500 camellias for the decorations. She also told Judy that she was organising the official opening of the Opera House by the Queen for the following month—from Albury.

Mercia explained her work as a member of the Australian Opera auditions committee, which had started ten years previously in cooperation with the Metropolitan Opera House in New York, giving young Australians a chance to work in New York. She casually mentioned that her friend, Lady Fairfax, was a director, and Sir Bernard Heinze was the chairman. Mercia also spoke of her involvement with the Opera Foundation committee, of which she was also a member, as well as 'Friends of the Ballet'. Mercia couldn't help herself, telling Judy that she had visited every opera house in the world, before exclaiming that the Sydney Opera House was 'magnificent'. (With Cindy receiving a letter of sympathy from the General Manager of the Sydney Opera House Trust after her mother died, Mercia was indeed involved with at least one of these organisations.)

Underneath the photo of Mrs Masson that appeared with the full-page article was a description of Mercia that was nothing short of remarkable. It states, among other things, that she held a Master of Arts degree and was born in Scotland. That her father was a famous Fleet Street journalist, who covered such events as the opening of King Tutankhamen's tomb, and that he was one of the few journalists who attended the first Communist conference in Moscow with Lenin in the early 1920s, and had accompanied Edward, the Prince of Wales, on his first tour to Australia in 1920.

Despite Mercia's ability to tell incredible stories about herself, her colleagues seem to have held her in considerable esteem. After her death, a previous chief of staff at the ABC recalled in an article for *The Journalist* that her main aim was to get a job done quickly, get her copy through, and dash off to another assignment. She was from the 'old school' of journalism, never tackling a job without equipping herself with background—and seldom did her copy require correction.

There was a strange postscript to this eulogy that possibly undermined its credibility. The eulogist wrote: 'As an example of her unostentatious nature, she was, by marriage, Lady Masson—a title she guarded as a close secret.'

A creative backstory, something that Mercia had learnt well.

74

TRAITOR

When Mercia was having treatment in St Vincent's in December 1974, a book was left for her at the front desk. It was a copy of the newly released *Nest of Traitors*, written by Nicholas Whitlam and John Stubbs. Cindy only found out about this at the second ASIO visit. She doesn't remember seeing the book in her mother's hospital room, but she does remember Mercia showing her a thin booklet titled 'Where is the Nest of Traitors', which had been written by Rex Chiplin back in the 1950s and had also been left for her at the hospital.

In the book, Mercia was named as Mrs A.

It had been nearly twenty years since the *Guardian* had first exposed her. This public identification of her as Mrs A again, when she had successfully created a new life for herself, must have horrified her.

Despite being ill, Mercia was still on several committees sponsoring and promoting music, ballet and opera. Just months before, and despite being so ill, she had hosted a large party of press, stage and television personalities at an event for 800 people at a private home in Bellevue Hill. The event was to celebrate and send off two young opera singers who had received scholarships to travel and study in Italy, and it included a sit-down five-course Italian-style dinner, an evening of Italian song and music from a Gypsy band, and even a water ballet performance in the long swimming pool at the front of the house.

All of those people, with whom she had successfully cultivated social networks, would find out about her past.

At the time, Cindy couldn't understand why her mother appeared so upset by a tattered twenty-year-old booklet. She was further confused when her mother said she couldn't do anything about it, because of who the father of the man who had left the book was. There was no further explanation.

Cindy put her mother's upset down to the cancer that was starting to affect her brain. Mercia's condition deteriorated rapidly after that event.

Cindy didn't read the book *Nest of Traitors*, but if she had, she would have seen her mother identified as Mrs A from the Royal Commission on Espionage. Following the incident at the hospital, it would have been perhaps the best opportunity for Mercia to tell Cindy about her work with ASIO, about their past, and about what she had been through. But the opportunity was lost.

Despite her fear about people knowing about her life as a double agent, and her appearance at the Royal Commission on Espionage, Mercia did share the fact with a select few.

The late John Tingle, a celebrated broadcaster in his day, told Cindy a few months before he passed away that he had worked with Mercia in the ABC newsroom, and that they had a good working friendship. He had even gone up to Killcare on a few weekends to help Mercia putty-fill gaps in the windows of the old house. Mercia had revealed to him that she had been Mrs A at the Petrov Royal Commission; she had told him this in passing, but with great secrecy and a sense of mystery attached to it.

Perhaps the Royal Commission and her past life working for ASIO seemed so long ago and so far behind her that she had felt confident to share this information with John Tingle. But for a book to suddenly be published revealing her to the world as a person who had betrayed friendships would have been difficult for Mercia, especially as she couldn't control the narrative.

After VENONA disclosed that there was a spy ring in Australia, ASIO had needed to identify the individuals attached to the code names and halt the leakage of classified material to the Soviets. By placing an agent who was already accepted in left-wing organisations into a position where they had access to classified material, they hoped they might get an approach from someone in the Communist Party passing information to the Soviets.

Rex took the bait. Ray Whitrod, in his interview with author David McKnight, confirmed that he vetted documents given to Rex by Mercia, classifying them as low risk—including some surveys of the Channel Country. Whitrod didn't think she had passed on the surveys but found out at the Royal Commission that she had. This explains the timeline of her passing the surveys to Rex—after she had left the department, and after Ray Whitrod had moved to the CIS.

The leaking of the draft treaty departmental minute to Rex Chiplin, and the subsequent publication of Rex's article 'Secret Treaty Sells Us to the US', came to dominate the testimony of both Mrs A and Rex at the Royal Commission.

Rex said that the meeting with his source who provided the treaty document would have occurred up to ten days before publication on 14 November 1951. Mercia's travel expenses and hotel register showed the Commissioners this would not have been possible. Mercia saw Rex on 5 November, when she handed him the vetted documents on coal production and American investments at the TAA lounge in Sydney. She afterwards reported to ASIO her movements, mentioning that she'd had a sleepless night. She then reported that she travelled to Newcastle early on 6 November and was there until 12 November, before travelling back to Melbourne, and then Canberra the following week.

But there's an interesting side note in this collection of dates and events. Mercia's typed travel itinerary showed that on 6 November she caught the 9.05 a.m. train to Newcastle, arriving at 11.30 a.m., and checking into the Great Northern Hotel that evening at 8 p.m. When she was questioned at the Royal Commission about an entry in her diary for 6 November, she agreed with her diary note that she didn't leave Sydney until *late afternoon* on the train to Newcastle. Justice Philp did note this at the time in the court room, saying she had been in Sydney all day on 6 November. Mercia left Sydney on the 5.50 p.m. train on 6 November, arriving in Newcastle at 7.40 p.m. and checking into the Great Northern at 8 p.m.

Mercia *could* have been in Sydney another day.

On the same general expenses form, Mercia's next travel allowance entry was 12 November, where she claimed for the Newcastle to Sydney leg. The next line on her travel expenses was nine days later, where she claimed expenses for travel from Sydney to Canberra on 21 November, and then on to Melbourne on 23 November.

A report had been issued to ASIO by Mercia in Sydney on 14 November. Then, to quote Justice Owen at the Commission:

There is a report which appears to have been made from Melbourne on 15 November in which there is a reference to these terms: 'I am booked for Canberra Wednesday and Melbourne Friday', referring to the following week.

The report from 15 November is not available to the public, but Justice Owen's comment that it 'appeared to have been made from Melbourne' is curious and raises the possibility that Mercia could have been trying to deflect from the fact that she was in Sydney from 12 November to 21 November.

Instead, the Justices found that the draft treaty exchange had happened in Canberra as Rex initially reported, with an unknown departmental official.

Ray Whitrod said in his report to ASIO that Mercia was suffering from nervous tension before she left Melbourne, and she herself had reported that she had a sleepless night before she travelled to Newcastle on 6 November. Perhaps this was linked to her giving the documents that had been vetted by security to Rex—but it could also have been because she was passing on a classified document that hadn't been checked.

On 4 March 1955, Max Julius presented an interesting accusation in defence of his client.

On the evidence it seems highly improbable and it seems that Mrs A's operation was part of an entire operation—that the handing of the document to Chiplin was itself a plant on him. It may have been some initiative on her part, something she did without instructions from Mr Whitrod—I do not know—in the hope that 'We will see what happens to it; will it go to the Russians?', or in the hope that somebody would be able to succeed in a charge against Chiplin of a breach of the Official Secrets Act in obtaining or communicating information from a Government source.

In his lengthy summation at the Royal Commission, the Communist barrister Max Julius argued that Mercia was the person who gave Rex the document, saying, 'She [Mrs A] has been playing a double game for the last six years at least, and perhaps longer—a most extraordinary role.' These pages are missing from Mercia's copy of the transcript.

He went on to say:

She is a very highly experienced operative, and an intelligent operative, and if she were doing this, if she had this aberration from her duty to the Australian Security Intelligence Organisation, if she did at this time feel that this was a document that should be published,

Your Honour could well expect that she would take steps to
ensure that there was no possibility of its being traced
back to her.

Following Mr Julius, Mr Windeyer finished the day off with a
number of points, in part saying that the document they held as an
exhibit—being the minute of comments about the treaty—did come
from the Department of National Development:

But it cannot be suggested that that in itself establishes,
or is any reason for supposing, that Mrs A was the person
involved in Chiplin getting it. The reason why Mrs A
was put into the Department of National Development was
because people thought there were leakages going on from
that Department.

Mercia could have given the draft treaty document to Rex, with or
without ASIO's knowledge. If she did pass it on to him, perhaps she
shared it to gain more credibility with Rex in the hope that she would
become a member of the CPA, as ASIO wanted—or perhaps her own
feelings for Rex led her to share an unvetted restricted document.

Another possibility is that it was indeed someone else in the
Department of National Development who gave Rex the document
to copy—with Rex then placing the blame on an undercover security
agent he had once considered a close friend, until she was exposed and
found to have betrayed his friendship.

In his interview with David McKnight, Ray Whitrod said he
thought it was likely that Mercia had given Rex the 'Friendship Treaty'
document, and that she had been under a lot of emotional pressure
at the Royal Commission when she denied it. When asked why
Mercia would have given it to Rex without her case officer knowing,
Ray Whitrod didn't know. He explained to David McKnight that he
questioned Mercia 'heavily' about it, but there had been an emotional
entanglement.

In 1961, when Ray Whitrod wrote his reference for Mercia, he saw her as loyal 'to the principles of democratic government', despite the emotional entanglement. Mercia had ultimately been torn between two loyalties, ASIO and Rex Chiplin.

Mercia underlined in her copy of the transcript one part of her cross-examination by Mr Hill at the Royal Commission. This read:

You asked me before if I thought this information was going to the Communist Party. <u>At the time I was trying to get my mind clear. I did not believe and I was not interested in whether this information was going to the Communist Party, because I believe that the rank and file of the Communist Party are mostly innocent people who believe in things, their way of things; but what did concern me was that something was going on that did not have Australia's interest at heart, and I believe quite strongly from what I have observed that that exists, and exists quite strongly, and it is quite outside the Communist Party.</u>

75

IN SPIRIT

A word that Cindy often uses to describe her mother is lonely. Mercia sought out social interaction, and most of her friends were men—older men. She had boyfriends at different times, and friends she would go out with; Mercia had a wide range of contacts, across all social spheres. But at home she was alone, especially when Cindy went overseas.

Cindy feels that, as a result of her mother being 'outed' as a spy at the Royal Commission, her mother turned to alcohol, and that her behaviour when intoxicated—and the embarrassment it caused—added to her isolation. Mercia was what would probably be referred to today as a functioning alcoholic; drinking was her friend, and her support. Her drinking embarrassed Cindy, and turned her away from her mother even more.

Cindy knew her mother was a very bright woman; but to end up a sick and lonely alcoholic, she feels, was tragic.

Mercia had been very close to the nuns of Our Lady Help of Christians. Cindy does still wonder if Mercia confided in them, and whether religion helped her.

The nuns lived at St Therese's Convent at the back of St Patrick's seminary, on top of the hill in Manly, and were a great comfort to Cindy, as she imagines they were for her mother. They would look after Cindy's children while she did the local Meals on Wheels, and she would have lunch with them all after she'd finished delivering the meals. The nuns were all elderly and Cindy remembers with a smile that they were probably glad to see the kids go. The old ladies would be exhausted.

After Mercia died, Cindy, filled with a range of emotions, had tried at various times to get more information about her mother, to find out who her mother was. But when the memories became too much, she would stop, put her quest aside and get on with her life. She describes it as being like doing a giant jigsaw puzzle, with most of the pieces frustratingly missing. She had to wait until another piece was found, before moving on—the messy puzzle always waiting to be completed.

※

In 2014 Cindy and her two sons, Kieron and Shaun, attended the launch in Canberra of *The Spy Catchers: The Official History of ASIO 1949–1963*. The book included an appendix on her mother, and had paved the way for her and Kieron to view Mercia's files. Cindy's daughter, Kelly-Ann, lived in Perth and was unable to attend.

Kieron drove the three of them down to the capital and they made their way to the motel where they planned to stay the night, before going to Old Parliament House. Cindy went to the launch with mixed feelings. She was curious, but the visits to the ASIO office to view her mother's files had been torturous. She had wanted answers and felt she had obtained only some. Her mother kept many secrets: a mother who was more committed to her work with ASIO than to her own daughter.

Cindy found the event interesting. It was good to meet the author, David Horner, together with the researchers she and Kieron had met when reading the ASIO files. Some people at the event were apparently related to other former ASIO agents, but Cindy doesn't remember meeting any of them, which she now regrets—some of them may have known her mother and been able to tell her a little more.

She was surprised when she read Sandra Hogan's book *With My Little Eye*, about the Dohertys, an entire family of spies in which the children grew up knowing that their parents worked for ASIO—and even helped with some of the espionage work. In this book, Cindy read that the mother, Joan, had been assigned to listen to Mercia's private conversations in a cafe during the Royal Commission. Mercia didn't suspect them, a young mother sitting nearby, surrounded by her children—nor that ASIO would have been spying on her. Cindy read that the Doherty family were at the book launch, but she didn't meet them, and still finds it inconceivable that the children were aware of what their family was doing. That thought is so foreign to her own experience.

Cindy, Kieron, and Shaun sat with Rhys Crawley and his wife and some of the other researchers at the launch. Rhys had been present in the white room at ASIO when Cindy and Kieron went through the files, and had seen the devastating effect the contents of the files had on Cindy. Chatting with one of the other researchers, Cindy realised the legacy of ASIO and its secrecy wasn't just confined to the past, but was impacting the present. This researcher was not allowed to discuss, even with close family, the work she carried out, what they were reading and compiling.

Keeping secrets is a large part of working for ASIO.

Cindy did eventually decide to get in touch with Mercia's first ASIO case officer, Ray Whitrod, who'd had an illustrious career and was then retired and living back in his home town of Adelaide. Cindy managed to obtain his phone number, but for Cindy it was a somewhat unsatisfactory conversation. He didn't share much about her mother, and he was surprised to learn that she was Mercia's daughter, telling her he was under the impression that Mercia had a son.

But then Mercia had also told ASIO, after her move to Melbourne, that she was a widow.

Ron Richards, when working in ASIO's Royal Commission division, was not aware of the surname Pearce, or its history for their agent.

Mercia had successfully managed to alter her marital status, being listed as a separated woman when she joined the CIS, and then as a widow with ASIO; no one seemed to have noticed. This was probably not helped by Mercia changing her daughter's name by deed poll.

When Cindy followed David McKnight's advice and approached the National Archives, there was an extended period before a reply came back, and then again before she received the telephone call from ASIO. Each of the two visits to the ASIO offices with Kieron was unbearably hard for her. Her childhood had been recorded and scrutinised; her life was not what she thought it had been. She couldn't get all the answers she needed from the ASIO file; there were extensive redactions, and whole documents had been permanently withdrawn, which meant considerable information had been withheld.

After their last visit to ASIO, Kieron wrote a reflective note regarding the question of which ASIO papers are released to the public, and which ones are not. Initially, he was against such heavily imposed secrecy, but after going through all of his grandmother's papers that he and his mother were able to access, he could start to see why much was withheld.

He wrote:

These papers are held to protect the people involved.
There's nothing sinister or evil, or even mildly explosive.
Really these secrets are kept because they are keeping
the integrity of all people involved as best as they can.
Everyone involved had their bad moments. Done something
they shouldn't have or acted in an inappropriate way. This
is what ASIO are protecting.

Reflecting now, Kieron regrets not getting enough time to read all the files on the table, and not knowing enough to make sense of what the files contained. They didn't understand it all. At the end of their second meeting, he and his mother were told there would be no opportunity to see the files again, ever.

Two days to understand his grandmother's life just wasn't enough.

The information about Mercia that is available to the general public relates to the Royal Commission and her work leading up to her evidence. There are glimpses of other work she may have been reporting on, but with so much redacted or permanently withdrawn, we will never know for certain what else she was doing.

ASIO did give Cindy the names of two undercover agents she could contact with any questions she had. One of these was Moya Horowitz. In an emotional turmoil, Cindy let these opportunities pass. Both of the women named on that slip of paper have since passed away.

Finding out that she was illegitimate came as a huge shock to Cindy.

Another revelation on perusing the ASIO file was coming across her mother's death certificate. Cindy suddenly realised that she herself didn't even have a copy of that document. The certificate showed Mercia's year of birth as 1919, as Cindy had recorded it in the hospital, but the year was wrong—it should have actually been 1913. The discrepancy around her date of birth was one of the first questions Rhys Crawley had asked at the first ASIO meeting. Mercia had managed to shave six years off her life—even managing to keep that small but important fact of her age from her own daughter.

The next surprise for Cindy was that ASIO had paid for her mother's funeral. The receipt sat in the file staring back at her as she tried to make sense of it. Cindy had been in touch with the Australian Journalists Association after her mother's death, and she had assumed that the AJA had paid for her mother's funeral, as they had when Russell Grant had committed suicide.

Another surprise was when the ASIO staff told her someone from ASIO would have attended the funeral, and every time she was in hospital, someone would have visited her. This explained why she didn't see the *Nest of Traitors* book at the hospital after Mercia received it, only the pamphlet. ASIO looked after her mother to the end.

Putting everything into context from the ASIO files, and what she has found out about her mother, Cindy reflects that everybody, including mothers and daughters, have difficult times, and theirs was a particularly distant relationship, compounded by the double life Mercia was leading. Her work with ASIO had been all-encompassing, with no time for child-raising. Mercia's relationship with her own mother had held little emotional attachment; she had been closer to her invalid father. Perhaps Mercia just didn't know how to interact in a loving way towards her child.

On one of the pages missing from Mercia's own Royal Commission transcripts, one of Mercia's ASIO reports was being read out in court, concerning a discussion she had with Rex after Mr Wilks's interview into the missing treaty document. Rex apparently said to her: 'If you don't know, you can't tell.' This statement could almost be one from Mercia to her own daughter.

After Mercia's death, ABC broadcaster John Tingle had told Cindy how thorough her mother had been in her work as a journalist. Cindy could relate to that; she describes her mother as being like a dog with a bone, seeing things through to the end. Cindy admits Mercia was a fighter for things she believed in. But did the end justify the means? Is that reason enough for a mother to shut out her only child?

As her mum lay dying in hospital, slipping in and out of consciousness, Cindy couldn't bring herself to touch her. She had no feelings of affection; she was there purely out of duty. It didn't feel natural for her to reach out and hold her mother's hand on her death bed.

Mercia was cremated, her ashes placed next to her mother, Lucy, in the rose garden at Botany. Once a year Cindy travels down from Killcare by train to Central Station and catches two buses out to the cemetery. She always takes flowers she has picked from the bush, plus a small bottle of cleaning fluid and some steel wool to clean the two metal plaques for her mother and grandmother until they shine.

Sometimes she walks through the cemetery and up onto the top of a hill, to the Presbyterian section of the cemetery with its sweeping views over Botany Bay. There, across from his own parents and next to his sister and her husband, lies Mercia's father, without his wife.

Remembering her visit to the clairvoyant all those years ago, Cindy feels that, if her mother was indeed seeking forgiveness, she doesn't think she can give it.

She has tried to find out about her mother—and has done so, to a degree. But Mercia and the people who knew her have now gone, and the closest Cindy feels she can be to her mother is when she holds Mercia's rosary beads. Many unanswered questions linger, but in the end it must be accepted that some things will forever remain a mystery when it comes to Mercia Masson, distant mother and enigmatic spy.

ACKNOWLEDGEMENTS

This book would not have been possible without the assistance of several people. The first person to thank is Mercia's daughter: thank you, Cindy, for opening up your home and memories for this book. To Kieron, thank you for your time and valuable input, sharing your experiences at ASIO and your subsequent investigations into your grandmother.

Thank you to Rhys Crawley for helping with terminology, and for your own recollections of meeting with Cindy and Kieron. An enormous thank you to David McKnight for sharing your interview with Ray Whitrod.

Thanks to the staff at the Australian Archives for looking after our history and helping search for obscure files in your priceless collection.

To all at Allen & Unwin, you are an incredible team to work with. Thanks especially to Courtney Lick, Elizabeth Weiss and Richard Walsh.

Lastly, thank you to my family, who listened patiently as I worked my way through copies of redacted files, interviews and old documents, piecing together the remarkable and turbulent story of Mercia Masson.